To Paula
Best wishes
Mark Kelly

AGHOWLE –
WHERE THE DIVIL ATE THE TINKER

GW00469613

Dear Paula,   Jan. 2018.
I think you will enjoy this
love Trish.

MARGARET CONNOLLY

AGHOWLE –
WHERE THE DIVIL ATE
THE TINKER

*The History of a Wicklow Townland
and
its Farming Community*

Foreword by Ken Hannigan
Edited by Brian Mathews

Applefield Publishing

Applefield Publishing,
Dublin, Ireland
applefield_info@yahoo.com

This edition 2017
First published in Ireland 2017 by
Applefield Publishing
Copyright Margaret Connolly © 2017

The Author asserts the moral right
to be identified as the author of this work

ISBN 978-1-5272-1719-5

Typeset in Adobe Caslon Pro

Printed and bound in Ireland by
Naas Printing Ltd.,
Naas, Co. Kildare, Ireland

This book is dedicated to all those past and present
who have called Aghowle their home

And is in memory of my parents
Patsy Connolly (1907-1994) and May Connolly (1929-2017)
Who gave my sisters and I
Life, Love, and a wonderful childhood in the townland of Aghowle

Table of Contents

Chapter 4
The Famine Years and its Aftermath, 1845-1850 58

Chapter 5
1850-1885: The Post Famine years 74

Chapter 6
1885-1899: Land Wars and Love Stories 87

Chapter 11
1950-1960: Changing Times in the Farmhouses 178

Chapter 12
1960–Early 70s: Arrivals and Departures 196

Foreword

Aghowle Upper and Aghowle Lower lie just four miles west of the village of Ashford, on the slopes of Carrick Mountain in Co. Wicklow, on what was formerly part of the Synge Estate. Although they are denominated separately for administrative purposes, the two townlands have mostly been regarded as a single locality. The entire area amounts to just over 800 acres. This book tells the story of the families who lived in this area and of the life they shared. It was a way of life that was to survive with extraordinary continuity over centuries up to living memory, but then disappear in a generation.

Margaret Connolly grew up on a small farm in Aghowle where ancestors on her grandmother's side had lived since the early 1800s, and to where her grandfather moved at the end of the 1800s after his family lands near Roundwood were submerged by the extension of the Vartry Reservoir. Margaret has an intimate knowledge of the families who farmed in Aghowle over the years, but also of the history of the wider area between Ashford, Roundwood and Glenealy. Her account is based largely on her own experience and on the recorded memories of her own family and others who lived in the area. It is backed by assiduous research among a wide array of documentary sources, some of them unique to Aghowle.

Aghowle was part of the rimland, lying between the rich agricultural lands of Wicklow's coastal plain, and the wild mountainous interior of the county, which was largely uninhabited. In Aghowle, as in many rimland areas of East Wicklow, the farms were small, typically less than 30 acres, and were let on short leases, usually from year to year, until the Land Acts at the turn of the 19th/20th centuries transferred ownership of the land to the tenants. The 19th century Ordnance Survey maps perfectly illustrate the intensity of cultivation in the area, with a regular patchwork of similarly-sized small fields on the lower slopes, giving way to open spaces on the upper slopes, where sheep grazed on common lettings and turf was harvested on turbary rents.

In the near-subsistence economy that prevailed in places like Aghowle, smallholders had a tenuous grip on their holdings and this account records the experiences of many who were forced to let go that grip and to emigrate. For those who stayed there was the realisation that the farm could not provide for the needs of a large family into adulthood, and the corollary that some family members would have to make their living elsewhere. It is a sad fact that the population of Wicklow as a whole declined by a third between 1841 and 1861 and that the smallest of the smallholders, those holding from one to five acres declined by 60% in the same period. Dublin's proximity to Wicklow also acted as a magnet. One seventh of the population of Dublin in 1841 had been born in Co. Wicklow. By 1851 this had risen to one fifth. For these people, there was at least the possibility of maintaining contact with their homeplace, and some of the warmest memories of Aghowle included here come from the second generation of families who left who came down every summer to live on the family farm. Without exception in this volume, their recollections are positive.

This volume also follows the fortunes of many who travelled further afield. Combining genealogical expertise with the networking possibilities presented by 21st century communications technology, the author has located the descendants of many who emigrated from Aghowle and neighbouring townlands and has pieced together the histories of these families at both ends of the emigration experience. It is remarkable to see the gravestones that mark the final resting place of Aghowle-born emigrants so many thousands of miles from their birthplace and to read the accounts of families for whom contact with their ancestral homeplace has been restored after a century and a half or more.

Margaret Connolly has performed a great service in gathering the recollections of individuals whose families have farmed in Aghowle for generations. Some of those whose recollections are included have passed on since the interviews were recorded, but the author's timely action has ensured that their voices live on. These accounts form the warm heart of this charming book and are eloquent testimony of the imperative for local historians of saving the oral record of their communities before it is too late. They describe a time when two men with scythes would mow a two-and-a half-acre field in a day (although this was regarded as a remarkable feat even then), when the rhythm of the farming year was punctuated by such annual events as the threshing, the sheep-shearing and the cutting and drawing of the turf, all undertaken on a communal co-operative basis.

Such activities were infused with a community spirit and a commonality of purpose. Most of these families were in similar circumstances and this fostered a common bond. Mostly, they lived off the produce of their own farms and most of their produce was consumed on the farm. The slaughter of a pig once or twice a year kept the family in bacon for the rest of the year.

Sheep were mostly kept for their wool and were rarely slaughtered. Cattle were kept mostly to provide for household needs. Such small surpluses as might accrue would be churned into butter and sold in the neighbouring towns where their sale helped to pay for the sack of flour that would be used to supply the family with bread. The positive aspects of these memoirs illustrate a co-operative society not far removed from De Valera's idyllic Ireland of cosy homesteads.

But of course, it was also a way of life that was precarious in many ways and was replete with danger and hardship. Several tragedies are recorded here such as illness, famine, eviction and fire. The accounts of the Big Snow of 1947 remind us of how isolated an area like this could become. The arrival of electricity in the 1950s must have had a transformative effect on the lives of inhabitants, although it is pointed out that for many years it was mainly a source of light and power and that most households were to survive for many more years without the use of the domestic electrical appliances on which the average household is so dependent today.

There is an elegiac quality about this book. It describes a society that has now largely vanished. This happened in the lifetime of one generation. Changes in the wider economy made the small working farms less viable. Economies of scale, and the onset of new agricultural policies, led to the consolidation of holdings. The farmlands were gradually sold to farmers who lived outside Aghowle and who farmed on a larger scale. Fields were consolidated. Coupled with this, state afforestation had turned much of the higher ground into plantation.

The farmhouses were mostly sold as separate dwellings or were replaced by new dwellings. Then, from the 1970s, the number of houses in the townland began to increase. By a strange irony, the number of inhabited houses in Aghowle is now on a par with what it was at the beginning of the 19th century but the nature of that habitation is very different.

All the working family farms that once occupied Aghowle have now gone. While some of the farming families still live in the area, the farmhouses in Aghowle are now mostly occupied by people who have moved to the area and whose work takes them outside.

The structure of the book, incorporating relevant world events, the townland as a whole and the detail for each house is an ingenious schema, made possible by the author's first-hand knowledge of the area, and the fact of the area being so small and so self-contained as to be capable of being comprehensively documented. Woven into it are local songs and poems, as well as some of the author's own poetic creations. The customs and traditions associated with the historical sites in the townland are recalled and provide something of a handbook for those who might wish to get to know the area.

    This volume is a major addition to the growing number of local studies of Wicklow. Anyone who reads it will surely be tempted to come and explore the area.

Ken Hannigan

Ken Hannigan is a retired Keeper in the National Archives of Ireland, a founder member of the Wicklow Historical Society, and joint editor of Wicklow History and Society, a volume in the Irish County History series.

Introduction

"They were great people that lived and farmed here
and soon there will be no one at all left to remember them"

For centuries, our Irish rural landscape consisted of a patchwork of small townlands of farming communities, in which families had lived and worked together for generations. As the land was passed down from one generation to the next, so too was the knowledge, the memories and the folklore of each of those little localities passed on and preserved for future generations.

In 1959, I was lucky enough to be born into such a farming community in the townland of Aghowle (pronounced *Ah-howl*), approximately four miles west and uphill from the village of Ashford in Co. Wicklow.[1] At that time, everyone in the neighbourhood knew the history of each house and farm, they knew each field by name and who had planted what crop in each of those fields for decades past. I grew up hearing of the landmarks in the vicinity of our farm referred to as Giffney's Bank, the Soldier's Field, Joe Ryan's Gate, Mooney's Ditch and Loughlin's Walls. Although all these families had passed and gone, some having lived in the previous century, they were still in a way very much present and part of our community.

Also from talk around the fireside, I grew to know the neighbours no longer with us such as the Rocher Doyle, old Jer and Sarah Farrell, Crofton Smith, and old Sarah Doyle. Regularly I heard, like a mantra, the repeated wise sayings of a man known as Old Faulkner. These people were spoken of as if they might walk through the kitchen door at any time and take a seat with us by the fireside.

At that time, almost everyone in the area was making a living from the land and although tractors had recently begun to replace horses and electricity had arrived a few years earlier than myself in the valley, the farmers were still continuing to farm in the tradition of their fathers and

---

1 There is a larger townland also bearing the name of Aghowle, in the south west end of County Wicklow, near the town of Shillelagh. The two townlands are not connected in any way, other than like many Irish place names, they share the same name.

grandfathers. The cows were milked by hand, in the summer time the fields were full of cocks of hay and families were almost self-sufficient with their own potatoes, vegetables and eggs. The housewives churned butter and made their own bread, often baking it on the open fire. The practice of each farmer killing a pig and curing the bacon, was just beginning to fade out. Many of the houses still had large open fireplaces on which hung the big black kettle constantly on the boil and ready to make tea for anyone who might enter through the kitchen door.

As a child growing up here in the 1960s I was unaware that I was living through the end of an era. I did not know that in just a couple of decades this way of life would have vanished completely from our townland and become a thing of the past.

While the old methods of farming were beginning to change all over the country, in our townland a number of factors converged to bring about a complete change in a very short period of time. It happened that most of the local farming families were coming to the end of their line, as they consisted of elderly bachelors, couples who were not blessed with children, or others like my parents, who had only produced daughters. In the past, these farmers' daughters would have aspired to become a farmer's wife, but now with the benefits of free education, they were looking at careers further afield. These factors, combined with major changes in the way farming was now being carried out and the economic shift away from agriculture brought about a situation where within a couple of decades, one by one all the farmyards in the townland became empty and fell silent.

There was no sound from the farmhouse kitchens of the housewives busy churning butter or making bread and at evening time, no parade of cows coming homeward for milking. There was no sheepdog lying in the sunshine by the kitchen door as he kept a watchful eye on the hens scratching around him in the farmyard dirt.

For although the land remained, it had changed hands and was now farmed in a larger more commercial way by farmers who lived outside the townland. In many cases, the little patchwork fields became merged into larger and longer strips suitable for growing barley or intensive grazing for animals - and here and there sites were sold off and new bungalows appeared on the Aghowle landscape. The little farmhouses too were sold on to families not connected with farming, but luckily their new owners were sensitive to their former history and wanted to give them a new lease of life whilst still incorporating the memory of their past. So, it came to pass in the later decades of the twentieth century that the townland moved on into a new era and almost silently a long tradition and a way of life, slipped from existence.

Then a few years ago, while reminiscing with Billy Smith, a farmer from the neighbouring townland of Ballycullen, whose family have farmed in the locality for many generations, he was recalling all the families he remembered that farmed here in the townland of Aghowle. He commented that *"they were great people who lived and farmed here and soon there will be no one at all left to remember them"*. This made me think that unless someone tried to record the former history and folklore of the area and its people, it would just fade away and soon be lost for ever. This is my attempt to record the history and the life of the farming community that once lived in the townland of Aghowle.

While this book is about a particular townland and its former farming community, no place existed in total isolation of its neighbours, therefore there are also references to the surrounding neighbourhood and the local villages and towns. In particular, the townland of Ballycullen is often mentioned and this reflects the close connections between the farming communities of the two townlands. For several centuries, under the landlord and tenant system, the lands in both of these townlands were leased as a single unit. Also, geographically a large portion of Ballycullen lies in the same valley as Aghowle, between Slanelough crossroads and Ballycullen crossroads.

This book is presented in two halves:

- The first half gives a description and general history of Aghowle and its environs, including events that impacted on the lives of the families that farmed here until the second half of the 20th century. It also describes the traditional farming methods used by the community here.
- The second half provides a detailed history of the houses of the townland and the families that occupied them. For identification purposes, the houses are numbered, and you will find references to such as "House No. 4" in the first half of the book.

Where the Divil Ate the Tinker? – An Explanation Note

The title of this book may seem a little strange to many people but is not intended to cause offence to anyone - it has its origins back in the year of 1798.

When I was a child, and someone inquired where I came from or someone made any reference to Aghowle, I became accustomed to hearing the following refrain:

"Ah, you're from Aghowle, where the Divil ate the Tinker". I learned quite early on that this refrain had a connection to the story of a man named Dinny Byrne, who was a rebel and on the run from the Yeomen during the 1798 Rebellion. The story goes that to avoid capture, young Dinny disguised himself as a tinker. At that time, a tinker was a skilled tinsmith who traveled through the countryside calling at farmhouses to mend pots and farm implements. Under this disguise Dinny made his way to Aghowle and hid out in a cave in the rocks on Carrick Mountain. The pursuing Yeomen heard of his disguise and that he was hiding out somewhere in the townland, so they surrounded the area but could find no trace at all of Dinny, who was safely hidden in the cave. This apparent disappearance into thin air mystified and greatly annoyed the leader of the Yeomen, who is said to have sworn and cursed Aghowle, as being the place where the Divil ate the tinker.

When one reads the harrowing accounts of death and destruction that the local people suffered at the hands of the Yeomen during 1798, it is easy to see how the story of Dinny Byrne, the man that managed to outwit them and cause them great annoyance, would have become a local folk hero. Thus, Aghowle where he made this great escape has remained associated in the local folklore as the place *"where the Divil ate the Tinker"*.

As time passes the number of families remaining in the locality that hold connections to our past are greatly reducing, so such oral history as the story of Dinny Byrne, unless it is recorded, will probably fade from memory.

On the other hand, the following happened to me a few years ago, while giving my mother's details to a receptionist in the outpatients' department of a Dublin hospital. When I gave the address as Aghowle, Ashford, she looked up from her computer screen, raised an eyebrow and asked, *"Is that the Aghowle, where the Divil ate the Tinker?"* I replied that it was and how surprised I was that she had heard of it and knew that phrase. She explained that she had grown up in the village of Rathnew in Co. Wicklow and that as a child she often heard her father refer to Aghowle, where the Divil ate the Tinker. She was not even sure that such a place existed, so she was delighted to finally find out that indeed it did and meet someone who came from there.

Chapter 1:

The Local Landscape and its Ancient Links

Description of the Townland

As previously mentioned, there are two townlands in County Wicklow bearing the name of Aghowle. One is located in the south west of the county near the Carlow border while the townland which is the subject of this book is situated further north and in the east of the county.

Although the townland lies in a very rural location at the foot of Carrick Mountain, it is surrounded by several villages and towns. The town of Wicklow is approximately 12 km away, the local village of Ashford is 6 km, the village of Glenealy lies about 8km away and the town of Rathdrum is at a distance of 11 km. Heading further up into the Wicklow hills the small village or hamlet of Moneystown is at a distance of about 3km and the village of Roundwood, which is one of the highest villages in Ireland, lies 11km from the townland.

A road runs southwest to northeast through the townland, designated as local road L5092. Along this road, the boundaries of Aghowle can roughly be deemed to be the crossroads at Slanelough (to the south) and the junction with Aghowle Lane (to the north).

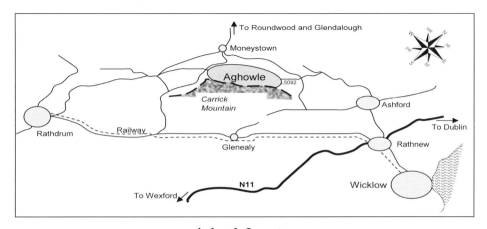

Aghowle Location

Officially the townland is sub-divided into Aghowle Upper and Aghowle Lower but mostly this distinction has only been used for official and legal purposes. In the past, when the townland existed solely as a farming community, the entire townland was commonly just referred to as Aghowle (although the farms and houses that lay in the lane at Aghowle Lower were looked upon as having their own little sub-community and were often referred to locally as "the people who lived in along the Lane").

In official designations, both townlands lie in: The Electoral Division of Ballycullen; the Civil Parish of Rathnew; the Barony of Newcastle and the County of Wicklow. Aghowle Upper is located at map co-ordinates 52° 59' 15" N, 6° 10' 43" W. Aghowle Lower, to the northeast and downhill, is located at map co-ordinates 52° 59' 32" N, 6° 9' 46" W.

The average altitude is around 200 metres (656 ft.). The highest benchmark in the townland is 714 ft. (217m) at the Wart Stone and the lowest is at Aghowle Lane, at 410.6 ft. (125m). Those are just the marked benchmark points – fields running up the side of Carrick Mountain would be higher.

The background Aghowle maps used in this section were created at the time of Griffith's Land Valuation (1848-1864), and are reproduced here with the permission of The Commissioner of Valuation.

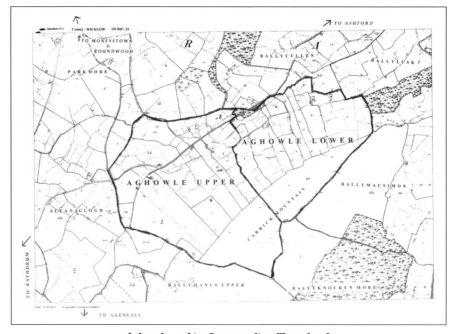

Aghowle and its Surrounding Townlands

The layout of our rural townlands often resembles a great patchwork of irregular strips of land, and so it is not surprising to find that the townland is surrounded by no less than 7 other townlands, namely Ballycullen, Slanelough, Ballymanus Upper, Ballylusk, Parkmore, Ballymacsimon and Ballyknocken More. Part of Carrick Mountain belongs to the townland of Aghowle and the remaining portion of the mountain belongs to the other townlands that surround it.

When the government officials set about making the first ordnance survey maps in the late 1830s, their description of the townlands of Aghowle Upper and Lower included the following information:

"The name of the townland, translated from the Irish language means apple field" - this would concur with the translation given by Liam Price in his *"Placenames of County Wicklow"* where he records Aghowle as *achadh ubhall*, meaning apple field or orchard.

The ordnance survey officials recorded that Aghowle Upper was about 6 miles west of the town of Wicklow and contained 488 acres Statute Measure of which 95 acres were uncultivated. The townland at that time was the property of J. Synge of Glanmore, as he was the local landlord. The land was described as gravelly and poor and produced indifferent crops. About one fourth was uncultivated and rocky and extended to the top of Carrickmaria Mt. (Carrick Mountain). The farms were held from year to year.

Their description of Aghowle Lower was that it was about five miles west of Wicklow town. The soil was poor and gravelly and did not produce good crops. A large portion of the South side was un-cultivated. The farms in general were small and let to tenants at will. Aghowle Lower contained 325 acres Statute Measure of which 26 acres was uncultivated [OSNB/W/p.180].

In the past, while our rural townlands varied greatly in their size and population, they would all have held a very strong sense of identity and pride of place for the residents who lived and farmed within their boundaries. Now with the passing of time and many changes in rural living, the townland is often seen as just a line on an address or a location on the SatNav.

Historical Features

Nowadays in our modern rural living, thanks to technology we are connected far and wide by unseen links such as satellite, mobile phones and internet access, to the vast global world around us. But as we drive through the countryside it is easy to miss the hidden links tucked away in our landscape, connecting us back in time to the lives of our ancestors. In and around the townland of Aghowle, we are lucky to still have several such connections back to the lives of those who lived here many centuries ago.

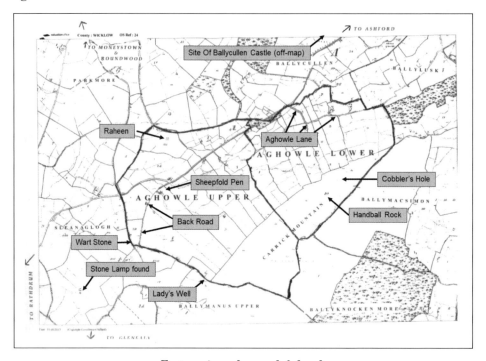

Features in and around Aghowle

In the features in and around Aghowle map the locations of physical and historical features related to Aghowle are shown. It also indicates the locations of the Back Road and Aghowle Lane, names which do not have any official existence, but are how those places have been known in Aghowle for centuries.

The Wart Stone

On the road south from Slanelough crossroads that heads towards Barnbawn and Glenealy, there is a granite stone known locally as The Wart Stone. This stone is located about ½ km from Slanelough crossroads on the left-hand side of the road where the boundary of Aghowle Upper meets the boundary of Slanelough. The large granite stone is set into the boundary ditch and contains a hollowed-out basin. While it is known locally as The Wart Stone, it is officially classified as a bullaun.

Bullaun stones come in a variety of shapes and sizes and are basins hollowed out in rock. They date back to at least the Bronze Age and some believe their existence may go back to even earlier times. Although their original use is still considered to be a bit of a mystery, in more recent times they have become associated with places of Christian worship like churches and Holy wells. The water that gathers in the bowl of these stones has often had holy or curative properties attributed to it.

They can be found dotted around Ireland and it has been noted that a high proportion of them are located in Co. Wicklow, especially in the areas near Glendalough. Judge Price, an historian who studied many of these Co. Wicklow bullauns, has speculated that the presence of these stones in the localities surrounding Glendalough could perhaps be connected to the boundary areas of the original monastic site, when it was believed to have extended to a much larger area than the current site [RAMPH/p.6].

The Wart Stone located at the boundary of the townlands of Aghowle and Slanelough

Judge Price noted that the bullaun stone at Slanelough does lie on the boundary line of the civil parishes of Derrylossary and Rathnew. This would have also corresponded to an outermost corner of the church parish of Glendalough. In the recent past some locals have speculated that perhaps this stone may have been used as a mass rock in Penal Times, but I do not know of any documented accounts to support this theory. There was reputed to have been a mass rock in the vicinity of Carrick but it is unlikely to have been this stone.

As children, hearing that the Wart Stone might have been where mass was celebrated in Penal times, my sisters and myself, decided to try and excavate behind the stone, in the belief we might uncover such amazing treasures as a silver or gold chalice, but of course the might of the solid lump of granite defeated our childish efforts and the perceived hidden treasure remained safe.

As trampled grass around the Wart Stone testifies, people still come to visit the stone and sometimes those with warts dip their hands in the water that collects in the basin (if there is any there at the time) in the hope of a cure.

My oldest sister Ann, recalls my father telling her that the water in the Wart Stone was considered to be holy water and that in times past, the local priest would bless the stone as he would ride by it on horseback. She also recalls hearing that the local people thought that as the stone used to be blessed by the local priest that perhaps the chalice used to say mass during penal times may have been hidden near the stone.

Raths and Fairy Forts - The Aghowle Raheen
Dotted throughout our Irish landscape are raths or ringforts. These are circular areas of hollowed out earth, reinforced by either stones or earth at the perimeter. It is thought that they probably date from the second half of the first millennium and there are several theories as to their use.

It is believed that they provided protection and shelter for people and livestock and that they were usually occupied by an important or prominent family in the community. It is also said that these enclosures may have been used to provide protection for livestock, especially during periods when raids and cattle stealing were rife.

Along with the practical explanation of their use, they are also associated with the fairies or little people in Irish folklore. It was commonly thought that the fairies lived in these ringforts and thus they were often called Fairy Forts. Because of this the local people treated them with great superstition and respect. In the past, local people would not have disturbed the fort itself or the earth around it or removed even a bough from the trees that grew there. To do so, would have upset the fairies and brought bad luck to yourself and your loved ones.

In more recent times, many people have overcome this superstition and while many of our forts or raths remain, quite a few have disappeared to make way for improved agricultural needs, new roads and commercial developments. However, in the townland of Aghowle, we are lucky to still have a rath.

When the ordnance survey men came through the locality to survey the area for their first maps, they were also charged with noting any remains of monuments, churches, graveyards, wells or other items of antiquity.

When Eugene Curry was surveying the local area in January 1839, [OSL/W/p.78] he noted that in the townland of Athghole (Aghowle) there was an ancient rath on the land of Garret Murrin and another little clump of stones on the south side of the glen near Matt Carey's house that was known locally as the Raheen.

The rath that Curry identified in his letters was marked on the first ordnance survey map in 1839 in the top field of what was then Garrett Murrin's (Moran's) farm. By 1854 when Griffith's land Valuation records were taken, this land belonged to Robert Moran and records show it changed hands several times during the following 60 years.

In 1914, Michael O'Brien and his family moved to live and farm in Aghowle and purchased the land surrounding the rath. This land then remained in the O'Brien family for over 70 years. During that time, the entire part of their farm that lay on the upper side of the Aghowle road became known as Brien's Raheen and the laneway that led to these fields was always referred to as the Raheen Lane, although within this section of their farm, each field also had its own individual name.

Of course, we will never know who originally occupied this fort or if it was used to shelter livestock and protect people and animals from local raids. But given its elevated situation on the brow of the hill, at the top of the valley, it would have had an excellent vantage over the surrounding countryside.

I am not aware of any superstitious stories relating to the little people who may have lived in this rath at Aghowle, but then the O'Brien family never disturbed or interfered with the rath. They did use it as a safe sheltered area in springtime during the lambing season and Miley O'Brien used to refer to it as *"the maternity ward"*. At one stage he kept an old van there, from which the seats had been removed and this was used as *"the labour unit"*. At evening time if he thought a vulnerable ewe was going to give birth during the night, he placed her in the van to protect her and her new lambs from bad weather and roaming foxes. As his flock prospered it would appear the "little people" were happy enough with the arrangement.

The rath and the surrounding land are now no longer in agricultural use, but is privately owned and planted with a commercial crop of trees. These trees have grown up around the rath and are now taller than the original trees that used to define its perimeter. It is therefore no longer easily visible on the landscape. Yet it still remains intact and is a reminder of habitation here over a millennium ago.

A section of the perimeter of the Aghowle Raheen still visible
underneath the planted trees.

Although in 1839, Eugene Curry also noted a little group of stones on the farm of Matt Carey in Aghowle Lower, which at the time was known locally as the Raheen, it would appear it was not thought significant enough to be marked by the Ordnance survey men on their map. I have checked with the farmers familiar with the land where Carey's farm would have been, but there does not appear to be any surviving visible remains or memory of these stones. The farm where they were noted in 1839 does appear again in this record of Aghowle's history, as the scene of the Carey family eviction in 1887 (see 1885-1899 Land Wars and Love Stories)

Irish Holy Wells - Lady's Well at Ballymanus Upper

It has been estimated that in the past there were probably in excess of 3,000 Holy wells throughout Ireland. While many of these have disappeared over time, some still remain throughout the country. Although they are now associated with the Christian religion, it appears their origins date back much further into our pagan past, when they were connected with Celtic spiritual beliefs.

After the arrival of Christianity to Ireland, these wells became part of Christian rituals. They are often found close to churches, abbeys, monasteries and graveyards - or at least to sites where once such religious connections existed. The Holy wells were usually dedicated to a saint, often with a local connection and as some healing properties were attributed to the water from these wells, it became common practice for local people to visit the well to pray and seek healing.

Usually, each well had its own Pattern (or Patron) Day. Visiting Holy wells took on a greater significance during Penal Law times as attending catholic churches was forbidden, so sometimes mass would be celebrated in secret at the Holy well.

In the past, the annual Pattern Day would have been a major event in the local parish with people from all around making their way to the site for ritual prayer. The Pattern Day was not always just about religious rites and prayers, but sometimes took the form of a day-long celebration, which is said to have included music, dancing, drinking and fighting.

This obviously did not meet with the approval of the leaders of the Catholic Church and in 1660 the synod of Tuam decreed that "*dancing, flute-playing, bands of music, riotous revels and other abuses in visiting wells and other holy places were forbidden.*" But it seems this fell on deaf ears and had little effect on those attending.

It is said that the decline in the tradition of the annual Pattern Day to the Holy well may be greatly attributed to the visitation of the great famine on our country. Also, in County Wicklow, it has been noted that in several cases the practice of gathering at the Holy well for the Pattern ceased in the year of 1798 when the county was in a state of unrest due to the Insurrection.

When I started my research into the history of the locality, I noted that on the first ordnance survey map drawn up in the late 1830s there was marked a well, known as Lady's Well, located in the townland of Ballymanus Upper, very close to where it forms a boundary line with the townland of Aghowle Upper. This location is now part of Coillte's planted forest, but given its proximity to our family farm where I grew up, I was surprised I had never heard of its existence from my father or the other elders of the community.

After finding that the map marked a well, I made inquiries from the older people still living around the locality, but no one had any recollection of a Holy well around Ballymanus Upper. Then, when researching through the Ordnance Survey letters written by the men charged with surveying this area of Wicklow [OSL/W/p.110], I found that Eugene Curry had noted on 24th January 1839, as he was surveying the Glenealy district, that there was a Holy well known as Lady's Well in the townland of Ballymanus Upper, at which a great Pattern was held annually on the 15th August down to the year 1798, after which it ceased. If pilgrimage to the well had ceased over two hundred years ago, this may help to explain why its existence had faded from the memory of the locality.

When I had first discovered the existence of the well on the Ordnance Survey map I had gone to the area of the forest where I thought it should be and could find no trace of it at all. Then about a year later, as if by magic, Lady's Well reappeared!

Lady's Well, Ballymanus Upper, in the early morning mist
Photograph courtesy of Séighean Ó Draoi

It seemed as if out of nowhere, the well was reopened, and the spot became marked with an official plaque containing the well's name and Pattern Day. A hawthorn bush had been planted, which would have been traditional at Holy wells. Soon the spot was further marked by visitors leaving coins and tying rags of cloth to the hawthorn bush. All this magic was brought about by the efforts of a small group of people based in the Wicklow and Dublin area who are endeavouring to preserve our ancient traditions and culture by marking the locations of Wicklow's Holy wells.

The people responsible for locating and re-establishing Lady's Well were: Rosaleen Durkin, Tom Hanrahen (RIP), Stephen Moss, Séighean Ó Draoi and Gearoid Ó Branagáin. Using the 1839 OSI map they located the remains of the original field boundaries and ditches around where the well had been and by water divining located the site of the well. Then on 15th August 2014 they visited the site of the well. Thus, after a gap of 216 years, the Pattern Day was re-established. Now each year, the August Pattern Day walk to Lady's Well has become a tradition again within the local community. Many of those who have attended in recent years belong to families whose ancestors have lived around here for many generations, so for some, they are following in the footsteps of their own ancestors who would have gathered at the well in centuries past.

As the Ordnance Survey letters noted that there was a great Pattern Day at this well up to 1798, one can imagine that on the morning of the 15th of August each year in times past, there would have been groups of people converging here from the local areas of Glenealy, Rathnew, Ashford, Rathdrum, Laragh, Moneystown and Roundwood. All gathering at the Well to pray, dance, listen to music, eat and drink and in the evening time they would have dispersed homewards again through the surrounding valleys and hills.

Plaque at Lady's Well, Ballymanus Upper
Photograph courtesy of Séighean Ó Draoi

Sheepfold at Aghowle Upper

On the Ordnance Survey 25-inch map (1897 – 1913) there is marked in one of the fields at Aghowle Upper, a small enclosure named as a sheep fold. This is another indication of the history of the farming community that lived here and the importance of sheep rearing in the area. A sheep fold is a circular enclosure or pen, used to hold sheep. They were usually built of dry stone and found in open ground, often on hillsides.

This sheepfold at Aghowle Upper was marked on the map a little way down from Carrick, in a field near the by-road (locally known as the Back Road), that leads out near the Wart Stone. At the time when this Ordnance Survey was carried out, the farmers of the area would have held grazing rights on Carrick and I expect all their sheep would have grazed together during the summer months on the mountain. Then at various times during the year, such as shearing or dipping time, the sheep would have had to be gathered together and each farmer separate out his own flock. So perhaps this might be a possible reason for the location of the sheep fold here. If sheep from the mountain were enclosed in the pen, then each farmer could identify his own marked sheep, separate them out and bring them home.

Stone sheep pen overlooking the Cloghoge Brook, Co. Wicklow
This sheep pen is similar to the one that existed at Aghowle Upper
Photograph courtesy of Christiaan Corlett

The field where the sheep fold is located on the map became part of the lands bought for tree planting by the Ministry of Lands in the 1930s. While no remains of the fold are visible today, I do recall back in the 1960s when as children we played in this area of the woods, there was still a partial circle of granite stones remaining at the base of the trees. The location of these stones would have corresponded to the location of the sheepfold on the OSI map.

A Local Castle at Ballycullen

When Eugene Curry was surveying this locality around mid-January 1839 after he had made detailed notes on the graveyard and ruined church at near-by Killfea, he went on to record that in the townland of Ballycullen he was shown pillars of the gateway that had led to Colonel O Toole's castle, but that the castle was now gone, the last portion of its walls had been levelled within the previous 10 years [OSL/W/p.78].

In Billy Smith's recollections on the history of the local area, he gives some further references to this castle at Ballycullen, which was known in more recent times as Pluck's Walls - see section "Billy Smith Reflects on Local History".

In the Ashford and District Historical Journal, published in 1993, there is also a reference to a building here as follows:

> *A few Antiquarian Notes*
> *"Squire Toole's house in Ballycullen". Traces of an old building on what was known as Pluck's field, on the left hand of the lane leading from road to Aghowle. This man was one of the O'Toole clan whose land became part of the Powerscourt property in the 16th century. The house is marked on Neville's map of County Wicklow 1755*

By kind permission of Sheila Clarke and the Ashford Historical Society

A Stone lamp at Sleanaglogh/Slanelough

Another local link to the past is a stone lamp that was handed into the National Museum of Ireland in 1930. This lamp was taken out of a wall in a farm at Slanelough, close by the boundary with Aghowle Upper. At the time, a family by the name of Bradshaw were living there. The Bradshaws had only recently come to live there, the farm having previously been owned by the Fannings of Slanelough who had lived there for about a century. This farm is also quite close to where the bullaun stone known as the Wart Stone is located.

• The following is from the notebooks of Judge Price, where he reprints an article from the Irish Times in 1930, which gives details regarding the stone lamp found at Slaeneglogh, which was the old spelling for Slanelough.

Extract from the Irish Times, 27th December 1930
IRISH Antiquities
Mediaeval Stone Lamp for Museum.
Dr. A. Mahr, Keeper of Irish Antiquities, announces that the Irish Antiquities Division of the National Museum, has obtained a very interesting antiquity in an early mediaeval stone lamp of unusual size, of the type which sometimes was supposed to be a cup (chalice) or the like. This valuable object was pulled out of an old wall in Sleanaglogh, Co. Wicklow and has been deposited by D. O'Dubhghaill …Dublin, to whom the Museum already had been indebted for several other additions [TPN/p.74].

Liam Price also made several entries in his notebooks about the bullaun stone at Sleanaglogh (Slanelough), in one such entry he recorded:

Sleanaglogh.
The Bullaun stone is locally called "the Wart Stone". If a person washes his hands in it, it cures his warts. The old woman who lives in the house nearest to it (about 200yds SW of the stone) told me this, she also said that people had told her that it had something to do with a church in the old days: but she said she never heard of there being a church there. Bradshaw's house where the lamp was found is the next house to the SW about 500yds from the stone.

The old woman Price referred to would have been one of the elderly Loughlin sisters, who used to live in the farmhouse nearest the Wart Stone. Both Michael Graham of Moneystown and Brendan Byrne of Garryduff recall the Loughlin family still living in this house during the 1930s. The Loughlins had lived here from at least the early decades of the 19th century. Price recorded that the woman had been told that the bullaun stone had something to do with a church in the old times, but it would seem there was no knowledge of any church there in the Loughlin's time living in the area, so if it had existed, it would have been sometime further back in the past.

One wonders if there could be any connection with Price's speculation that the bullaun stone at Slanelough might have been connected to the original outer boundaries of Glendalough's monastic settlement, the reference to a possible church associated with the stone and the finding nearby of a medieval stone lamp?

Carrick Mountain - A Presence on the Landscape

Throughout this book there will be many references to Carrick, or Carrick Mountain, referring to the clump of granite rocks at the top of the hillside on the south-east side of the valley.

Around 1930, the Ministry of Lands with responsibility for state forestry purchased a portion of the farm land in Aghowle which led up to the base of Carrick Mountain. As the trees that were planted grew up around the mountain, it became only partially visible and in time one might almost pass through the townland without noticing it. Recently, as this section of the forest has reached maturity, the felling of some of those trees on the slopes beneath the rocks, has brought the mountainside back into view again. Its reappearance serves as a reminder that in the past it was a focal point on the landscape and very much part of the everyday life of the local community.

Those for whom the word mountain conjures up an image of high snow-capped alpine peaks, or even our own County Wicklow's impressive Lugnaquilla, could be forgiven for scoffing at the grandiose term of Carrick Mountain. Technically, Carrick is marked on the map as 1,250ft, or 381 metres, hence just about makes it into the official height requirement to be classified as such, but among the locals it has always been referred to as Carrick Mountain. In fact, according to some local folklore sources there is a story that some of the local people built a cairn on top of the highest peak so that it could reach the required height to be classified as a mountain.

It should also be noted that when observing Carrick Mountain from Aghowle, you are already standing at a height of something around 200m, hence Carrick only seems half as high as its actual height above sea level.

When Eugene Curry of the Ordnance Survey team was surveying the area in January 1839, the mountain without its present cloak of trees surrounding it, would have appeared more impressive than today and he noted the following:

> *"A stupendous rocky peak at the east brow of the hill that separates the parishes of Rathnew and Glenealy on the west"* [OSL/W/p.78]

View from the Aghowle Valley towards Carrick Mountain,
which is currently partially obscured by the Coillte forestry plantation.

He noted that some people call this Carrick Mac Reilly and that it was also
known as Carrick Mac Roille and Carrick Moroille, while the western part
of the mountain is known by its Irish name of Sliabh na gCloch, meaning
the rocky mountain.

Almost a hundred years later, Judge Liam Price recorded the following
in his note book, relating to a possible burial cairn on the mountain:

> *We went up Carrick Mountain from the deserted farmhouse which is in the*
> *neighbourhood of where Lady's Well must have been – and A. Farrington*
> *showed me where the ruined cairn is. It is on the peak which is on the*
> *boundary between Aghowle Upper, Ballymanus Upper and Ballyknocken*
> *More – at the angle. This is the boundary between Killiskey and Glenealy*
> *parishes. The peak is about ¼ mile south of the highest peak marked 1252ft*
> *on the map. This peak is very little lower. The cairn is almost entirely ruined*
> *and in fact might not be noticed, but the stones as Farrington pointed out*
> *could not be there naturally as all the peaks are naturally scraped clean by*
> *glacial action. The ruin of the cairn is about 12yds in diameter, approximately*
> *circular: it appears to be of 2 to 3ft in depth.*
> *This looks like a ruined burial cairn: but any human or pottery remains*
> *must have disappeared long ago, completely disintegrated by moisture and*
> *air [TPN/p.281].*

I am aware that in recent years, several people have gone in search of this burial cairn and followed Judge Price's directions, but have been unable to locate it.

Carrick Local Folklore

The presence of Carrick Mountain on the landscape also seems to have influenced the folklore of the area, as can be seen from the following two pieces submitted to the Ashford and District Historical Journal in 1991:

The Giant Jack Stones

There was once a giant who lived in a cave up in Carrick. Every day he worked his fingers to the bone to get some money to pay his debts. Now he had a wife who liked to play Jack Stones (this is a type of bowling). She played it all day long. The poor man's dinner was never ready and he had to make it himself after a hard day's work. One day, he couldn't keep his anger in. He walked over to the wife and shook her. The stones and rocks fell out of her hands. They fell all the way down the hill. And that is why there are so many rocks at the bottom of Carrick.
Esther Doyle (11)
Drumdangan, Glenealy

Cobbler's Rock

Once upon a time there was a beautiful lady who lived in Glenealy near Carrick Mountain. One day a cobbler from the village asked for her hand in marriage. When she refused, he left the village to live in a cave, now called "Cobblers Cave". As time went by he lost his mind and instead of mending people's shoes, he mended the shoes of the fairies. He lived among them for many years and when he died they mourned for many days. It is said if you go up to Cobblers Rock at night you can hear his hammer tapping against a Fairy shoe and the cry of the Fairy Folk.
Tara Dignam (11)
Mullawn
Ballymanus
Glenealy

Reproduced by kind permission of Sheila Clarke and the Ashford Historical Society

Dinny's Cave / The Cobbler's Hole

In the story of Dinny Byrne's escape from the yeomen in 1798, it is recounted that he hid in a cave in the rocks on Carrick Mountain. This cave is also referred to in Larry O'Brien's ballad of Dinny Byrne and is also mentioned in Billy Smith's recollections of the local area. In my childhood I recall the older people of the area referring to Dinny's Cave on Carrick and they also spoke about the Cobbler's Rock. It would appear to me that these two places are in the same location.

There is also a reference to the Cobbler's Hole in the Schools' Collection (1937-39) of the National Folklore Collection. In a copybook submitted from the Glenealy and Ballylusk school the following is recorded:

> *The Cobbler's Hole*
> *This place is in the peak of Carrickmacreilly at the north end of the hill and is said to have been occupied by a cobbler about one hundred years ago. Part of the cave fell in about fifteen years ago* [NFC/SC/GS].

Carrickmacreilly was an old name for Carrick Mountain, but still seems to have been in use in the Glenealy area at that time.

In the same copybook entry, the pupil had also recorded a piece about the Handball Rock:

> *At the back of Carrickmacreilly is a long and excellent natural Ball Alley in olden times players came from all over the country to play matches there, it is yet fit for playing, it is a splendid cliff.*

Eric Bradshaw, who was born in Aghowle Lower, House No. 4, recounted to me in June 2017 his memories of The Cobbler's Hole. The Bradshaw's farmland stretched up to the foot of Carrick and as a child in the 1950s Eric would have had to go up onto the mountain in search of sheep that would have strayed from their farm. He recalled seeing the entrance to the Cobbler's Hole, but he was reluctant to venture into the dark interior. He remembers the older local people telling him that a cobbler had lived and worked there in times past and that the people of the area would drop in their boots to the cobbler as they walked over the mountain on their way to Glenealy village. Then by the time they were returning over Carrick the cobbler would have their boots mended and ready for collection.

Carrick is now mainly used for leisure pursuits and has gained an international reputation as a location for mountain biking, but in the past, it would have been the scene of much more everyday activities. Sheep and goats grazed on its slopes up until the early decades of the 1900s and the local farming community used it as a short cut to the village of Glenealy to do their shopping, attend mass, or to catch the train at Glenealy station. I have been told that up to the 1930s, it was a great place for social gatherings on a Sunday afternoon, when the younger generation of the area would make their way up the hillside and many a romance is said to have blossomed there.

Gathering on the rocks at Carrick, c. late 1920s
Back L-R: Kate Horan? Liz O'Reilly (Aghowle), Cis Giffney,
Front: Molly O'Reilly (Aghowle)

The Handball Rock at Carrick

In my gathering of the local history I had heard stories of a smooth rock face, on the Aghowle side of the hill that functioned as a handball alley, with challenge matches between the lads from the Aghowle and Ballycullen side playing against the men from the Glenealy side of the mountain. Most of the people now still living in the area were a little vague as to the exact location of this handball rock. But in the springtime of 2016, as the forestry workers began to fell the mature trees on the slopes beneath Carrick, what should come back into view but the rock face that was known as the Handball Alley.

The rock face is a tall smooth surface, and while the ground in front is now covered with the remains of trees and branches, it can still be clearly identified where the base of the handball alley would have been. There is evidence that efforts were made to create and define a flat stone base beneath the rock. Also visible is evidence that the handball players had patched holes in the rock face with small stones to prevent the handball becoming lodged.

A stone patch on the face of the Handball Rock on Carrick Mountain.
Photograph courtesy of Séighean Ó Draoi

There is a photograph of the handball rock in the colour section of this book.

Carrick and the Weather
Carrick was also a trusted weather forecaster for the local community and the carrying out of many a farming activity was dictated by observing the colour of the sky above the mountain and the formation of the clouds as they were passing over it. If the sound of the train carried over the hillside from Glenealy as it was passing through Kilcommon then rain was due and it would not be the day to go mowing the meadow. When it did rain, the way the mist or fog formed on the top of Carrick, would be observed

by the local people to tell them if it was just a passing shower or "*it was down for the day*".

It would appear that the people on the Glenealy side of the hill would also have observed the clouds over Carrick as a means of weather forecasting, as Liam Price recorded in his note book [TPN/p.378] that a man from Ballymacsimon knew the following rhyme:

> "*When Carrigmareena wears a black cap,*
> *Coolnakilly may look out for that*"
> (meaning rain)

Chapter 2:

The Townland of Aghowle in the 17th and 18th Centuries

It is difficult to say when the area of land lying in the valley on the North-West side of Carrick Mountain became known as the townland of Aghowle, but it is thought that in Ireland the defining of specific areas of land into divisions known as townlands began sometime before the Norman Invasion. But in many cases the actual recording and mapping of these townlands did not take place until the 17th century.

The name Aghowle is from the Irish *Achadh abhall* meaning the field (or place) of the apple tree. We don't know when the area actually got this name, but it perhaps implies that sometime in the distant past, the slopes beneath Carrick Mountain were once covered in apple trees.

Like many other Irish townlands, it has been written in records down through the years with a wide range of different spellings. From the early 20th century, it seems to have settled on the current spelling. But I did notice in my research, that some of the local families that had long established connections here, still favoured the older form of spelling, *Aghoule*, even up until the mid-20th century and in some cases, that is what is recorded on their headstones.

Aghowle on the Map

The first comprehensive land survey and mapping of Ireland was carried out in the 1650s under William Petty. The method used to survey the land throughout the country was by laying down chains and thus it became known as the Down Survey. On the Down map the townland of Aghowle is clearly marked and named as Aughole.

Aghowle Tax Payers - Home is where the Hearth is

Another official record of Aghowle's existence during the 17th century is a tax record, known as The Hearth Money Rolls. This method of taxation could be compared to the current Property Tax, in that a household was required to pay a twice-yearly tax levelled on the standard of their dwelling house, which was defined by the presence of a fireplace - hence it became known as the Hearth Tax.

For assessing the amount of tax due it was noted if a house had a hearth but no chimney, a hearth with a chimney, or more than one hearth. The householder was taxed accordingly. The surviving tax records for 1669 show that the townland of Aghowle, spelt as *Aghoole* at that time, had 9 houses liable for the Hearth Tax [NAI/HMR]. All these houses were under the classification of one fireplace with a chimney. The nine householders were named as:

James Byrne	Roger Moore	Adam Welsh
Own Byrne	James Callaghan	Richard Mainwaring
John Byrne	Bryan Cullen	Edm. Purcell

This would indicate that in the mid-17th century there was a well-established community in the townland and these houses with a chimney and hearth would probably have belonged to people who were farming here.

Certain dwellings would have been exempt from the tax e.g. if they were very basic and of little valuation or if the inhabitants were very poor and in receipt of alms. It is likely that there would have been more than just these 9 recorded houses there at the time - many of the small land holders and the labouring classes would have existed in tiny makeshift dwellings with no formal fireplace and hence would not have been recorded on the Hearth Money Rolls.

In later land records from the 19th and 20th centuries, the number of houses in the neighbouring townland of Ballycullen was usually greater than the number of dwellings in Aghowle. But at this time, it appears that there were only two households in Ballycullen liable for tax, namely Col. Toole and Teig Kennan. The dwelling held by Col. Toole may have been Ballycullen Castle, as it is said to have belonged to a Colonel O'Toole.

A Gift for Cromwell's Man
By the second half of the 17th century, much of the land in Ireland was held by protestant landlords. I do not know who held the lands at Aghowle at the start of the 17th century, but there is a record of its ownership by the middle of the century, when it was held by the Wingfield family of Powerscourt in Enniskerry.

Records for Powerscourt Estate show that after Cromwell invaded

Ireland, 1649-1653, that he took 7 outlying townlands from Sir Edward Wingfield of Enniskerry and granted them to one of his officers, Sir Charles Meredith, as payment for his services. Two of the 7 townlands given were Aghowle and Ballycullen.

A document in the Powerscourt Estate papers (held in the National Library of Ireland) show that on the 2nd July 1680, King Charles II, took back the 7 townlands from Sir Charles Meredith and granted them back to the Wingfield family [NLI/EP/P/Ms 41,997/2].

> *Ms 41,997 /2*
> *Conveyance of lands of Ballynillon, [Ballycullen] Aghole, [Aghowle]*
> *Kilcoyne, Ballygaughan, Ballaghn, Castlemcadam and Knocknota,*
> *county Wicklow by Sir Charles Meredith to Folliott, 1st Viscount (2nd*
> *creation). Lands had previously been held by Sir Edward Wingfield,*
> *(grandfather of Folliott) and were conveyed by order of Letters Patent*
> *of Charles II; 1 membrane [in secretary hand] 2 July 1680*

At this time, the Wingfield family of Powerscourt Estate in Enniskerry owned considerable lands in Co. Wicklow, mostly based in and around the Enniskerry area but they also held some lands in other outlying areas in the county. It would appear that they chose to lease on some of those outlying parcels of lands to smaller landlords, who would then sub-let individual holdings to tenant farmers.

A lease also held in the National Library of Ireland records that on 17th Day of February 1698 Edward Wingfield of Powerscourt Estate, leased the lands of the townlands of Ballycullen and Aghowle to a person named Francis Toole [NLI/Ms/43,005/1].

This lease contains the following information:

> *Aghowle Upper, 488 acres, valued at £150 - 10 shillings*
> *Aghowle Lower, 325 acres, valued at £109 - 5 shillings*
> *Ballycullen, 1,237 acres valued at £505.- 5 shillings*

The lease gives a very detailed description outlining the Wingfield's ownership of all the lands, dwellings, mountain, mineral rights etc. within the two townlands.

Landlord and Tenant in the 18th Century

There are not many surviving records from this period to give us a window into life in the valley around this time. Deeds held in the Land Registry office in Dublin show that while the lands of Aghowle and Ballycullen remained in the ownership of the Wingfield family of Powerscourt Estate, the name of the intermediate landlord changed quite a few times during this century. This would have led to a difficult situation for the small tenant farmers of Aghowle, as they were at the mercy of their landlord and in most cases their lease was renewable from year to year. They lived with the daily struggle of trying to provide for their family and meet their yearly rent - or face the prospect of eviction onto the roadside. One imagines that each time there was a change of landlord for the tenants, there would follow a period of uncertainty and vulnerability as they waited to see what rent and conditions their new landlord would impose.

One record I did find relating to the landownership at Aghowle during this period was the following notice that appeared in Saunders' News-Letter, dated 20 November 1775:

> *To be sold, for payment of the debts of the late Laurence Toole of Wicklow, Esq: the lands of Ballycullen and Aghoule, being a lease for a long term of years, whereof 143 years are yet unexpired, subject to the yearly rent of 50l. now let to solvent tenants at above 320l. yearly profit rent:*

The notice went on to state that the lands at nearby Ballymaghroe, which was a fee-farm lease, was also offered for sale and noted that the tenants there held 31-year leases, and many were due to expire shortly, "*and the lands will then rise considerably*".

A Glimpse of Life in the County during the 18th Century

A number of surveys were carried out in Ireland in the 18th century. These surveys looked at distribution of the different religions throughout the country as well as looking at the general economics of the individual counties.

Three of these surviving surveys for Co. Wicklow are detailed in an article by Brian Gurrin in Analecta Hibernica No. 39 (2006) published by the Irish Manuscripts Commission. The article is entitled: *Three eighteenth-century surveys of County Wicklow*. If one looks at the information collected from these surveys, relating to the landscape, economics and farming practices in Co. Wicklow around 1740, we can get some idea of everyday life for the farming community here at that time. The survey makes a distinction between farming in Wicklow's lowlands and farming in its hills. The area around Aghowle could be seen as sitting on the borderline for these two areas. The following information is transcribed directly from this publication:

> *The near neighbourhood of the metropolis gives the country man an*

easie opportunity to convey thither ye product of his farm. Wicklow veil, bacon and ale are noted for their goodness and so is their butter and cheese, the effect of cleanliness. Wheat do's well on the lowlands & rye affords a great crop on ye sides of the hills. The latter is the bread of the common people.

Forest and fruit trees thrive well here, and evergreens seem natural to the soil. The arbutus and myrtle shew to great advantage in some places & the product of hops & orchards are encouraging to the young planters in others.

The linen manufacture has begun to take root and already thrives. Flax do's well & spinning wheels and looms are in motion.

There is not any limestone in the whole country, but marle lately found in good plenty by the sea gives the husbandman a good fund of manure. Bees answer well & yield good quantities of honey

From a separate section:

About 4 miles east of Glen da lough is Roundwood, on the great road between Rathdrum and Dublin. The country about this is rough and course (and) lies high and expos'd and is not very fruitful. Yet(it) produces good rey (rye), potatoes & oats and by enclosures & good husbandry of the farmer, it is daily improveing. The bulk of the labourer and inferior people are Papists, who are numerous here and in the neighbouring mountains.

Local Family Records from the 18th Century

While the above surveys give us some idea of the type of farming carried out in rural Wicklow at that time, I was curious to find if there was any information on the actual families that were living and farming here in the 18th century. But as the state registration of births, marriages and deaths, did not commence in Ireland until 1864, the only possible records we would have of these family events are in the surviving registers of the church records.

In many cases the surviving catholic parish records do not go back much further than the state records and those that do go back as far as the start of the 19th century usually did not record the townland in the parish that the family resided in, thus making it difficult to identify individual families with common surnames.

In general, the surviving Church of Ireland records often date back a little further than the Catholic records and sometimes did contain more information on location.

The townland of Aghowle lies in the Church of Ireland parish of Killiskey, whose surviving records commence in 1819, while the local Roman Catholic parish for the townland was the parish of Wicklow town until 1864, when Ashford got individual parish status.

I was delighted to discover that the Catholic parish of Wicklow has surviving records for an eight-year period covering 1747 to 1754 and then from 1776 onwards for baptisms and 1797 onwards for marriages [NLI/ PR/W].

I am greatly admiring of the local priest from that time who, in the mid-1700s and in the shadow of the Penal Laws, not only diligently recorded in the church register the baptisms and marriages he performed, but also in many cases he recorded the townland the family lived in. This was exceptional, as in most catholic registers the practice of recording actual addresses did not come into general practice for about another 100 years. He somehow also managed to keep the registers safe for future generations, for which I am grateful.

Searching through these records for the period 1747-1754, I could see that in the little farmhouses and cabins of Aghowle and Ballycullen, family life was busy with couples marrying and babies being born.

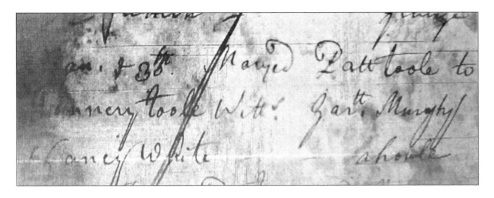

1753 - Jan 30th Maryed Patt Toole to Honery Toole
Witt. Garth Murphy, Nancy White, Ahoule
Copy of entry from the register of the Roman Catholic parish of Wicklow
By kind permission of the National Library of Ireland

Some of the family names recorded, such as Toole and Byrne, match those recorded living here a century earlier in the Hearth Money Rolls and other family names appearing in the register can be traced forward through the next two centuries to families still living here in the mid-20th century.

Some examples of Aghowle families recorded in the church registers were:

- In the marriage register, Pat Toole of Aghowle (then spelt as Ahoule) married Honor Toole in January of 1753.

- The baptism register shows that Silvester Byrne and his wife Catherine of Aghowle had three children baptised, Garrett in 1749, Bridget 1751 and Edward 1754. Luke Byrne and his wife Mary baptised their daughter Nelly in 1750.

- Another Aghowle family to appear in the baptism register is the Moran family. Simon Moran and his wife Rose have two children baptised, Mary in 1749 and Darby in 1753. As will be seen in the land records for the first half of the 19th century, the Moran families would remain established in the townland and are by the 1830s leasing a considerable number of farms in the townland.

Looking through the parish register for the 7-year period 1747-1754, I found baptism records for 20 individual families in the townland, with the Byrne surname the most common family name. At the time the priest did not record the mother's maiden name, so the following are the names of the 20 fathers that appear in the baptism register between 1747 and 1754:

James Byrne	William Byrne	Pat McGrath	Murtagh Murphy
Luke Byrne	? Doyle	Reddy Monohan	Garrett Murphy
Maurice Byrne	George Crohill (possibly Croughil)	Hugh Mourn (Moran)	Pat Toole
Silvester Byrne	Daniel Farrell	Simon Mourn (Moran)	Thomas Tourney
Simon Byrne	Laurence Kere	James Murphy	Larry Tyre

From these parish records, one could presume that there were probably more than these 20 families living in the townland of Aghowle in the mid-18th century. It is unlikely that every Catholic family living in the townland had a child baptised in this 7-year period and some entries did not identify the family's address. Also, these records do not include any Church of Ireland families that may have been living here at that time.

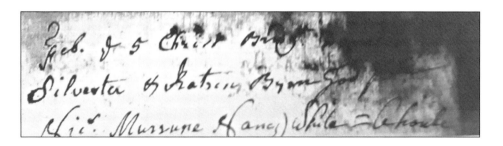

1751 – Feb 05 Christ. Bridget daughter to Silvester & Katrin Byrn God ___?
Nic.Murrune & Nancy White – Ahoule
Copy of entry from the register of the Roman Catholic parish of Wicklow
By kind permission of the National Library of Ireland

The next surviving baptism register starts in 1776 and looking at the first few years of these records, I find that it is the families in Ballycullen, more so than Aghowle, that are now busy bringing new lives into the parish.

It was with sadness I noted the following baptismal records for three baby boys born in Ballycullen between 1776 and 1778:

> *Mathew Cullen – baptised July 1776*
> *Thomas Doyle – baptised May 1778 (Thomas's godfather was recorded as*
>   *Gregory Cunniam)*
> *Maurice Cran (Crean?) – baptised July 1778*

In just over two decades, these three boys' names will appear again in our local history. They were part of a group of Ballycullen men shot dead (on the word of an informer) by Yeomen during the 1798 rebellion. Thomas Doyle's godfather, Gregory Cunniam, is recorded as having his premises burned down and another member of Mr Cunniam's family was tortured and killed.

Who Fears to Speak Of '98?

In 1791, the Society of United Irishmen was formed with the aim of uniting Irish people of different religious persuasion to campaign for greater economic and political independence from Britain.

Within a few years, the government became very concerned about this new movement and set about establishing Infantry and Calvary forces drawn from people within the local community, to try and suppress the United Irishmen organisation. The membership of the United Irishmen in Co. Wicklow was said to be the strongest rebel force in Leinster and the British government became very concerned about the situation in the county. Given its proximity to Dublin, they feared the Wicklow rebels might launch an attack on the capital.

Towards the end of 1797 the government launched a severe campaign to suppress the United Irishmen. To help the local Yeomen forces in Wicklow, militia units from other counties including Antrim and North Cork were drafted in and by April 1798 these forces were carrying out a widespread campaign of torture, house burnings, floggings and executions throughout the county. The following month saw an all-out rebellion throughout the country. The major battles and massacres from this period were well recorded and documented, but many of the small incidents throughout the countryside did not make the major headlines. However, in one publication titled Insurgent Wicklow 1798: *The Story as Written by REV.BRO. LUKE CULLEN O.D.C. (1793-1859)*, we get details of many such incidents that took place throughout County Wicklow. Brother Luke Cullen gathered these accounts from local Wicklow people in the decades after the Rebellion, while they were still within their living memory.

1798 -Murders at Ballycullen and Aghowle

Insurgent Wicklow 1798 describes many atrocities that took place in Wicklow in local areas such as Newtownmountkennedy and around Killiskey. I was quite surprised to find that the townlands of Aghowle and Ballycullen also featured as places where torture, house burnings and murders had taken place at the hands of the Yeomen.

The following is a transcript from chapter four:

> *In the latter end of May '98 a party of Wicklow local cavalry burned down the premises of Gregory Conyam(Cunniam), a farmer of Ballycullen (Ballincullen, S.W. of Rathnew). On their return, they met a man named Wn. Conyam of the same place. They hanged him (that is, they half hanged him, a term well known then, for half hanging and flogging generally succeeded each other) and burned straw under him to extract a confession and shot down his throat. (This Ballycullen is near Glanely and those men were of the same family of Mr. Danl. Conyam that Capt. Sir Charles Coote's division roasted to death on the bridge of the latter place in 1641.*
>
> *Hugh Magrath of the same place gave information on the following men in June, '98 James Murphy, Thos Doyle, Matthew Cullen, Maurice Crane and Patrick Magrath, brother of the informer, all of Ballycullen. They were shot at their own places.*

McDonnel McKitt of Munduff (near Ashford): his whole premises burned in May '98: himself transported for 14 years. Luke Kelly of Ballinlea on the same day; his premises were burned. This was near Eccles of Cronroe. Wn. Pluck of Ballycullen; his place entirely burned and himself most barbarously used. (T.C.D. Mss)

Also in chapter 4 is the following account of what happened in Aghowle in December of 1798

A man named Harry Hetherington gave information to the Wicklow cavalry in Dec. '98 that some men who had lately returned home from the mountains had formed a place of retreat in a large turf clamp at the residence of Wm. Murphy of Aghole (S. Of Ballycullen). To that place a party of the Wicklow Corps rode under the command of one of the Revels of Seapark and one of the Wrights of Dunganstown to the above place where they found Wm. Murphy and three sons– John, Patrick and David; the latter was an idiot. They met with him first and discharged some shots at him. He escaped their fire and ran to his mother for protection. She clasped her arms about him thinking that her maternal solicitude would protect him from their fury. But no, they clove open his head awhile in her arms. The shock to her intellect was terrific. She lost her reason that instant and exhibited her want of reason in the collection of the brains of her idiot son awhilst her husband and other sons were being butchered by her side.

The turf clamp was now assiled and Murtagh Doyle, Wm. Coffey, John Byrne, Garret Byrne and Garrett Vesty Byrne nine in all; after shooting them, they set fire to the clamp of turf, the house and every particle about the place.

Also recorded is a list of chapels that were burnt down during this time, including Ashford Chapel which was burnt on 25th Jan. 1799 and Glenealy chapel which was burnt in Feb. 1799.

In the following transcript from chapter 5 there is a description of some executions that took place in the town of Rathdrum, including another reference to a resident of Aghowle;

About the same time a batch of men were brought up to the Fairgreen of the same town and shot. One of them named Murphy either from

This church at Ashford was built around 1812
to replace the church which was burnt down in 1799

Ballycullen or Aghole not, immediately complying with the order to
kneel down on his coffin (for they were honored in this instance; there
were shells brought to the place of execution to place the bodies in. This
order was from the commanding officer there). He was ordered with
a stern and peremptory voice to kneel down. On such occasions the
loyalists all thought they had a right to command and several voices
cried out, "Kneel down on your coffin". He gave a look of indignation
around him, leaped on the slight shell and drove the lid down to the
bottom and firmly stood for their fire. (T.C.D. Mss)

A footnote appears at the bottom of the page, regarding the above account, stating that the man named Murphy who refused to kneel on his coffin, may have been from Trooperstown and not Aghowle.

These accounts tell us that this period must have been a horrific time for the families who were living in Aghowle and Ballycullen during 1798.

I have been unable to definitively identify the location of William Murphy's house in Aghowle where the nine people were murdered in December 1798, as there were not maps that identified the location of dwellings in this area until the 19th century. The local church records from the mid-18th century identify that there were at least three Murphy families living in Aghowle at that time. The Glanmore tenant records taken in 1832 do not show any Murphy families remaining in the townland by that time [NLI/Mss11996-11997].

However, in June 2017 I was given a piece of oral local history that might have some connection to these murders. Eric Bradshaw who grew up in house no. 4 at Aghowle Lower in the 1950s, gave me the following information. The Bradshaw's farmland ran from their farmhouse up to the foot of Carrick Mountain. On their farm there was a laneway that ran about halfway up towards the mountain and then stopped. The laneway was not used on the farm and Eric was always told that five men had been shot on this laneway. On the 1839 OSI map the laneway is shown and also a dwelling at the Carrick end of the lane. In the Griffith's Valuation land records for this farm in 1854 this dwelling is not recorded or included for valuation, which would indicate it was not inhabited at that time. One wonders if the local memory that five men were shot on that laneway might correspond to the shooting of the 5 men in the turf clamp in December 1798?

The above account states that the men who were hiding in the turf clamp had lately returned home from the mountains - it is assumed that they all were men from the locality. Three of the men have the surname Byrne, which was of course very common in this area of Co. Wicklow - the church records show there were at least 6 Byrne families living in Aghowle around 1750. One of the other men was named Doyle, again a common name in this part of Co. Wicklow. The fifth man in the turf clamp was William Coffey, this was a less common name, but church records show there was a family of this name living in the townland of Ballymacsimon, which is just the other side of Carrick Mountain. This Coffey family is recorded as living in Ballymacsimon in the latter half of the 18th century and there is an entry for a William Coffey of that townland baptized in 1752. There is also an entry in the church records for a James Coffey of Aghowle baptized in 1772 [NLI/PR/W]. As Aghowle and Ballymacsimon are very close to one another, it is likely that the Coffey family in Aghowle were connected to the Ballymacsimon family.

In Ballycullen the Cunniam family, who had their place burnt and also a member of the family tortured and murdered, were a long-established family in the community with connections back to Cromwell's time. As mentioned above, a member of this family was murdered by Cromwell's men, on the bridge in Glenealy in 1641. Descendants of the Cunniam family

Laneway at Aghowle Lower heading towards Carrick Mountain.
Eric Bradshaw recalls from his childhood that it was said that 5 men had been shot on this laneway.

remained farming in Ballycullen well into the twentieth century. The last member of this family, also named Greg Cunniam, is still well remembered by many of the local people. He features in Billy Smith's reflections – see "Billy Smith Reflects on People and Places around Ballycullen".

The other home in Ballycullen that was burnt belonged to the Pluck family. The remains of the castle at Ballycullen were known as Pluck's Walls, but I don't know if the home that was burnt was connected to this location. Around this time there were several Pluck families living in the surrounding townlands. The above account of the Aghowle murders states that 9 men in all were murdered and Mr. Pluck and some friends had them interred. But it is not known if it was the Ballycullen Plucks, or one of the other Pluck families in the area that organized the burial of the men. Nor is it known where they were buried.

Of the five men named who were shot at their homes in Ballycullen, I found baptismal records in the local parish register for Mathew Cullen, Thomas Doyle and Maurice Crean, all in their early twenties at the time of their deaths. I did not find records for James Murphy or Patrick Magrath, but both family surnames do appear in the register in the later years of the 18th century.

The above accounts describe harrowing and cruel acts of violence against the local United Irishmen and their supporters, but of course there were two sides to the conflict. The local militia and the law-abiding citizens that they were trying to protect also suffered at the hands of the rebels. In his book The Rebellion in Wicklow 1798, Ruan O'Donnell records that from mid-July 1798, the execution of Loyalist prisoners became common in Wicklow as veterans of the Wexford campaign returned home to Wicklow. He gives an account of the cold-blooded killing of three men in woods belonging to Mr. Acton, near Clara Bridge. Two of the men Joseph Ellison and John Bolton were wood rangers and lived locally.

In the old graveyard in Glenealy there is a headstone for Thomas Hodgins of the Wicklow Cavalry who was shot on 02nd of September 1798 as he was ascending Glenealy Hill. Thomas was from Dunganstown and was a member of the same cavalry that rode to the Murphy home in Aghowle. Two of the commanding men mentioned in Luke Cullen's account of the incident were also from the Dunganstown area, and would have been neighbours of Thomas Hodgins. One imagines they would not be very sympathetic to a group of rebels who were hiding out a few miles from where Thomas Hodgins was shot.

Where the Divil Ate the Tinker – Dinny Byrne's Great Escape
In the light of such horrific events in the locality, it is perhaps easy to see how the story of the rebel Dinny Byrne, who managed to outwit the Yeomen in the townland of Aghowle, became part of the local folk history

and how two centuries later the phrase "*where the Divil ate the Tinker*" was still being recited with a sense of pride and defiance.

In the Poetry Appendix, there is a ballad written by Larry O'Brien, a native of Aghowle (See section "*The Ballad of Dinny Byrne*"). This ballad fills in the background to the origin of the story of Dinny Byrne, who hid out in a cave on Carrick and evaded capture by the Yeomen.

O'Brien's farmhouse (House No.5), like most of the others in the valley, faced up the hillside towards Carrick Mountain and the fields of their farm ran up to the bottom of the rocks. When Larry was a boy in the 1920s, the local farmers would still have held grazing rights on the mountain. He would have spent many a summer's day up on Carrick and I am sure the older farmers would have often recounted the story of Dinny Byrne as they passed by Dinny's Cave. While Larry, like many of his generation, had to emigrate to England to find work, he always remained an Aghowle man at heart and all during his lifetime he returned to the O'Brien family home every year. As this ballad shows, the history and folklore of his childhood always remained with him. There are several other poems by Larry in the Poetry Appendix.

Chapter 3

The Townland in the Pre-Famine years

The people of the valley must have entered the 19th century under the dark shadow of recent events, after all the upheaval of the 1798 Rebellion throughout the county of Wicklow and the horrific deaths on their own doorstep, along with the trauma of having their two local catholic churches burnt down. In the early years of the 19th century throughout the county, the aftermath of the Rebellion was still being felt and it was not until 1803 that the last of the rebels who were hiding out in the mountains were captured or gave themselves up.

While the district was recovering from these recent traumatic events, a nearby landlord was expanding his domain and in time this was to have a lasting influence on the townland of Aghowle. At the time, Francis Synge and his wife Elizabeth were living at Roundwood Park (about 8 miles from Aghowle) where they held extensive lands around the Roundwood district and stretching down to the Devil's Glen.

In the early years of the century, Francis Synge made the decision to relocate his main residence from Roundwood Park down to the Devil's Glen. At the time, there was a large house in the glen known as Glenmouth, but Francis had more grandiose plans for his new residence in the glen. He employed the architect Francis Johnson to extend and remodel Glenmouth house. This work included adding towers at each of the corners and covering the roof with a crenellated parapet. This new gothic style of residence he renamed Glanmore Castle and once completed, Francis Synge and his family moved into residence here.

Although only about 6 miles from his former residence at Roundwood Park, Francis felt that this new location was less remote and nearer to society. But his main reason for relocating down to here was said to be that he felt his lands around Tiglin were a much better base for his main farming activities. He believed if he took his stock that had been born and partly reared on the poorer upland mountainous areas of his estate down to the more fertile lands around Tiglin that they would thrive and flourish.

Glanmore Castle, Home of the Synge family
Photograph by kind permission of Sheila Clarke

Aghowle Joins Glanmore Estate

As part of his relocation down to the Devil's Glen, Francis Synge also set about increasing his lands in the surrounding areas. One of the parcels of land that he acquired the lease for was the townlands of Aghowle and Ballycullen, details recorded in an estate notebook indicate that the lease of Aghowle Upper and Lower was signed on the 15th August 1810 [NLI/ Mss11996-11997].

This change of landlord would have been a major event in the lives of the local tenants. For the previous century or more, the tenants of Aghowle and Ballycullen had been under a series of intermediate landlords or middlemen who may not have even resided in the county and so the tenants most likely had gone through a great deal of uncertainty and change during this period. But now they were to become part of a large local estate whose landlord lived and farmed just a few miles away. They were to remain part of Glanmore Estate for over a century and while the plight of the tenant farmer was always difficult and uncertain, I feel during this time they probably fared better as part of the Glanmore Estate than if they were tenants to a smaller landlord or an absentee landlord. In general, the Synge family appear to have been reasonable landlords and while we will see their financial management was not always sound and led to near disaster, they are said to have treated their tenants better than many of the other landlords at that time. There was one recorded exception to this, which is covered in detail further on in this story.

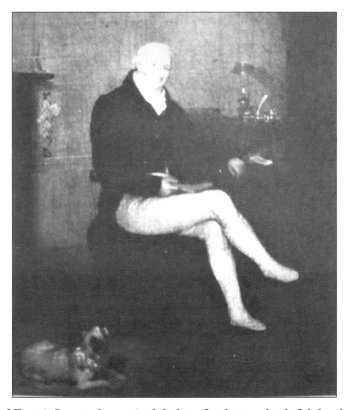

Landlord Francis Synge who acquired the lease for the townland of Aghowle in 1810
Photograph by kind permission of Sheila Clarke

As the fate of tenant farmers was very much dependant on the fortunes of their landlords and the Synge family now held the entire townland of Aghowle, the story of the local farming community here over the next century is closely related to the story of the Synge family and Glanmore Estate. Therefore, for this period of the townland's history, we will follow both the story of the landlord's family in Glanmore and the story of the tenant farming families living in the townland of Aghowle.

In the years following the Synge family's move down to Glanmore, Francis put much effort and finances into developing the demesne around his home, as well as extending his portfolio of properties in other counties.

Between 1816 and 1824, Francis Synge planted a total of 162,300 trees in the following areas on his estate: Killiskey, Clora, Rathnew and Ballycullen [ITCT/p.120].

New Landlord at the Castle

In December 1831, Francis Synge died at Glanmore Castle aged 70. In the weeks following his death, a person now unknown was given the task of going to Glanmore and taking an inventory of the estate. This task was recorded in several small notebooks which have survived to the present day and are held in the National Library of Ireland [NLI/Mss11996-11997].

Within the pages of these note books, we get details of the local tenants and how much land they held, as well as getting a glimpse of everyday life inside the local landlord's castle. Details of the tenants for the townlands of Aghowle and Ballycullen show that there were several tenants who held lands in both townlands. This probably stems from the fact that the two townlands had previously been leased as a single unit.

The list of tenants for Aghowle, taken in January 1832, is given as:

Thomas Moran	Nich. Ward	Widow of Luke Byrne
Dennis Moran	Laur. Toole	Widow Toole
John Moran	Frank Byrne	John Relish (recorded elsewhere as John Rutledge)
Simon Moran	Ter. Reilly	Adam Woodward
Denis Byrne	James Reilly	Nich. Moran (3 holdings)
Pat. Byrne	Ephr. Falkner	Garret McDaniel
Thomas Shannon	George Croqhal	Mat. Carey

As some of these 21 tenants, such as members of the Moran family, held leases in both Aghowle and Ballycullen, it is difficult to say which townland they resided in. As well as the tenant farmers recorded for the townland, it is very likely that there were also a number of labourers living there as well at that time but as they usually subleased a small dwelling or cabin from a tenant farmer they do not appear on the official list of estate tenants.

These labourers would have lived in very small basic dwellings probably with mud walls and consisting of 1 or 2 rooms, and if lucky they might have had a small garden to grow vegetables. The tenant farmers would not have been much better off than these labourers and would have lived in a two or perhaps 3 roomed dwelling with a thatched roof. Inside these dwellings they would have had a small few basic pieces of furniture and a pot or two which they would have used for cooking their food over an open fire.

The Synge family would have lived a lifestyle like many other families of the big houses of the time but were probably not living in the grandeur of some of the larger estate houses, such as Powerscourt. But to the tenants living on the estate, life inside Glanmore Castle must have seemed extremely luxurious.

In the surviving notebooks of the inventory for Glanmore Estate taken in early 1832, just after Francis Synge's death, we get a glimpse of life inside the castle.

For example, the contents of the cellar are recorded as
- *4 doz. port wine*
- *1 bottle sherry*
- *2 bottles of Claret*
- *8 bottles of cape madeira*
- *2 bottles of rum*
- *3 bottles of whisky – common*

The "plate" is also listed in detail and contains such items as silver tea pots, creamers and sugar bowls, silver servers, 6 pairs of plated candle sticks, various dozen silver spoons, knives, etc. and the entire plate is valued at £135. For many of the estate tenants that would be equivalent to 6 or 7 years rental of their farms. There is also a list of the domestic staff inside the house and the names of 50 staff employed in the running of the estate farm.

Among the listings for the farm animals are: 4 carriage horses, 4 mares, 5 colts, 3 cart horses, 4 mules and 3 asses. In the garden, various garden tools etc. are listed and also recorded are 1,383 flower pots of various sizes, which would reflect Francis Synge's labours in creating extensive ornate grounds around the castle.

Francis Synge was succeeded as landlord of Glanmore by his eldest son John. John came into his new position as the local landlord with some unusual beliefs and philosophies for a man of that time. He was educated at Trinity College Dublin and then Oxford College in England. After his formal education was completed, John went on a European tour for several years.

While on his travels he became very influenced by a famous Swiss educationist called Pestalozzi who practiced a child-centred style of education, which was very different from the norm of the time. John was also influenced by a group of people who followed a particular religious philosophy. These followers, who were mostly based in Devonshire in England, would later become known as The Plymouth Brethren.

When John Synge had returned to Roundwood Park from his European travels, he brought with him a printing press and set up a Charter School in Roundwood where his Pestalozzi style of education was taught. John married Isabella Hamilton in 1818 and the couple lived at Roundwood Park for 9 years. But Isabella suffered from ill health and in 1827 the family moved to Devonshire where it was thought the milder climate might suit Mrs Synge better. It was also thought that their move there was greatly influenced by John's wish to be with the people who followed the same religious beliefs as himself.

When his father Francis died in December 1831, John and his family came home to take over the running of Glanmore Estate. He said at the time, that whether it was his wish to run the estate or not, he felt duty bound to labour at it for a few years as he owed it to those that depended on the estate. As it transpired, he threw himself into running the estate and remained at Glanmore until his death in 1845.

As soon as he got settled into his new role, John Synge set up a Pestalozzi school on the estate and also set up his printing press in the Castle grounds, so he could print educational materials for the school. This school would have been for the children of the tenant families on the estate and perhaps he may also have allowed some the other local children to attend as well. It is difficult to know whether many of the children of the families living in Aghowle at that time would have attended the Pestalozzi school. As children of the estate they would have been encouraged to and I imagine the education provided there might have been free of charge. But most of the families living in Aghowle at that time were Roman Catholics and the education provided would have a strong protestant religious aspect which the Catholic families might have found objectionable.

Pestalozzi School Room, Kilfee, circa 1825, founded by John Synge (1788-1845)
Pestalozzi School Kilfea
Image courtesy of Sheila Clarke

The Catholic tenants may have preferred the option of sending their children to a hedge school. Around this time, there was such a school in Moneystown, which had 60 pupils attending, 30 boys and 30 girls and almost all the pupils were Roman Catholics. The teacher was a Mr. Prendergast and the school consisted of one room which was said to be in a very poor condition. Also, the children attending here would have had to pay a fee which was used to pay the master's wages [THSOW].

But the choice of which school the children of the townland attended could also have been influenced by the distance from their home, the cost involved and the quality and usefulness of the education provided. Of course, many families did not send their children to school at all at that time and of those that did send them, attendance was often poor as the children of large families were frequently needed at home to mind siblings and carry out housework as well as helping to farm the land.

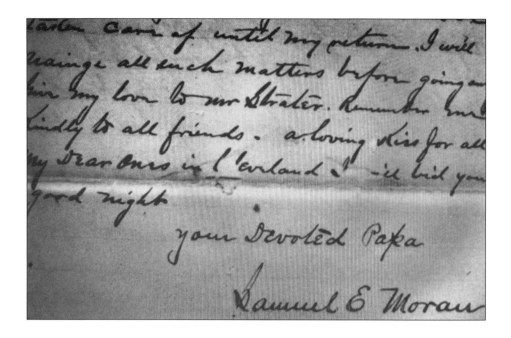

Extract of letter written by Samuel Edward Moran in 1885
Courtesy of John Moran, Ohio, USA

However, there are indications that at least some of the tenant children received some schooling at this time. The above image depict an extract from a letter written by Samuel Edward Moran to his children in 1885. Samuel was born in Aghowle in 1836 and would have been about eleven years old when his family emigrated in 1847. The family settled in America. From the penmanship of this letter it would appear that Samuel would have attended either the Pestalozzi school at Glanmore or the hedge school at Moneystown.

A Missionary Man comes to save the Aghowle tenants

As well as providing a school for his tenants, John Synge also brought over from England a person who followed the same religious philosophy as himself to minister to the Glanmore tenants.

In 1832, which was the year that John Synge took over as landlord of Glanmore Estate, there appeared among the local tenants a missionary man called William Graeme Rhind who had come to save their souls, improve their economic earnings and look after their physical and spiritual well-being.

Mr Rhind and John Synge had met when they were both students at

Captain W.G. Rhind, who ministered to the Glanmore tenants between 1832 and 1838

Oxford College and became friends through their shared religious beliefs - both men were influenced by the teachings of the Plymouth Brethren. When John Synge became landlord of Glanmore, he invited Mr Rhind, who was living in London at the time, to come live on the estate at the landlord's expense and in a sense to act as a missionary for the tenants.

Mr Rhind was a married man with two children at that time and he and his family moved into Clorah cottage at the edge of the Devil's Glen. Then for almost 7 years, the family lived among the Glanmore tenants and administered to their needs while John Synge reimbursed Mr Rhind for his work.

"Faithful Unto Death: A memoir of W.G. Rhind" was written in 1863 and part of this memoir covers the time he spent living on the Glanmore Estate. From this memoir, we can get an insight into the everyday life of the local tenants of the time and how Mr Rhind's presence here had some beneficial influence on the residents of Aghowle and the other people living on the estate [FUD/pp.39-50].

The memoir contains a letter written by Mr Rhind in 1835, regarding his time so far at Glanmore. The following extract describes his observations after his initial visiting of the cabins on the estate and outlining what he intended his plan of action to be:

1st To give, as much as possible, employment to those in health.
2nd To administer to the sick, both by medicine and other necessaries.
3rd. To keep up, by visiting, a friendly intercourse with the people at large.
Relative to the first measure, I have found it answer behind my

expectations: and I have now, during six to nine months in the year, seventy families employed in knitting, spinning, weaving, &c., and, as an encouragement to them and now decided comfort to ourselves, from my wife to the youngest little one and each of our servants, we all wear home made things as much as possible. My travelling cloak and bag are linen painted: my summer light dresses are unbleached linen; my table –cloths are diaper [at the time this was a name for linen with a diamond pattern on it], spun and wove close to us and our blankets also: and soon, I shall have my own shirts.

This may, to some minds, seem trifling, but the poor people do not think it so: and when I tell them my little girl is wearing their home knit stockings, one can see how happy it makes them.

Thus, seventy families are clothed by their own industry, – and often times I am made their savings bank, until their earnings reach seven or eight shillings, for a little pig &c. Thus also the shops are aided; the shoe maker, a poor Protestant man and true Christian, is also aided; and the great wheel goes around easier and better; for I do not <u>oblige them</u> to take their earnings out in clothing, yet nine tenths prefer it.

If they are sick I visit them and if in need I aid them; and during the confinement of mothers and families, if my funds admit to it, I give them extra aid –not in money (this, as much as possible, I avoid), but in flannels, baby clothes & c.

2. To administer to the sick, medicine and other necessaries. The kind Christian friend, on whose estate I am residing, very handsomely allows me sufficient entirely to support a weekly general dispensary and one of daily call at my own house; to this all are welcome- his own tenants and all around. Being originally fond of medicine, & c. and the Lord having greatly blessed the means hitherto, the people are quite satisfied with my practice and where the case is behond my knowledge, the physicians of the two neighbouring towns, distant five miles [presumably here he is referring to towns of Rathdrum and Wicklow] each most kindly attend to any cases I send them gratis and admit them into the hospitals if cause require.

The centre of my practice comprises the workmen and tenancy of my above mentioned friend… and comprises a great many of "nobody's people" as they are emphatically called in this country. Being the tenants of little landlords almost as poor as themselves, or cabin keepers by the roadside, who are neglected to a proverb; and of whom it may be said no man careth for me. I also vaccinate their children.

3. And lastly, I have endeavoured, by friendly visiting amongst the peasantry, to keep up a social intercourse and know their wants; and either in one capacity or another, I know almost everyone about me and thus am enabled to visit equally Roman Catholic and Protestants; and it is a fact to my mind of importance, that rarely a Roman Catholic dies around us, who, at last, has not heard some blessed portion of the gospel of Christ ... as yet little visible fruit has been manifested in direct conversion.

From this description, we learn that Mr. Rhind had managed to get 70 families on the estate active in the cottage industries of weaving, spinning and knitting. As sheep rearing was a significant part of the local farming here at that time, he was enabling them to make use of the resources they had to hand. Also, it is possible that some of the local farmers may have grown flax at that time.

From the 1839 OSI map which was drawn up around the time of Mr Rhind's departure, I have estimated there was at that time at least 20 dwellings in the Aghowle townland and as it is stated that about three quarters of all the families on the estate were engaged in Mr Rhind's enterprises, it seems likely that quite a few families living in Aghowle would have participated in his industrious enterprises.

I have been told by several sources that at some time in the past there was a little community of dwellings up towards the foot of Carrick Mountain where craft people like weavers, hatters, cobblers, etc. lived and worked but no one I spoke with could estimate when these dwellings were there. Perhaps they may have been related to Mr Rhind's cottage industries or perhaps they belonged to a previous era.

Mr Rhind's letter refers to the local shoemaker being assisted by the extra money earned from the tenant's involvement in these new industries. This may refer to John Storey, who was a protestant shoemaker living in the Ballycullen area at that time. Mr Storey was leasing a small cottage and 8 acres of land on the Glanmore Estate. If so, the extra income would have benefited the rearing and education of Mr Storey's children. Later on in the story of this century we can read details of one of Mr Storey's sons, John, who emigrated and rose to the height of his career as a sea captain and also of Mr Storey's daughter Jane, who married a school teacher and went on to live at house no. 5 at Aghowle Upper.

Mr Rhind also refers to his assistance to mothers during their confinement and his vaccination of their children. From my researching of the church records and the history of the Aghowle families, I know that several of the families living here during Mr. Rhind's time would have had babies and young children. For example:

- Thomas and Ann Moran who lived at Aghowle Upper had 7 children, the younger members of their family were born during the 1830s, their photograph appears a little further on in "The Moran Family Who Never Forgot Their Townland".
- Francis and Mary Byrne (my great-great-grandparents, see house no.10) at Aghowle Upper, had several children born in the 1830s.

Some of these children, including my great grandmother, Bridget Byrne born 1835, may have benefited medically and materially from the good Mr Rhind's ministrations to the local mothers and their babies.

From Mr Rhind's memoir regarding his time at Glanmore estate, we learn that he administered medical aid to everyone who called to his house at Clorah and that *"sometimes, quite a long row of old women, huddled up in their cloaks and squatted on the ground, might be seem in the front of his house, awaiting his return"*.

There is also reference to the local people bringing their sick animals to him and often they were restored to full health.

Before he left Glanmore in 1838, cholera had arrived in the neighbourhood and many shunned the cholera sufferers but Mr Rhind was always willing to visit them. The following is a description taken from his memoir of one such visit that he made:

> *On one occasion, people came from a distance, saying, that a man was dying of it* [cholera] *and they described it as of the most malignant kind. Committing himself to the Lords care and asking the prayers of the Christian friends he was leaving, Mr Rhind set out for the dwelling where the poor man lay.*
>
> *There outside the house he found the terrified relations and neighbours. Not one would go near him* [the cholera sufferer] *all were panic stricken.*
>
> *When their kind visitor signified his intension of seeing him, they cried "And will your honour have a glass of whisky first"*
>
> *Telling them that he never resorted to these things, but calming trusting in his God, he entered the cabin. There lay the poor sufferer, almost purple in colour and racked with agony.*

We also learn from the memoir that when Mr Rhind decided to leave his position on the Glanmore estate to return to England, that he had a handbill printed of his farewell address to the tenants. This most likely was printed on John Synge's printing press at Glanmore Castle. The following is the opening sentences of this address:

> *My dear Friends – after residing in your midst for nearly seven years, I cannot leave you without a few words at parting. Be assured, I feel deeply at separating from you, for though not your countryman by birth, yet I always feel a love for you and an earnest desire for your welfare and that of your families.*

From here the address ran to several pages and mostly took the form of a sermon on how they could save their souls and reminding them of the religious teachings he had imparted to them over his time among them.

It is clear that his presence in the local community would have been beneficial to many of the families living here at that time. But as one of his main aims was to convert people (especially the Roman Catholic Irish people) to his particular brand of Christianity, it is likely he may have left feeling a little dejected. For it seems likely he did not manage any conversions at all during his stay.

But these Irish catholic people had managed to hold fast to their beliefs during the Penal Law times, so they were unlikely to convert for one English preacher who came to live in their midst. It is probable they thought him a good man, who was trying to help them economically and medically and they would have politely listened to his Christian preaching, without any intention at all of paying any heed to it.

The Slate Quarry

As well as providing education and religious instruction for his tenants, John Synge also tried to provide them with some local industry on his estate. There was an old slate quarry about half a mile from the Castle, which he tried to turn into a profitable business. He brought over slate workers from Wales who were skilled in cutting roof slates. He laid metal lines to carry the slate in trucks from the quarry to a stream where a watermill had been built, so that the slate could be made into roofing slates, flags and gravestones. He had a system where the trucks of dressed slate ran down by gravity to the road into Wicklow, from where they were taken to the port for shipping [MUJ/p.11]. As well as the Welsh slate workers, this enterprise would have given good employment in the local area while it was operational.

The Slate Quarry at Glanmore 1840
Copy of illustration by kind permission of Sheila Clarke

But unfortunately, it was found that the grain of the slate was not suitable for cutting and the resulting roof tiles were too small and as the demand for gravestones was not sufficient to keep the enterprise in business, it had to close.

The following extract taken from a publication titled *Industrial Resources of Ireland 1845*, indicates that when the material for this publication was compiled the quarry was operational and the quality of the slate was thought to be equal to the Welsh slate.

In Wicklow, at Rathdrum and at Glanmore where Mr. Synge is now carrying on operations at a considerable scale, giving employment to upwards of 100 persons and bringing into the market slates of a quality and appearance fully equal to those imported from Bangor [IROI/p.242].

A Glimpse into the life of the local tenant and labourer in the 1840s

A few years after Mr Rhind's account of his time on the Glanmore Estate, we get another insight into the everyday life of both the tenant farmer and the agricultural labourer in this region of County Wicklow. In the early 1840s the British Government set up a commission of inquiry into the *Law and practice in respect of the occupation of land in Ireland*, this is often referred to as The Devon Commission. Government representatives interviewed people who were involved with farming in different areas throughout Ireland. Two of those that were interviewed in Co. Wicklow gave evidence relating to the local Ashford area. They were Charles Jeston Case who lived at Clorah on the Glanmore Estate and as he was Mr John Synge's land agent, some of his evidence would have related to the local tenants. The second person was Mr Simon Moran who held several leased farms in the Ashford area including lands at Milltown, where he ran a mill [EPPI/DIPPAM/pp.696-708].

The evidence was given in October 1844 at Bray Co. Wicklow:

Evidence given by Mr Case

Mr Case gave evidence that he held land locally and that he was also the land agent for Mr John Synge, a position he had held for the last 7 years. He said there was a great difference between the quality of the land in the mountainous higher regions of the county and the land which was down nearer the coast. He stated that there was good opportunity to improve the land for tillage by drainage and clearing, but in his time here, he had not seen much of this type of work carried out.

He stated that the average size of the farms was from 20 to 50 acres and that some were up to 100 acres, but that there was also quite a few farms less than 10 acres. The land was generally in mixed tillage and with some grass land, dairy stock and fattening stock.

Mr Case had been on Mr Synge's estate since 1837, where there were 86 tenants and in that time, there had not been more than 4 changes of tenants. He also gave evidence regarding loan funds, which he was not happy about, as often the tenants were getting money from these loan funds at very high interest rates, which they did not fully understand. He said that usually the farmers could not improve their land as they had no capital to do so and that no assistance was given by the landlords. Although he did point out that Mr Synge had a system of giving his tenants a barrel, or a barrel and a half, of lime per acre, if they paid their rent by the due date.

He also stated that the subdivision of farms was usually prevented by the landlords, even where the tenant had adult sons who wished to lease a portion of the farm.

The officials asked Mr Case what was the situation for the labourers and were they allowed land to grow potatoes for themselves. Mr Case replied that in this part of the county, the situation for the labourers was very bad. Generally, they were not allowed land to plant potatoes and had to buy them. He said he would pay his labourers on a Saturday evening, so they would have money to buy potatoes and by that time of the week they would generally have little or none left and would have to go directly to the market to purchase some. The labourers were usually paid 10d. a day without diet, or 5 or 6 d. with diet and they would have to pay 10d. or 1 shilling a week for their cottage. On the other side of the county the labourers were allowed con acre to sow their own potatoes and were better off in that respect. He said the labouring classes were dreadfully bad off and often had only half an acre of land, but they were the most peaceable people in the world. He felt the only way their lot would be improved, was by improving the country in general.

Mr Case said he was a farmer himself and as well as collecting the rent for Mr Synge, he tried to advise the farmers on the best use of their land and how to rest it between crops. But that his advice was often not heeded to, as the tenants tried to get as many crops as possible out of the land, so that they could pay their yearly rent.

When asked about what happens when a tenant falls into arrears and the bailiff comes in, he said that generally the cost of the bailiff was charged to the tenant, but that Mr Synge always got him to charge the Bailiff's costs to himself.

The officials inquired if there any other work available for the labouring classes and he replied that there was Mr Synge's slate quarry and that employed up to 50 people, the labourers were paid 10d. a day. The slate was cut for flags, chimney pieces, headstones and gravestones.

Slate from the quarry was used to build the farm buildings at Glanmore.
The remains of these impressive buildings are still visible at the roadside today

Evidence from Mr. Simon Moran

Simon Moran also gave evidence to the commission at Bray on the same day. Simon was connected to the Aghowle/Ballycullen Moran family, but exactly where he fitted into their family tree is not known. At this time he was living and farming in the Ashford and Milltown area.

Simon was a Catholic tenant farmer and he appears to have been quite successful in his enterprises while showing great concern for his fellow countrymen. He was listed as one of the elected guardians who was present at the setting up of the Rathdrum Workhouse and was also actively involved in local famine relief during the Great Famine. His son Patrick Moran became the first Roman Catholic Bishop of Dunedin, New Zealand.

When Simon Moran died in 1859 his obituary in the Freeman's Journal dated 31st May 1859 stated "he died universally esteemed and chiefly mourned by the poor, who had lost in him a kind-hearted friend and one of the best of employers.

At the start of his evidence to the Commission Si`mon Moran stated that he held 112 Irish acres of land and that in the past he had been a Tithe Commissioner and land valuer and also a land agent for a number of properties.

When asked about his knowledge of local tenants being dispossessed of their houses or land, Mr Moran said that there were two landlords who lived near him and it was horrifying how they had disposed the finest set of labourers that ever existed. There had been a number of houses thrown down on the property of the late Robert Hall, the houses were in the townland of Ballylusk, [this townland borders Aghowle Lower] while the owner Mr Hall himself lived in Tipperary.

It appeared the previous owner of the land sold on the lease to Mr Hall and around that time the labourers built their houses on the lands, they were mud houses with gardens, one even had three or four acres attached. Mr Robert Hall let the houses stand for some time, but then at some stage, he took it into his head to throw down the houses, even though the tenants were paying rent to Mr Hall's agent, a Mr Coates.

When asked by the commissioner if the tenants owed any rent, Simon Moran said he could not say, but that the tenants were ejected and the houses thrown down and no compensation was given to them. Mr. Coates was no longer the agent; the estate was now in chancery and there was a good agent in place. The land the houses stood on was added into the adjoining farm and the person who was leasing this land was ordered to throw down the houses.

When asked what was the other incidence of tenants been disposed locally, Mr Moran said that there had been a comfortable class of labourer living on the estate of Mr Carroll of Ashford and their houses were thrown down 3 or 4 years ago, when the poor law was coming into operation. It seems the tenants were leasing the houses from a middleman, but that Mr Carroll had some dispute or issue with the middleman and it was resolved by passing on the leases of the labourers houses to Mr Carroll, who then ejected the tenants and knocked down their houses. The disposed tenants went to live on the commons near

Rathnew. The commons land was occupied by many such people and it had been donated for such purposes by a very generous lady and without it, Mr Moran did not know what would have become of these poor people.

He said that these labourers from Ashford who had been ejected were fine hardworking men, who had worked on the farms of local gentlemen in the area and had constant work, except during the winter months.

When asked how he thought the situation of the tenant farmer in this area of Co. Wicklow could be improved? Mr Moran said by giving them proper leases, that many of the local Tory landlords only gave a few leases to their own sort. He said there were many farmers in Co. Wicklow who would work hard to improve their land and invest in it, if only they had the security of a lease and not fear been ejected off their own land. He said this improved work would benefit the labouring classes as well and the want of this security was a social evil in the country.

He said that as well as security of lease, the tenant would greatly benefit from knowing if he did have to leave, that he would be compensated for any improvements he carried out to the property and land at his own expense. He felt this type of security for the tenants would improve the country within 10 years. Mr Moran said there was very little agricultural education available for the sons of the farming classes, but he did not know whether they would avail of it anyway, as they seem to think the already know best."

Honest William Power of Ballycullen

As can be seen from the evidence given to the Devon Commission, the situation for small tenant farmers and agricultural labourers in Co. Wicklow was not an easy one, even before the arrival of the Great Famine.

As reports were reaching people here of potential new opportunities in the faraway lands of America, some of those who could scrape together the money for their passage were taking their chances and heading into the unknown, with the hope of providing a better life for themselves and their families.

In April 1845, the Power family were farming in the neighbouring townland of Ballycullen and one branch of this family, William Power and his family, were setting out for America.

For William Power, a chance occurrence on a street in Dublin as he and his family were making their way to the ship for departure, resulted in the family starting life in America considerably better off than when they left their home in Ballycullen. The following is a report from the Freeman's Journal dated Wednesday, April 23rd, 1845.

Curious Fact – Reward of Honesty
On Saturday last a rich farmer named Patt O Brien, of Corra Collen, Kings County, lost a pocket book containing the sum of 354 pounds 10 shillings, some mems. and a Bank of Ireland Debenture for 312 pounds, in Dame Street. He instantly reported the case to Mr. O Connor, superintendent of police, at the Castle and offered a 30-pound reward. Mr O Connor sent some of his men in search of his property. In the mean time a very poor man, named William Power, of Ballycullen, Co. Wicklow, who was on his way to America, with a long helpless family, found the pocket book and property. He could read and write well, he examined the contents and instantly repaired to Mr. O Connor and lodged it with him, although not knowing who the owner was, nor had the poor man many minutes to delay in the city.

Mr. O Connor sent for the owner of the money and told him to pay for the reward which he offered for the recovery of the money: but the owner refused to pay the reward when his property was safe. He then offered 10 pounds, which Mr. O Connor would not allow Power to accept.

The superintendent very properly insisted on getting the 30 pounds for poor Power, as the property was restored to the owner. Mr. O Brien then paid the 30 pounds. Much to the credit of Power he said the sum found would be of use to him, but he could not expect salvation if he kept it.

By the time the poor man reached the quay the steamer was starting for Liverpool and he went on his way rejoicing and blessing Mr. O Connor for the (to him) small estate which he was the means of procuring for him.

To put the above in context, the value of the lost cash and debentures which Patt O'Brien lost would be equivalent to approximately €95,000 today and the £30 reward that William Power received would equate to around €4,500. In the Griffith's Land Valuation records in 1854, Judith Power of Ballycullen, who I believe to be the widowed mother of William Power, is leasing a house and 1 acre of land for £1 a year, while John Power of Ballycullen (who may have been William's brother) is leasing a house and a large farm of 52-acres for a fee of £18 per year.

It is easy to see how a man less honest than William Power, coming upon the money, might have weighed up the situation and thought to himself that within an hour he would be safely on a ship sailing away from Ireland forever. His chances of escaping detection would be very good, and he could start a new life as a rich man. Let us hope that William Power was rewarded for his honesty by finding prosperity and good fortune in the new life he and his family were heading to.

Chapter 4

The Famine Years and its Aftermath, 1845-1850

Death of John Synge and an Estate in Debt

During his time at Glanmore, John Synge continued the work which his father had started in developing the grounds around the Castle and into the Glen. He created many walks and pathways throughout the Glen, with built-in viewing places for visitors to admire the fine vistas. Although he was a religious and moralistic man, he nevertheless spent money he did not have in order to create a grand demesne and keep up a certain standing in society. There was now a depressed economic market and the income from his tenants was falling but he did not seem to comprehend that the estate was drifting daily into greater debt.

It is said that when he died on 29th April in 1845, that the bailiffs were in the house at the time and that the only money there was seven shillings and sixpence. The story is told that the bailiffs were so annoyed with the situation that they tried to seize John Synge's corpse in the hope of selling it for dissection. Fortunately, some of the family managed to recover it on the avenue and he was safely buried in Nun's Cross churchyard [MUJ/p.11].

In 1845, the Aghowle tenants, along with the rest of the families living on Glanmore estate were now facing a very uncertain future as their landlord was dead and the estate was bankrupt. As this was on the eve of the Great Famine, the general situation in the county and the country was to get considerably worse over the coming years.

John Synge's eldest son Francis inherited Glanmore and its substantial debts. Two years later, the High Court sought the sale of all the Synge properties. The case was transferred to the Encumbered Estates Courts, where cases moved very slowly - probably because so many other estates around Ireland were in the same situation as the Synges. Francis and two of his sisters were allowed to live in Glanmore Castle as tenants while the matter was awaiting settlement. As this uncertainty coincided with the years of the Great Famine it must have been a very worrying and bleak time for both the Synge family and their tenants. I have not read or heard any oral historical accounts of harsh treatment of the Glanmore tenants during the famine years. As everything relating to the Synge estate was on hold or proceeding through the courts at that time, it may have worked to the tenants' advantage and they might have been left alone until matters were settled. It does seem that the Synge family had good local support in their efforts to retain their estate. As the Encumbered Estate Courts came near concluding their processing of Glanmore, Francis Synge offered £40,000 to buy it back. But the offer was refused, so the estate went up for public auction.

Portrait of Francis Synge, who inherited Glanmore Estate in 1845
Courtesy of Sheila Clarke

At the public auction in December 1850, Francis lost part of the estate containing Roundwood Park and the surrounding lands but for the sum of £25,000 he managed to buy back Glanmore Castle plus Tiglin and its surrounding lands, including the townlands of Aghowle and Ballycullen. Some furniture from the Castle was also sold off but with the help of various members of the Synge family, most of it was retained. There is a story that this was achieved with the help of the local blacksmith, who was a very large man and he was supposed to have backed any prospective bidder up against the wall and blocked them from bidding. The story is also told that the night after Francis managed to buy back Glanmore, there was a party and a torchlight procession at the foot of Ballymaghroe hill [MUJ/p.12]. So, it would seem the tenants were pleased that the Synge family were reinstated as their landlord again.

The Great Famine – A Local Perspective
In 1845, when John Synge died and Francis Synge was taking over his father's indebted estate, the country was on the brink of a major disaster as the potato blight was reaching its shores. In the following years, thousands of Irish people were to die of starvation and many thousands more were to flee the country. The regions worst affected by the famine were in the west and south of the country.

Relatively speaking, Co. Wicklow was to survive better than many of the other counties. Yet while the official numbers of people who died from starvation in Co. Wicklow were low, there was still much hardship and suffering among the county's poor and destitute. The number of recorded deaths in the county for 1847 was 2,776, two and a half times as high as that recorded for the pre-famine years. For the remainder of the decade the death rate in Wicklow continued at twice the annual pre-famine average. In 1847, figures from the Relief Commissioners for Co. Wicklow showed that 20% of the population in the south of the county were receiving food rations or soup, while the figure was 13% in the north of the county. Also, by the middle of January 1847 all the workhouses in the county were reported to be full [RHJ/2009/pp.14-18].

To get a picture of how the locality around Aghowle was affected during the famine years we can look at some details that have survived from the 1841 and 1851 census records [EPPI/C1841/51]. The actual census records for individual people have not survived, but details of the number of houses existing and people living in each townland have survived. Although the numbers between 1841 and 1851 may have altered for a variety of reasons, major factors would have been the starvation effects of the famine, along with the resultant migration to Dublin and emigration abroad.

In the table below, we can see how the population and number of dwellings of Aghowle and most of the neighbouring townlands were greatly reduced during this period.

Townland	1841 No. of People	1851 No. of People	1841 No of Houses	1851 No of Houses
Aghowle Upper	79	50	11	9
Aghowle Upper	96	66	14	11
Ballycullen	326	238	51	38 (1 vacant)
Ballymanus Upper	77	28	16	5
Ballymanus Lower	25	48	7	7
Barnbawn	75	62	10	9
Drumdangan	142	59	23	9
Garryduff	115	7	19	2 (1 vacant)
Sleanaglogh	70	62	9	9
Parkroe	90	54	12	10
Parkmore	125	89	19	14 (1 vacant)
Moneystown South	46	34	8	4
Moneystown North	123	97	19	19 (1 vacant)
Moneystown Hill	59	53	10	7

When you compare the figures for 1851 with those recorded in 1841 it shows that for the townland of Aghowle the overall population decreased by approximately 30% and the number of houses by 20%.

Drumdangan experienced about a 60% drop in its population and its houses. In the townland of Ballymanus Upper, the population and the number of houses both decreased by approximately 65%, while in Ballymanus Lower there was a substantial increase in the population although the number of houses remained the same, so perhaps there might have been several young couples starting their families around this time.

Garryduff was especially badly impacted, being almost uninhabited by 1851, having dropped from 115 people living there in 1841 to just 7 remaining in 1851 and of the 19 houses there in 1841 only two remain in

1851 and just one of those was occupied. The townland of Garryduff was owned by Lord Fitzwilliam, who held considerable lands in Co. Wicklow and it is well documented that around this time, he cleared many of the tenants off his estate by assisting them to emigrate. I have not found any oral or documented evidence of the Garryduff tenants being part of this clearance, but it is a possible factor.

In the above group of townlands, both the overall population and number of occupied dwellings were reduced by approximately one third from 1841 to 1851. Over any 10-year period some fluctuations could be accounted for by births and deaths and people moving to farm or work in a different townland or further afield. Also, there may be some people marrying and moving from one townland to another. But such dramatic changes in some of the above townlands between 1841 and 1851 could only be attributed to the impact of the famine on Ireland and the subsequent emigration in the years that followed.

While we cannot now know the personal stories behind all these figures, I have been able to trace the stories of several local families who would have appeared in the above 1841 census records, but who had emigrated or otherwise left their townland by the time of the 1851 census.

Famine Time Emigration – The Stories of Three Local Families
This section tells the stories of three families that had to leave Aghowle due to the Famine and traces where they ended up.

The Moran Family Who Never Forgot Their Townland
Thomas Moran and his family left Aghowle Upper during the time of the great famine to migrate to Canada. Thomas was a member of a large family group of Morans' who were well established in the townlands of Ballycullen and Aghowle at that time. Church records show that in 1821, Thomas Moran married Ann Fanning in the neighbouring parish of Glendalough. From my research, I believe Ann was a member of the Fanning family that lived and farmed at Slanelough at that time. The Fanning's farmland lay just across the townland boundary from Aghowle Upper, about half a mile from where Thomas Moran lived. It is known that Ann originally came from Co. Wexford, but how the Fanning family came to live at Slanelough is not known.

Between 1822 and 1839, Thomas and Ann Moran had seven children: Mary, James, John, Jeremiah (Darby) , Thomas, Samuel and William. In 1832, Thomas is recorded as the leaseholder of 33 acres of land at Aghowle.

We don't know much else about Thomas and his family during these years except that in 1842, he appears in the petty court records for Co. Wicklow, where he is taking a case against another member of the family, one John Moran also residing at Aghowle Upper, for wilfully and maliciously throwing his turf in a heap and damaging them and for cutting part of his turf bank [FMP/IPCR]. This case would appear to be a dispute between two members of the same family regarding who had the turbary rights for the turf bank. Perhaps another member of the Moran family had died or moved away and both Thomas and John were claiming a right to his turf bank. In the days when turf was the main source of fuel to provide heat for the dwelling house and the means of cooking for the household, the cutting and saving of one's turf would have been essential for the family's survival.

Around the year 1847, Thomas and his family made the decision to leave their 33-acre farm at Aghowle Upper and emigrate. It is not difficult to see why the family may have taken this course of action. The country was experiencing the worst year of the Great Famine and thousands throughout the country were dying of starvation and many others were struggling to survive. The future that lay ahead for the entire country was bleak and uncertain. For Thomas, the future of the lease on his home and his farm was also very uncertain as Francis Synge, his landlord, was now in great debt and only a tenant on his own estate. If the estate was to be sold, who knew what plans a new landlord might have and how he might treat the existing tenants.

Coupled with these factors was the fact that Thomas and Ann had 7 children, 6 of them sons. As these sons reached adulthood, their 33 acres at Aghowle would not be able to support all these young men, especially if they married and set up families of their own. Also, in many cases the tenants were not allowed to subdivide their existing holdings. As mentioned, Thomas was a member of the larger Moran family who held leases for quite a few of the holdings in Aghowle and Ballycullen and were perhaps a little better off than many of the neighbouring tenant families. They may have been fortunate enough to be able to afford the option of emigrating, while many of their neighbours would just have to sit it out and hope for the best.

A great, great grandson of Thomas Moran, named John Moran, who resides in Ohio, America, has provided me with the following summary of what is known from oral family history of the emigration route the Moran family took and their early years in America.

Thomas Moran, from Aghowle, who was born around 1782, along with his wife Ann and their 7 children, emigrated from Ireland around 1847. Oral family history records that they came first to Canada and then down to America where they settled in Canandaigua, New York, a little east of Niagara Falls. Their exact date of arrival into America is not known, but the family are recorded here in the 1850 census records.

The Moran family settled and prospered in their new country and census records show that the professions of Thomas and Ann's sons included farmer, clothing merchant and hackney driver. A few years after their arrival, Thomas's wife Ann died in 1854 and in 1874, Thomas Moran passed away, both are buried in Calvary cemetery in Canandaigua.

John and his family kindly supplied me with the photograph below of the children of Thomas and Ann Moran taken in America, it is thought it may have been around the time of Thomas's death in 1874. These children were all born in the Moran's home in Aghowle, during the 1820s and 1830s and their baptisms are recorded in the local church register. This is the earliest photograph I have found of people born in the townland.

C. 1874 - The seven children of Thomas and Ann Moran in the USA.
These children were all born in Aghowle between 1822 and 1839.
Photograph courtesy of John Moran Ohio USA.

John has also given me the following photograph of Thomas Moran's grave. After over a quarter of a century living in America, Thomas's grave inscription does not give any details of his American residence, but instead documents the small Wicklow townland over 3,000 miles away where Thomas came from:

The fact that Thomas's grave inscription does not just record that he was a native of Ireland or of Co Wicklow but specifically mentions Aghowle, shows the strong connection the family still retained after many years living in America to their place of origin from which they had departed in 1847 - a little townland beneath Carrick Mountain, where only about 20 houses existed. But when one considers that the Moran family were established in the townland for at least a century prior to Thomas's emigration, perhaps it is not that difficult to understand their strong identification with their birth place.

The recording of "Ahowle" on Thomas Moran's grave in 1874, enabled myself and Thomas's great, great grandson, John Moran, to connect nearly 140 years later and for John's family to be able to establish the exact location of the birth place of their Irish ancestors.

Today the American descendants of Thomas and Ann Moran, who are now into their 7th generation, still cherish their Irish ancestry - their children bear Irish names such as Kathleen, Sheila Kevin and Alan and they compete in

Thomas Moran's grave, courtesy of the Moran family, USA.
Thomas's wife Ann's grave inscription records she was
a native of Pallace, Co. Wexford.

Erected by his sons

To the memory of their dear father
Thomas Moran

Who departed this life
April 22 1874
Aged 92 years

A native of Ahowle,
Co. Wicklow,
Ireland

Irish dancing competitions. See the story of House No.6 for an account of the visit in 2017 to Aghowle of John Moran, Thomas and Ann Moran's descendant.

The Fanning Family: Neighbours in the Workhouse
The story of the second local family, the Fannings, who emigrated in the aftermath of the famine, is somewhat different to the story of the Morans' emigration. While Thomas Moran and his family were probably reluctant to leave their home and farm and head to a new faraway country, they had made the decision that it was probably the best option for the future of their family. The Fanning family of Slanelough, on the other hand, did not have any option but to take the emigration route.

In his book, *From Shadow to Sunlight*, the author, Kevin Byrne, has traced the history of the building that now houses St Colman's Hospital in Rathdrum, from its opening in 1842 as the Rathdrum Workhouse to the present day. Much of the following information is taken from this book.

When the workhouse in Rathdrum was opened in 1842, it was intended to cater for 600 inmates, but in February 1850 there were 1,317 inmates. As the country was in such a devastated situation following the Great Famine, the prospects of the inmates of the country's workhouses being able to return to independent living seemed very remote, so in many cases the workhouse Board of Guardians began to look for solutions to the situation. One such option put forward was to assist the able-bodied inmates to emigrate and hopefully have a chance to start a new life abroad [FSTS/p.20].

Among those that came to this decision was the board of the Rathdrum Workhouse who voted in favour of the option of emigration and they chose Quebec in Canada as the destination. They engaged a shipping contractor named James Miley of Dublin and he was paid £4-4-0 per adult and £2-2-0 for each child under 14 years, while infants under 1 year travelled free. As most of the inmates were destitute and had inadequate clothing, items such as shoes, coats, etc. were also supplied for the needy. Each emigrant was given £1 per adult and 10 shillings per child to assist them in the initial days after their landing in Canada [FSTS/p.20].

In *From Shadow to Sunlight*, the author has listed those selected from the Rathdrum Workhouse for emigration to Quebec from July 1850 to May 1854. For the 351 persons selected, he has recorded their names and ages and the area within the Rathdrum Union where they had lived prior to entering the workhouse. The emigrants came from many different areas of the Union and among the locations listed in proximity to the Aghowle area were Glenealy, Roundwood and Moneystown.

While looking through this list I noticed that there was a family group with the surname Fanning listed from the Moneystown area. The family members listed were Joseph aged 40 and 7 of his children, aged from 18 years down to 4 years of age. They had been selected to emigrate to Quebec on board the Agenora ship on 10th June 1851:

> *Fanning Family: Joseph 40, Catherine 18, Mary 16, John 16, Michael 10, Anne 8, Rose 6 and Bridget 4* [FSTS/p.27]

The surname Fanning was not a common name in County Wicklow at that time - in fact in 1831, there was only one family of this name listed for all of Co. Wicklow in the Tithe Applotment land records and that family was leasing land in the townland of Slanelough, then known as Sleanaglogh, which borders the townland of Aghowle [NAI/TAB].

These land records show there were three members of the Fanning family listed as tenant leaseholders; Robert, William and Bryan and the following information is recorded:

> *William Fanning – 45 acres of arable and 47 acres of rough – annual rent £39,*
> *Bryan Fanning – 30 acres of arable and 33 acres of rough– annual rent £28,*
> *Robert Fanning – house and land, [acreage unspecified], annual rent £30.*

I was curious to establish if the Fanning family listed for emigration from the Rathdrum Workhouse in 1851 were part of the Fanning family that lived and farmed in Slanelough at that time.

Back in the 1840s, Moneystown and Slanelough were part of the Roman Catholic parish of Glendalough and in searching through the parish registers for Glendalough I found baptism records that matched six of Joseph Fanning's children who later appear in the registers for the Rathdrum Workhouse [NLI/PR/G]. These children were born between 1832 and 1848 and the records confirmed that the family had been living at Slanelough when these children were baptised and that their parents were Joseph Fanning and Rose Reilly. The baptism records also show that members of the extended Fanning family living at Slanelough, as well as their neighbours from Aghowle and Slanelough, were baptismal sponsors for Joseph and Rose's children.

Also noted for the Fanning family of Slanelough, from a separate source, was a grave inscription from Glendalough graveyard:

> *Erected by William Fanning of Slaneaglough in memory of his son John Dep. 3rd November 1823 aged 20 years* [FMP/CMOD]

For some reason, Joseph and Rose Fanning's family appears to have fallen on hard times, as the registers for the Rathdrum Workhouse show that in the summer of 1849, seven members of Joseph Fanning's family were admitted to the workhouse [WCA/WR]. They were Joseph's wife Rose and their younger children, John, Ann, Rose, Biddy, Essie and baby Margaret, who was about 9 months old at the time. A note in the margin beside the entry for the children's mother, Rose, records that she died while in the workhouse, but the date of her death was not recorded.

In 1844, the Guardians of the Rathdrum Workhouse purchased land nearby at the end of the Union lane, for a graveyard. During the famine years, over 1,000 bodies were buried here in a communal grave. Joseph Fanning's wife Rose would have been buried in this graveyard and as the death rate was still very high in the immediate years after the famine, it is likely she was buried in this communal grave [FSTS/p.72].

The two youngest Fanning children who were admitted in 1849, were Esther born November 1845 and her sister Margaret born September 1848, these two children do not appear with the rest of the family on the emigration list. So, one wonders had they, like many others, died in the workhouse in the meantime? If so, they may also lie with their mother in the communal famine grave.

The workhouse register also shows that at some separate but unknown date, Joseph, his son Michael and daughter Mary were also admitted into the Rathdrum Workhouse. John, the elder son of Joseph and Rose, was admitted to the workhouse at the same time as his mother and younger sisters and was about 5 years older than his brother Michael. However, an entry in the register shows that John was classified as crippled, so 9-year-old Michael would have been the only able-bodied son in the family to assist Joseph.

I did not find any entry in the workhouse registers for the oldest child, Catherine Fanning aged 18, who is recorded with the rest of the family on the emigration list. But perhaps she had already managed to gain work somewhere before the rest of the family fell on hard times and were admitted to the workhouse. When her family were offered assisted passage,

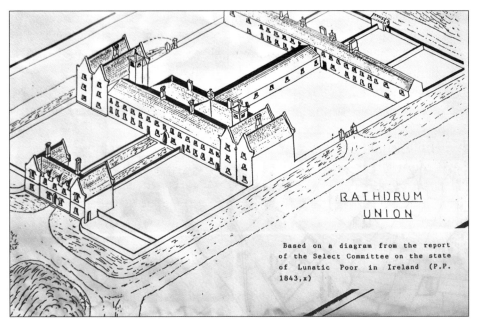

Illustration of the Rathdrum Union Workhouse 1843.
Reproduced from **From Shadow to Sunlight** *by kind permission of Kevin Byrne*

perhaps she opted to emigrate with them, as her mother was now dead, and she could help her father care for her younger siblings.

Records show that in 1851 Joseph Fanning and his remaining 7 children were part of a group of 144 inmates chosen from the Rathdrum Workhouse for assisted emigration to Canada. On the 10th June 1851, they left Dublin on board the Agenora, arriving 6 weeks later in Quebec on 24th July 1851. The emigrants were transported to Dublin by cart, at a cost to the workhouse of 10 pence per person. [FSTS/p.20]

It must have been a poignant sight to witness the procession of these carts laden with the emigrants making their way from the workhouse through the town of Rathdrum as they began their journey to the ship in Dublin. One wonders, along the way, were these cart loads of people looked upon with sadness and pity - or perhaps to those as destitute as themselves, they were envied the chance that they were getting of a better life elsewhere. For those left with nothing in the world, setting out into a total unknown must have been a very frightening and bewildering prospect.

As the minutes of the Rathdrum Workhouse board meeting show, this fear was too great for one of those travelling. 25-year-old Mary Duffy from Ballyarthur refused to leave Wicklow, stating "she would not be able to cross the sea". Another member of the group, Jane Allen, aged 26, from Dunganstown South, dressed in her emigrant outfit, jumped ship in Dublin before it set sail. It is not recorded whether, at this stage, she was in possession of her emigrant landing money of £1 or if she decided to take her chances penniless on the streets of Dublin [FSTS/p.22].

Records in Quebec show that the Agenora arrived on the 24th of July with 133 emigrants from the Rathdrum Union. It is not recorded if deaths occurred during the voyage, or if only 133 passengers set sail from Dublin. Sometimes emigrants that had been chosen were deemed unfit to travel by the medical officer [ITC/1851].

I do not know if all the Fanning family survived the trip, or how they fared after arrival. As there were many emigrants arriving into Quebec around this time, conditions in the area were not favourable for the new arrivals and there was no prospect of work locally. Those that had been given landing money fared better, for at least they had the means to get to more remote locations where there was some chance of finding employment.

As of yet, I have not been able to find out what happened to Joseph Fanning and his family after arrival. Many of the emigrants to Canada would have made their way down to America, where prospects were better. Let's hope that the Fanning family and the rest of the emigrants from the Rathdrum Workhouse got their chance of a better life.

One wonders what circumstances led to Joseph Fanning's family ending up in the workhouse. From the Tithe Applotment Land records of 1831 the Fanning family at Slanelough appear to be relatively large leaseholders, although it is noted that at that time, Joseph does not appear as one of these named leaseholders. On the Griffith's Land Valuation records in 1854 there is just one remaining member of the Fanning family recorded as the leaseholder, namely Robert Fanning who has a house and 86 acres of land at Slanelough.

Records from the County Wicklow Court Petty Sessions may help to give us a little more background on Joseph Fanning [FMP/PCR]. In August 1839, Joseph Fanning took a case against John Murray for absconding from his service. This would indicate that although he is not recorded as a lease holder in the 1831 land records, that Joseph was farming in his own right in 1839 and employing a workman.

A second entry in the Petty Sessions records relating to Joseph Fanning was found for January 1842, when he took a case against Letitia and Mary Fanning, for wilfully trespassing on his land and stealing a quantity of his cabbage, turf and grass, contrary to the statute. The outcome to this claim is unknown as the only information recorded is "no appearance". Letitia was the wife of Bryan Fanning of Slanelough and Mary Fanning may refer to Robert Fanning's wife, as he married a Mary Maher, but as Mary was such a common name, it might also refer to some other member of the Fanning family living at Slanelough at this time.

This case to me would appear to be a dispute over land ownership. I don't think Letitia and Mary were taking the produce because they were hungry and destitute, but rather they and their branches of the Fanning family might be claiming a right to the part of the land that Joseph was farming and the products it produced. If this was the case and Joseph lost his claim on the land he was farming, he might have had to survive finding work as a general labourer to provide for his large family. As the lot of the agricultural labourer became extremely difficult during the famine years, it is a possible explanation for the family ending up in the workhouse.

If this was not the case, but he continued farming at Slanelough in his own right, perhaps some misfortunes befell him like many others around the time of the famine and he might not have been able to meet his yearly rent and faced eviction. From the records the remaining member of the Fanning family, Robert Fanning, appears to be farming a large farm here in 1854, but we do not know how Robert himself was surviving during the years of the great famine. Perhaps Robert might have been struggling himself to provide for his own family and meet what would have been a considerable yearly rent and he may not have been able to give any assistance to Joseph, Rose and their 9 children if they were in difficulties. We know from many accounts of life in Ireland around this time that labourers and also many tenant farmers were frequently only one step away from the door of the workhouse.

As a child in school, 1 learned about the time of the great famine in Ireland and about the people that died and those that left on board the emigrant ships in the years directly following the famine. At the time, I thought it was a very tragic period of our history, but it seemed to me to have happened in the distant past. Now when I reflect on the plight of the Fanning family of Slanelough and the 351 persons who were shipped out from Rathdrum Workhouse in the years immediately following the great famine, I feel a stronger connection to that time - especially when I realise that the Fanning family lived literally just a few fields away from the farm where I grew up.

The workhouse records show that Mary Fanning was 16 years old when she and her family left the Rathdrum Workhouse on board a cart bound for Dublin port. That would have been the same age as my great grandmother

Bridget Byrne, who lived a few fields away from where Mary grew up. Given that they lived in such a small farming community, it is likely that Mary Fanning and my great grandmother, Bridget Byrne, would have been childhood friends.

The Mystery of the Disappearing Croughals

Rental records from the Glanmore Estate in 1832 list 21 families who were leasing lands at Aghowle at that time. While researching these 21 named families I was curious about one particular entry for a man named as George Croghal who was leasing approximately 8 acres of land. I was intrigued by this surname as it was not a name I had come across anywhere in my research of County Wicklow families and I did not find this name again in the land records for the tenants who were recorded living in Aghowle in 1850 and 1854. Nor did it appear to be a corruption or spelling variation of any of the other local names found in the area at that time.

Upon further investigation, I found that in the local church records there was a William Crohill baptised in 1758. He was a son of George and Elizabeth Crohill of Aghowle. Given the very unusual names of both Croghal and Crohill and finding them both in the townland of Aghowle, I feel this is the same family name and it shows they were living in Aghowle as far back as 1758. The local church registers show entries for the Croghal/Croughal family located around the Aghowle area up until the late 1830s. As the name had disappeared from the land records relating to Aghowle from 1850 onwards, I did not know why this family with the unusual name had disappeared from the townland.

Then in 2016, a message was posted on a County Wicklow genealogy message board and the mystery was solved [AWMB]. A woman with the surname Croughwell, living in America, was trying to find out more about her ancestor George Croughwell/Croughal who had emigrated from Wicklow around the time of the Great Famine. She had very good information on George's year of birth and his parents' names, etc., from records her ancestor had to fill out after his arrival in America and later when he was applying for naturalization. Pooling our information and checking the local church registers, we were able to establish that her great-great-grandfather, George, was the son of Thomas Croughal of Aghowle. Thomas was born in February 1800. Croughal was a very unusual name in Co. Wicklow and it appears in the church and land records with a variety of spellings. This was not unusual for those times e.g. another more common local name, Moran, can appear as Murrin, Murine, Morn, Moren, etc.

Upon emigration, many Irish family names were slightly changed as they were recorded officially on entry into their new country, by people not familiar with the Irish names, or the Irish accents. Often these officials wrote down what they thought the name sounded like, thus Croughal appears to have become Croughwell.

I now know that George, along with his brother and sister, migrated from Wicklow to America around 1850.

George Croughal/Croughwell's descendant was able to share with me some information relating to his life after he emigrated. She kindly supplied me with a newspaper article relating to George and I have reprinted an extract of this article below.

> *George Croughwell was about twenty-three years of age when he came to this country. His educational advantages were limited, but he was naturally industrious and observing and as he found himself dependent upon his own resources, he soon found employment. Later he entered the works of the Glass Company at Berkshire, Massachusetts and for fifteen years was in the employ of this concern, engaged in the manufacture of clay crucibles for holding the molten glass. Mr. Croughwell was an excellent workman and the conscientious way in which he performed his duties soon won for him the respect and confidence of his employers. Politically Mr. Croughwell was a sound Democrat and in matters of religion was a devout member of the Roman Catholic Church.*

George married an Irish girl named Ann Devlin and the couple had 11 children, the youngest was just 1 year old when he died in 1877, aged 50 years.

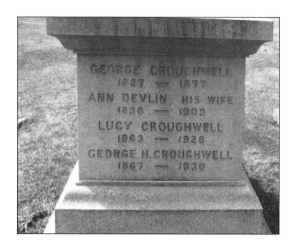

George Croughal/Croughwell's grave in Fairview cemetery, Dalton, MA.

Photograph courtesy of George's descendant Robin Croughwell, USA.

Chapter 5

1850-1885:
The Post Famine years

As the country entered the 1850s following the famine years, it was in a devastated state with many people trying to put money together to emigrate. Those that had survived the famine and were either too determined to stay in their birthplace or too poor to leave, settled down to try and rebuild their lives.

Revival of Glanmore
For the local people of the Aghowle area, the reinstating of Francis Synge as the owner of Glanmore Estate in December 1850 brought some stability. It is said that Francis was a good and hardworking farmer and he set himself the task of reviving the family estate. Under his management, the estate had recovered well by the mid-1850s.

Stables and farm Buildings erected by Francis Synge
using slate from the Glanmore Quarry
Photograph by kind permission of Sheila Clarke

In the following years, Francis continued to put all his energy into improving Glanmore. As the slate from the quarry was found to be unsuitable for roofing slates, he decided to utilise it instead in the extensive new farm buildings he was erecting. Parts of these impressive buildings can still be seen standing by the roadside at Glanmore today.

On the estate he had a large productive walled garden, a carpenter's shop and a forge. In addition to providing employment for local people in the area, he also provided lodgings and employment on the estate for young labouring men.

He held a bible class for these young lads on a Sunday morning and then marched them down to the local church service. Francis was a very strict religious man and followed his Brethren beliefs which would have differed greatly from the beliefs of his tenants. But as he was a hardworking and good landlord, he was well liked by his tenants and the local people. A story is told that on one occasion when there were very few buyers at the local fair, Francis himself stepped in and bought all the animals and was cheered as he headed for home with the stock [MUJ/p.21].

A Glimpse of life in the Locality
This section contains excerpts from Newspapers and Court records c.1860

This notice appeared in the *Wicklow People* Newspaper in March 1858 and gives us an insight into an aspect of dairy breeding in the district of Ashford at that time. One wonders if any of the Aghowle tenant farmers could have afforded the 5-shilling fee to bring their cow to Satin Jacket, especially as Mr Clements was not going to be accountable for accidents to cows.

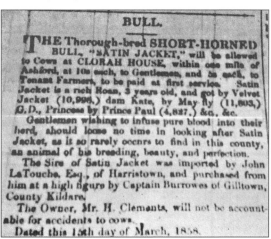

BULL.

THE Thorough-bred SHORT-HORNED BULL, "SATIN JACKET," will be allowed to Cows at CLORAH HOUSE, within one mile of Ashford, at 10s each, to Gentlemen, and 5s each, to Tenant Farmers, to be paid at first service. Satin Jacket is a rich Roan, 3 years old, and got by Velvet Jacket (10,996,) dam Kate, by May fly (11,803,) G.D., Princess by Prince Paul (4,827,) &c. &c.

Gentlemen wishing to infuse pure blood into their herd, should lose no time in looking after Satin Jacket, as it so rarely occurs to find in this county, an animal of his breeding, beauty, and perfection.

The Sire of Satin Jacket was imported by John LaTouche, Esq., of Harristown, and purchased from him at a high figure by Captain Burrowes of Gilltown, County Kildare.

The Owner, Mr. H. Clements, will not be accountable for accidents to cows.

Dated this 15th day of March, 1858.

Wicklow People Newspaper March 1858

BULL,

The Thorough-bred SHORT HORNED BULL, SATIN JACKET, will be allowed to cows at CLORAH HOUSE, within 1 mile of Ashford, at 10s each, to Gentlemen and 5s each to Tenant Farmers, to be paid at first service.

Satin Jacket is a rich Roan, 3 years old and got by Velvet Jacket (10,998) dam Kate, by May fly (11,803,) G.D., Princess by Prince Paul (4,827) &c, &c.

Gentlemen wishing to infuse pure blood into their herd, should loose no time in looking after Satin Jacket, as it so rarely occurs to find in this county, an animal of his breeding, beauty and perfection.

The sire of Satin Jacket was imported by John LaTouche, Esq., of Harristown and purchased from him at a high figure by Captain Burrowes of Gilltown, County Kildare.

The Owner, Mr Clements, will not be accountable for accidents to cows. Dated this 15th day of March, 1858

Remember to keep holy the Sabbath

Petty Sessions 20th September 1858 [FMP/IPCR]
In the petty court in Bray town, John Maher, of Ballymanus/Carrig Mountain, was charged with challenging James Timmons of Slanelough to fight at Ballymanus, on Sunday 5th September, when they were on their way home from Prayers. (Presumably they were walking back over Carrick after Sunday mass in Glenealy). The case was dismissed.

Petty Sessions 18th October 1858 [FMP/IPCR]
Constable Joseph Young charged Nicholas Ward of Aghowle Lower, with the following crime; that on Sunday 19th September at Aghowle Lower, he found Nicholas Ward employed stacking corn and thereby committing a breach of the Sabbath. The case was dismissed.

At that time Nicholas Ward was leasing a house and 20 acres of land at Aghowle Lower. On this particular Sunday he was probably trying to save his corn so he would be able to pay his rent to the landlord and have some food to feed his livestock over the winter months.

Auction of Farm Produce, Animals and Implements

The auction notice reprinted below appeared in the Wicklow Newsletter Newspaper on 27th August 1864. It would seem to indicate that one of the local Aghowle farmers may have moved from the area or had perhaps died, as the list of sale items goes beyond just farm crops. It also includes a horse and cars, a donkey and varied farm machinery.

HAY, OATS, POTATOES, &C.

TO BE SOLD BY AUCTION,
On SATURDAY, 3rd SEPTEMBER, 1864 at
UPPER AGHOWLE,
near Giant's Grave

5 Cocks of prime Well Saved Hay, 15 Stacks of Excellent Oats,
Half an Acre of White Rock Potatoes in drill,
a useful Farm Horse, rising 7 years' old:
1 Car and Harness;
I Jaunting Car, Harness and Cushions;
a Donkey, 5yrs. old; 1 Plough, by Paul and Vincent;
1 Harrow, 1 Ladder, 1 pair of Wheels, nearly new;
Beam, Scales and Weights.
Sale at 12 o'clock. Purchasers to pay Auction Fees.

HENRY Mac PHAIL, Auctioneer Wicklow

It can be noted that the Giant's Grave[1] is referenced as a landmark for finding Aghowle Upper.

Emigration in the 1860s

Although Glanmore Estate was profitable again and the local tenants were possibly in a better position than many other tenants of the time, still their lot remained a difficult one. They did not own their farms and most of them only held a one-year lease. Their whole existence was dependant on their land producing sufficient to keep their family and pay their yearly rent to the landlord.

As most farmers married and had large families, it became even more difficult when their children reached adulthood, as the small holdings they had could not support all members of the next generation. Most of the

---

1   The Giant's Grave is a pair of standing stones in a field close to Moneystown.

adult children either went out to work locally as agricultural labourers or looked for other employment further afield. For those thinking of moving away to seek work elsewhere, there were options of emigrating to England, America or even Australia. The following are the stories of three young men who left the Aghowle locality individually during the 1860s to seek employment or pursue a career elsewhere.

William Hatton: From Aghowle to a Californian Cattle Ranch

In the early 1860s, a young boy of just 13 years old left the townland to pursue a life at sea. He was William Hatton of Aghowle Lower house no.4. The Hatton family farmed 40 acres of land and had 8 children, William being the 4th oldest. Not much is known of his time at sea, but after 7 years William decided his future lay on dry land and he headed to California which was seen at that time as a place of great opportunity.

William Hatton
Courtesy of Elizabeth Barratt, Carmel Valley

He first worked in Salinas and then moved to the Carmel Valley. Here he took a position working on a large dairy ranch but in a short time became a ranch owner himself and also married around this time. The Hatton family very quickly established themselves as one of the most successful and prosperous families in Carmel Valley. This was due to William's hard work and skill at introducing innovative methods into the dairy industry. His influence was so significant that today the local historical society in Carmel Valley has considerable material in its archives relating to William Hatton and his family. Talks and lectures are given on the Irish boy who left County Wicklow at the age of 13 and went on to make a significant contribution to their community.

This is probably best illustrated by the following article, which was written in 2014 by Elizabeth Barratt of the Carmel Historical Society. Elizabeth has a particular interest in William Hatton and was most helpful to me in my research, sharing with me information and photographs relating to William and his family, from local history sources in Carmel. In turn, I was able to share with Elizabeth information on William's Irish background and his farming family in Aghowle.

FEBRUARY 2014 THE CARMEL VALLEY HISTORIAN
PAGE 5
Carmel Valley Pioneer William Hatton
By Elizabeth Barratt
(reproduced here by kind permission of Elizabeth Barratt)

Born the fourth of eight children on June 9, 1849 in County Wicklow, Ireland, William Hatton sailed away from his homeland at age 13 as an apprentice on a merchant ship. In 1869, at the end of his seven-year term at sea, he spent a year in Charleston, South Carolina where he worked as an agent for the United States Revenue Service. It was here that he met his future wife, Kate Harney, whom he would later marry in 1875.

Hatton came to California in 1870 and in time came to Carmel Valley where by 1884 he had acquired from Mrs. Dominga Doni de Atherton a 1,000 acre portion of the western most section of Rancho Cañada de la Segunda, near the mouth of Carmel Valley. This ranch, called the St. John Dairy Ranch, would become popularly known as the Hatton Lower Dairy. Old photos of the lower dairy, where The Barnyard Shopping Center is located today, show barns, corrals, a windmill, a ranch house, cookhouse, cheese house and other outbuildings.

Hatton at this time also became the manager of the Pacific Improvement Company's dairy ranch at Rancho Los Laureles and managed Mrs. Atherton's ranch as well. By 1888, he either owned or managed most of the dairies and cattle ranches from Highway 1 to past Carmel Valley Village. As one source claims he was "running nearly all the beef on the Valley floor all the way to Rancho Tularcitos." By 1889 he had purchased another large parcel of land near the mouth of the Valley from Joseph W. Gregg.

Carmel Valley old timer Joe Hitchcock wrote of Hatton's ranch, "Starting at Highway One was the St. John Ranch, which terminated at Cañada de la Segunda, approximately where Valley Hills Shopping Center is now located. Hatton had two dairies on the tract, there were two artesian wells on the tract, which he irrigated to grow alfalfa and rye grass. He had 2,200 acres in all on which he kept 600 cows."

During the twelve years he managed the Pacific Improvement Company's Del Monte Dairy at Rancho los Laureles, Hatton brought modern innovations to the dairy business. He introduced Durham cattle into the Holstein herd to increase the stock breed and improve the butterfat content in milk. He installed modern milk vats and cheese presses. Monterey Jack Cheese was made on the premises, sometimes marketed as Del Monte Cheese and sold to the famous Del Monte Hotel in Monterey to serve to its guests.

In time, William and Kate had nine children, seven of which survived: Anna, Harriet, Sarah, Edward, William Jr. , Frank and Howard. On October 22, 1894, just prior to completion of the Hatton's new 18-room Victorian home (at what is now the entrance to Carmel Knolls subdivision) he died at age 45 of Bright's Disease. His funeral was said to be the largest Monterey County had ever seen. The Southern Pacific ran a special train for persons who came from out of town and all Monterey businesses were closed during the funeral.

As can be seen from this article, William became a very successful dairy rancher and business man. It is not known whether this was due to his aptitude for learning and innovating or from the basic farming skills and work ethic he brought with him from his family farm in Aghowle. But for the 13-year-old boy who grew up on a 40-acre tenant farm in Aghowle Lower, where his father Edward Hatton probably milked 5 or 6 cows, William Hatton did remarkably well.

Captain John Storey: From Aghowle to the Antipodes

The story of the second young man who left the local area about the same time also tells of a young boy starting out for a career on the high seas. John Storey was the son of the local cobbler who lived at Ballycullen, about a mile from William Hatton's family home at Aghowle Lower. John was born in 1845, just a few years older than William and was about 17 when he went to sea. Unlike William, John Storey had a lifelong career at sea. He completed his training and returned to Ireland in 1871 to receive his Masters Certificate. In August of the same year he married Mary Anne Free.

William Hatton's home in Carmel Valley California
Courtesy of Elizabeth Barratt

By this time, John Storey's sister Jane was married and living in house no.5 at Aghowle Upper. It would appear that John and his new wife may have stayed for a while with Jane and her family at Aghowle. Birth and baptism records show that John Storey's wife Mary Anne gave birth to their first child a year after their marriage, while staying with Jane at house no. 5 Aghowle. Their daughter Alice was christened in Nun's Cross church in September 1872 and quite soon after that, mother and daughter joined John on a voyage back to Australia. He went on to captain many ships around New Zealand and Australia. He used to take his pet dog and cat with him on his voyages and sometimes his wife and children also went along.

Luckily, his family were not aboard in 1877 when Captain Storey was commanding a barque named *Planter* carrying coal from Newcastle to Adelaide. On that journey, they ran into extreme weather and the vessel

Captain John Storey c.1928
Photograph courtesy of the Smith family
New Zealand

began to take on considerable water. Captain Storey decided they would have to beach the vessel on a nearby island. While making for the island, they were forced to abandon the vessel and launched a boat to take the crew and the captain, along with the ship's dog and cat, to the island. But this boat was over-turned by a large wave and they were all thrown into the water, struggling to make land.

John Storey became trapped under the upturned boat for a considerable length of time but his dog stayed with him. He eventually freed himself and he later wrote that as he struggled to swim ashore, his dog caught his clothing in his jaws and assisted him to safety, thus helping to save his life. When he reached the beach, he collapsed and was unconscious for 20 minutes, but when he came around his faithful dog, *Sailor* was still sitting beside him. After a number of days, all the crew and Sailor were rescued from the island and Sailor lived with the Storey family into his old age.

John Storey died in 1929, aged 84, and was an active member of the Ancient Mariners' Reunion Association right up until his death. A year before his death, on the 28th of April 1928, The Sydney Morning Herald ran a feature on Captain Storey, recounting his many adventures at sea and concluded the feature by saying *"still hale and vigorous, carrying his 6ft 2in with an almost soldierly bearing, Captain Storey thinks nothing of a journey of 900 miles to attend the yearly outing of the Ancient Mariners"*.

Garrett Short - From Aghowle to the most polluted town in England
The third young man who left the local area around the same time as William Hatton and John Storey did not travel as far as his two neighbours. He was Garrett Short who lived at Aghowle Lower, House No.1 and his home was only a few hundred yards from William Hatton's family home. Garrett was born in 1848 and was the third of six children born to Patrick

and Margaret Short. In these tenant farming families, as the older children reached adulthood they would have been looking for some way to earn their own living and to contribute to the rearing of the younger children. Often one or two of the children would remain at home to help run the family farm while others would look for employment locally, move to Dublin or look at the option of emigrating. It was to England that Garrett Short set out in search of employment.

In the early years of the nineteenth century, life in England changed dramatically due to the Industrial Revolution. People poured in from the rural agricultural countryside to find work in the new industrial towns and cities. One such town that was undergoing great expansion during this time was the town of Widnes in Lancashire.

In 1847, the first chemical plant was set up in Widnes to produce alkali for the new manufacturing industries. Soon it became a central location for more chemical factories and the town grew rapidly as workers flooded in to find employment in these new industries. The demand for workers became so great that people from Ireland started to make their way there and later in the 1880s, workers began to arrive from Poland and Lithuania. By the late 1880s it is said that the town existed under a cloud of smoke and chemicals and it gained the reputation of been the ugliest, dirtiest, most polluted town in England at that time.

Sometime between 1866 and 1871, when Garret would have been around 20 years of age, he left the green fields and fresh air of the family farm in Aghowle to seek work in the chemical industry in Widnes. In the English 1871 Census, Garrett is recorded as living in Widnes, where he is boarding with an Irish family named Cassidy from Co. Offaly. Also living with the Cassidy family is their 19-year-old niece, Catherine. It appears romance blossomed for Garrett while boarding with this family and in the summer of 1871, he and 19-year-old Catherine were married in the district of Prescott in Lancashire.

According to the census records taken ten years later in 1881, Garrett and Catherine were still living in Widnes, with Garrett being a chemical labourer in the manufacturing industry. Also recorded were the couple's two daughters, Margaret aged 7 and Mary aged 5. Garrett's youngest sister Margaret had also come over from the farm in Aghowle to live with the family.

Unlike many that moved to England and settled there permanently, Garrett and his family returned to live and farm at Aghowle. By 1883 they were back in Aghowle, as the land rental records show that he took over the lease for the house and family farm at that time [VOI/CB/AU]. They were now returning with four young children.

The move must have been quite a transition for the family. While Garrett was returning home to the familiar place where he was born and reared, his wife Catherine was arriving with a young family to an unknown rural location. Their children must have found their new surroundings quite strange. The only home they had known until this time was the bustling and heavily polluted town of Widnes.

Now they found themselves in a small thatched farmhouse, looking out on the little green fields that stretched up to the foot of Carrick Mountain. Maybe for the first time in their lives, they were experiencing the freedom of open spaces and fresh air. We can follow the fortunes of Garrett and his family after they returned to Aghowle in the story of house no.1 in the second half of the book.

Changes on the Estate
In 1861, Francis Synge of Glanmore Estate married Editha Treull from nearby Clonmannon House. Editha, like Francis, was a very religious person and a member of the Plymouth Brethren and she practised homeopathy. Francis and Editha did not attend the church services at Nun's Cross Church, but chose instead to attend meetings of the Brethren at Kilfea school house. Editha was in favour of modernisation and brought many changes to the Castle at Glanmore. She also took a great interest in the running of the estate school at Kilfea and even gave a room in the castle to its new teacher, who was of mixed race and from the West Indies [MUJ/p.20].

By the 1870s, Glanmore Estate was again prosperous. All the work and dedication that Francis Synge had put into rebuilding the indebted estate had paid off. The tenants were probably counting their blessings that the estate was back in profit and was being run efficiently by a fair-minded landlord.

Unfortunately, in 1878 this situation was to change. Francis Synge became ill and rather than seek medical attention for him, his wife Editha undertook to treat him herself, by praying for him and administering homeopathic potions. This proved unsuccessful and Francis died. Francis had willed the estate to Editha for her lifetime and then it was to return to the Synge side of the family. It is said that Editha was greatly affected by her husband's death and those around her became very concerned for her health and wellbeing, suggesting she move to London for a while.

When she returned from London a year later, she came back to Glanmore with a new husband. He was Major Theodore Webber Gardiner. Major Gardiner shared his wife's religious beliefs and was a member of the Exclusive Plymouth Brethren. The Major was not a man of money and had no knowledge of farming in Ireland. So, without the influence of a dynamic landlord the estate started to go into a decline from this time onwards and the estate tenants, including the farming families of Aghowle, were again facing an uncertain future.

1880-1885: Impacts of the Land League

At this time throughout Ireland many tenant farmers were finding themselves in difficulties. Agricultural prices throughout Europe had been dropping and there had been a number of bad harvests due to wet weather, especially in the west of Ireland. As a result many of the tenants in that part of the country were facing eviction due to being unable to meet the high rents set by their landlords.

Charles Stewart Parnell, president of the National Land League

Thomas Shannon of Aghowle, worked on Mr. Parnell's estate when he was in prison in 1882

In response to this situation, tenants were urged to form together to resist eviction and to campaign for reduced rents and the right to buy out their farms. From this movement, the National Land League was formed in 1879 by Michael Davitt. At its inception, Charles Stewart Parnell was elected to the position of president. As Parnell's estate was at Avondale Rathdrum, less than 8 miles from Aghowle, it is likely that the local people would have followed this new organisation with great interest.

We know from the obituary of Thomas Shannon (of Aghowle Lower, House no. 2) that he was an active member of the Land League and when Parnell was imprisoned in 1882 for his involvement with the organisation, Thomas Shannon was one of the people who volunteered to work on Parnell's estate at Avondale.

Two of Charles Stewart Parnell's sisters, Fanny and Anne set up the Ladies Land League in 1881. The function of this organization was to support the work of the National Land League and to help raise funds. Many branches of the Ladies Land League were set up around the country and the wives and daughters of tenant farmers joined these branches. It is not known whether a branch existed in the Ashford or Glenealy area, or if any local Aghowle ladies joined. But it is likely that if a local branch existed, then Thomas Shannon's wife Catherine would have joined. There was a branch in Roundwood and some of its records still exist in the National Library of Ireland.

The records for the Roundwood branch show that in 1882 over 70 women in the surrounding district of Roundwood joined the league [NLI/LNLL/R]. The catchment area extended as far as Parkmore, which is one of the townlands that borders Aghowle Upper, and some of the members listed from around this area included: Mary Kiely of Parkmore who was assistant secretary; Martha Davis of Moneystown who was treasurer; Miss Lucy Byrne; Miss Kate Byrne and Miss Alice Byrne all from Moneystown and Miss E.A. Kiely from Parkmore.

The correspondence shows that as well as collecting funds, the ladies of the Roundwood League were also active in supporting a local woman named Mrs Carroll who was being evicted from her farm at Castlekevin, where her family had farmed for over 80 years. The letters from the Roundwood branch to head office give details of the local tenants attending Mrs. Carroll's eviction and helping to transport her furniture to a neighbour's house, where she was afforded temporary accommodation. The Ladies of the Roundwood branch also organised the delivery of a land league house for Mrs Carroll, which was wooden in construction and easily erected. Mrs Carroll's house was sent down from Dublin by train, with a man who would help erect it.

The national organisation of the Ladies Land League only survived for a short while, before it was asked to disband. It is thought that the men of the Land League felt that the Ladies branch had become too active and militant! In the years of the late 1870s and into the 1880s the scenes of tenant evictions throughout Ireland became commonplace.

Chapter 6

1885-1899:
Land Wars and Love Stories

Eviction of the Carey family at Aghowle Lower
Following the death of Francis Synge and the marriage of his widow
Editha to Major Gardiner in 1879, the situation changed for the families
of Aghowle, along with the rest of the Glanmore tenants. Francis had
been a dedicated and hardworking landlord who had returned the estate
to profitability in the 1850s and 1860s. When Editha married Major
Gardiner, who had no knowledge of running an Irish estate, the couple
relied on other people to keep the estate running. The agricultural economic
situation was not good at that time and the Glanmore Estate rental records
for the year 1886 show that this was reflected in the yearly rental accounts,
as they recorded a number of the tenants were in rent arrears. The yearly
accounts for 1886 also show that in that year, Edward Synge was appointed
as agent for the estate. [NLI/HP/GEA]

Edward was a nephew of Editha's late husband Francis Synge (and a
brother of the playwright John Millington Synge). Edward Synge was at
that time a land agent based in Co. Cavan and operating in several counties
around the west of Ireland, where evictions were commonplace and where
Edward was said to have a reputation as a harsh land agent. As the estate
at Glanmore was to be returned to the Synge family on Editha Gardiner's
passing, no doubt the Synge family would have had a strong interest in
keeping it as profitable as possible in the meantime.

One of the tenants that had accrued rental arrears by 1886 was Hugh
Carey of Aghowle Lower. Hugh was leasing a house and 53 acres of land
and was a single man in his sixties. Living with him on the farm were his
two elderly unmarried sisters, Mary and Bridget. Bridget was born with a
mental disability and she had been cared for all her life by her family in
their cottage at Aghowle. In those days, her mental disability was classified
medically as an imbecile - this term would later be dropped from general
medical use.

Hugh was working the family farm which his father, Matthew Carey, had farmed before him. The Glanmore Estate rental records taken in 1832 show that Matthew's holding was 32 acres at that time, while the land records taken in 1854 show that by that time, Matthew Carey was the leaseholder for the house and 53 acres of land. Previously, the local parish church records show that Matthew and his family had been well established in the locality in the early years of the nineteenth century. There are records for the baptism of 8 children born between 1803 and 1820 to Matthew Carey and his wife Eleanor/Elizabeth Doyle [NLI/PR/W].

It would appear that as time moved on, Hugh took over the lease after his father Matthew died and eventually there was just Hugh and his two elderly sisters left living in their home at Aghowle Lower by the year 1886. It is likely that, as he approached old age with no family to assist him, farming the 53-acre holding and meeting the yearly rent of £25 would have become very difficult for Hugh Carey and by 1886 the rental records show that he was in arrears.

The following article appeared in the Freeman's Journal dated 22nd October 1886:

Wicklow Thursday

Today, at 12 o'clock, the interest in a farm belonging to Mr Hugh Carey, Aghowle, was set up for auction for the recovery of rent, in the Wicklow courthouse. The farm is situated about 4 miles from the town of Wicklow, on the property of the late Mr Francis Synge, now owned by Major Gardiner, who married Mr Synge's widow. In the writ of sale, however, it was not Major Gardiner's name was entered, but Henry Alexander Hamilton, of Balbriggan. The farm was put up to auction by Mr Kennedy, sub-sheriff, who read out the particulars and terms of sale.

Before the auction began, Mr M'Carroll asked who was the landlord in this case, was it Major Gardiner?

Mr Kennedy – I can not exactly say, but it is Mr Henry Alexander's name is entered as plaintiff in these proceedings

Mr M'Carroll – if Major Gardiner were the landlord perhaps if Mrs Gardiner were written to she might interfere and stay the sale, which deprives an honest man of his home?

Mr Kennedy– I believe it is Mr Hamilton who is the landlord. I regret I have no power to stop the sale.

The farm was then put up, when a man in the court offered £5

Mr M'Carroll asked- What is the name of this man?

No answear was given.

Mr M'Carroll – Who offers £5

The Bidder – I am a representative of Mr Hamilton.

There was no offer from anyone on Mr Carey's behalf and representative of Mr Hamilton was accordingly declared the purchaser of Hugh Carey's farm for £5.

It is not known what transpired between 22nd October 1886 and 22nd July 1887, but it would appear from the above newspaper report that Hugh Carey and his sisters had lost the right to their house and farm, although they remained there until July 1887.

Edward Synge was the agent for Glanmore Estate at the time and it was he who was responsible for their eviction. It is said that he had experience of evictions in the west of Ireland, where he would use the element of surprise and organise the eviction party to arrive at the house by an unexpected route and at an unexpected time.

In the early morning of July 22nd, 1887, Edward Synge organised his eviction men to set out from Tomriland crossroads to head for Carey's house in Aghowle [TSBS/p.196]. The following is the report of the eviction as it appeared in The Freeman's Journal on July 23rd, 1887.

EVICTION ON THE ESTATE OF MRS. GARDENER, OF GLANMORE CASTLE, COUNTY WICKLOW

(From our correspondent)

Wicklow Friday

The eviction of Mr Hugh Carey, of Ahowle, on the above estate, took place today, under circumstances of the most distressing character. The tenant himself advanced in years, was the mainstay of two aged sisters, one of whom is an imbecile. The eviction was carried out by the sub Sherif, Mr Davidson, of Bray and the agent, Mr Synge, of Cavan.

About one o'clock when it became known that the tenant was evicted Cannon Dillon, Rev F M M'Enerey, C.C, Rev Father O'Brien, C.C. Messers Joseph M'Carrol, Peter O'Brien, Christopher Murray, Garrett Byrne, &c drove to the scene. Large crowds had by this time assembled. After the eviction, eight policemen under head constable Kelly, arrived.

A meeting was subsequently held and speeches were delivered by Messers Joseph M'Carroll, Peter O'Brien, M Cooney, Murray, Garrett Byrne & c denouncing landlordism and expressing the deepest sympathy for the evicted. A vote of thanks to Mr Hutton [Hatton] a protestant neighbour of Mr Carey, for offering a house and shelter to the victims, was passed with acclamation.

The Mr Hutton mentioned in the above report refers to the Careys' close neighbour, Edward Hatton. As the Hatton family were Church of Ireland religion, it seems it warranted particular mention that they offered shelter to the evicted, even though they were of a different religion. This would seem to be in keeping with the very close community spirit that existed in the farming community in the townlands of Aghowle and Ballycullen, where the tenant farmers of both religions farmed and socialised together. The Hatton family had farmed beside the Carey family for over 40 years.

The laneway that connected the Hatton farmhouse to the Carey Farmhouse at Aghowle Lower.

The above report from the Freeman's Journal gives us a good description of the eviction of the Carey family and the rallying of the community in the immediate aftermath. But the following two accounts below gives an even more distressing report of what happened to the three elderly Careys on the evening and night following their eviction. These articles were printed in the Flag of Ireland newspaper one week later on the 30th July 1887. This newspaper was published by a branch of the Irish National League and this is reflected in the content and tone of the articles.

Eviction in County Wicklow

The eviction of Hugh Carey on Friday, though heartrending in the last degree, was followed by scenes still more harrowing. After the eviction, the poor imbecile sister sat at the door of the little room once her own, beside her the other aged sister, trying to soothe the poor creature. Apparently feeling that something awful had befallen, but without understanding its cause, she clung to the old place; nor could anything induce her to leave the old spot.

As the evening wore on the two sisters remained in the same position, more like statues than human beings. The kind offer of Mr Hatton, Mr Carey's protestant neighbour, of a house and shelter, could not therefore be accepted, as Mr Carey himself, though advanced in years, refused to leave his sisters.

At last all three retired to a broken shed and there, without door or roof, the three victims of eviction spent the night, true at all events to Irish brotherly and sisterly affection. The evictor is Mrs Gardner, of Glanmore Castle.

Elsewhere in the same edition of the Flag of Ireland newspaper:

One More Horror

Mrs Gardiner of Glanmore Castle is spoken of as a Christian Lady if so how can she explain leaving Hugh Carey and his two aged sisters, in an old broken down shed, with the rain pouring through the roof, large portions of which have long since fallen to pieces?

Even that part of the roof remaining, being sodden scraws, admits the rain like a sponge. No chapter of the most tear moving romance, that was ever written, not even Dickens death of Little Nell - is more touching than the story of this pitiable eviction in the County Wicklow.

To read of a poor old imbecile woman sitting down and refusing to stir from the home where her darkened reason had ever found a loving shield and devoted family sympathy and the aged brother and sister, feeble and faint though they were, staying faithfully by her and herding in a shed which a wild animal would scarcely deem a shelter, reads more like a tale got up to move one's dormant pity than an incident of everyday life in Ireland in the jubilee year of Queen Victoria.

It starts the question whether we who prize ourselves on living in a civilised and religious age are not after all the victims of some delusion and whether we are really not less hardened in heart and less mindful of the bond of our common humanity than the brutal crowd who turned down thumbs long ago in the Colosseum and beheld with equanimity the spectacle of men and women hopelessly battling with the beasts of the jungle.

What is there about landlordism that it seems to have the power of making all Christianity a sham and a cold cynicism the only rule for the guidance of human society? For the people who have so long tortured the lives of the Irish peasantry the Sermon on the Mount would seem to have been preached in vain.

It is not known how many nights the three Carey siblings spent in the shed, but it is recorded that the local people came together and managed to build a house for the family, in one day.

[AJTT/p.79] No details are recorded as to the nature of this house, whether it was a dwelling built of whatever materials were available to the local neighbours, or if it might have been a wooden hut obtained from the Land League. There are accounts from around this time that describe how the Land League would sometimes supply a pre-packed wooden hut that the neighbours could erect for an evicted family. Nor is the exact location of the Careys' new abode known. It was most likely located somewhere at Aghowle Lower close to their former farm and among their lifelong neighbours and friends, who had come to their aid. Reports of similar situations from around this time, record that often the new dwellings were erected where there was sufficient space by the roadside and in a location that the landlord could not claim that it was on his property and could therefore not look for rent from it, or have the right to knock it down.

I have identified a possible location where the house for the Carey's may have been built. As one enters Aghowle Lane, just before where the river used to cross the lane, on the right-hand side, is a small area of waste land.

This area lay on the outside of the boundary ditch of the land that the Carey family had held. Three local sources, Terry Timmons, Dick Mahon, and Eric Bradshaw, remember the remains of a dwelling there into the 1950s, but it was not recorded as a dwelling, occupied or unoccupied, in the 1901 census, the last of the Carey family died in 1900.

A few days after the eviction, Edward Synge had the house from which the Careys were evicted, knocked down. This no doubt would have been very distressing for the family, in particular for Bridget, who could not fully comprehend what was happening. A death certificate for Bridget Carey shows she died exactly three months after the eviction. Her brother Hugh, who registered her death, recorded she died at Aghowle on the 22nd day of October 1887 and under the section for cause of death, he had recorded "*shock from eviction*".

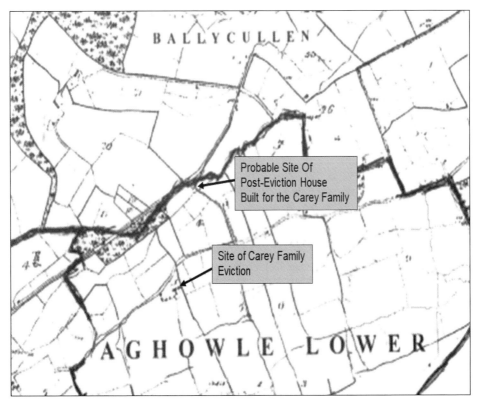

Carey Eviction Sites

Death Certificate for Bridget Carey, who died three months after the eviction

As the two remaining Carey siblings had no means of income and it would appear no remaining family in the locality, they would have been destitute following the eviction. Newspaper records show that they did receive grants of money, from the Irish National League, usually for the sum of £2, at various intervals, but they must have been greatly reliant on the generosity and care of their neighbours and friends in the local area.

One person in particular appears to have been very supportive to the family. He was Thomas Shannon, who lived in Aghowle Lower, close by the Careys' farm. Both the Shannons and the Careys would have been living and farming at Aghowle Lower for several generations. Thomas Shannon was an active member of the Land League and his obituary in 1925, in the *Wicklow People* newspaper, made special reference to his assistance to the Carey family at their time of need. When the Careys were evicted in 1887, Thomas was farming 22 acres of land and had 6 young children to provide for.

Four years after the eviction, in June 1891, Hugh Carey, then aged 70 years, passed away. His death record shows that he was still residing at Aghowle and that he had been suffering from paralysis for 18 months. His death was registered by his neighbour Thomas Shannon, who was present at his death. The dog licence records, [FMP/IDLR], also indicate that in the years following the eviction, Thomas Shannon had continued to renew the dog licence for Hugh Carey's black sheep dog, so while Hugh no longer had any farm stock or need of a sheep dog, it would seem that Thomas Shannon wanted to ensure that Hugh, who had so little left in the world, could still enjoy the companionship of his dog for his final years. With the support and generosity of his neighbours, Hugh Carey passed his final years where he had lived and farmed all his life, in the valley beneath Carrick Mountain, in the company and care of his elderly sister Mary, surrounded by his neighbours and friends and with the companionship of his sheep dog.

It also appears that the care and kindness of the Carey's neighbours continued on after Hugh's passing. A death record dated nine years later, shows that Hugh's sister Mary was still residing at Aghowle when she died at the age of 80 in May 1900. Again, the death was registered by Thomas Shannon who was present at her death. But for the support of their neighbours and friends, it is likely that the Careys might have had to end their days in the Rathdrum Workhouse.

It is said that the Carey eviction cast a shadow over the good name of Synge as landlord in the locality. Previous generations of the Synge family were reputed to be fair landlords and were generally well liked by their tenants. It is not known if Editha Gardiner was involved in the decision to evict the Careys and the mode in which the eviction was carried out or if Edward Synge had full responsibility, but perhaps the previous generations of Synge landlords might have handled the situation differently.

A poem I wrote in relation to the Carey eviction can be found in the Poetry Appendix (See poem "The Eviction").

The Annual Accounts for Glanmore for the year 1886-1887 show that Edward Synge had just taken over as agent that year and an expense of £6 was recorded for the cost of producing notices to inform the tenants of the appointment of Edward Synge as Agent. Also noted was that a Mr. Murphy received a salary of £2 "*for warning the tenants*".

It was not uncommon during the years of the Land War for a repossessed farm to remain empty for some time, as the locals would not take up the lease. This was usually out of loyalty to the evicted family, or out of fear of reprisals from supporters of the evicted. The surviving Glanmore estate rental records would indicate that Hugh Carey's farm remained unoccupied into the 1890s and for nine years after Hugh had died [NLI/HP/GEA].

The first reference I found of this in the Glanmore rental records was in 1899, when there was a note that Carey's evicted farm had been re-leased. This would have been 12 years after the eviction. It is not known whether the land lay idle for this period or whether the landlord or someone connected to the family may have had the use of the land in the intermediate years. But the surviving records would indicate that no rental income was received from Carey's farm before 1899.

I have not come across any reference to other high-profile evictions on the Glanmore estate in the years that followed the Carey eviction. Perhaps they had decided to handle matters differently from then on.

There are surviving rental records for the Glanmore estate for some of the years between 1886 and 1918 and within these records are some interesting notes written in red pen in the margins, relating to rent due and arrears owed from various tenants.

Some examples of these include notes for rental due in September 1887, just two months after the Carey eviction. It would seem that a lot depended that year on the tenants getting a good sale for their hay. The first note related to Bryan Reilly, who was a close neighbour of Hugh Carey at Aghowle Lower: *"horse died will pay after sells hay"*.

While the same year beside some tenants in nearby Tomriland the following notes were recorded:

- John Coleman – *"promises further payment on sale of hay"*
- William Coleman was receiving a reduction in his rent *"allowed at Mrs Gardiner's written request"*
- Nicholas Neill in the same townland *"bullock died, promises to pay when hay is sold"*

The tenants' dependency on their harvest to meet their rent requirement is also highlighted in another rental record where it is noted that - *The tenant promises to make a further payment in about a month's time when she threshes her oats.*

In 1913, the compassion of Mrs Gardiner, perhaps mindful of the Carey eviction many years earlier, is reflected in the following note relating to the widow of Patrick Carr of Ballycullen, whose rent was £2-10 shillings – *This tenant is very old and very poor, and the landlord does not wish for her to be pressed for the rent due.* The census records taken two years earlier in 1911, show that Mrs Ann Carr was widowed and was living in Ballycullen in a two-roomed thatched cottage which had only one window to the front and that in 1911 she was aged 78 years and the only other person residing with her was her 80-year-old unmarried sister.

An Ill-Fated Love Story

Just a few years after Aghowle was making newspaper headlines in relation to the eviction of the Carey family, the townland found itself appearing again in local and national newspapers. This time the story was regarding a relationship between a young man from Aghowle and the daughter of his employer. The details of this story could have been taken from the plot of a novel by Thomas Hardy or Jane Austen.

It involved a relationship between a young Catholic farm labourer and the daughter of his employer, who was a Protestant landowner. The year was 1891 and the young man in question was John Doyle, 25 years old at the time and from Aghowle (house no.9). For the previous year, John had been employed as a farm labourer on the farm of a Mrs Sarah Haughton in the townland of Roscath, about 8 miles from Aghowle.

Mrs Haughton had married in 1873 but within five years she found herself widowed while still in her 20s. She was left to run her late husband's farm and rear her two small daughters on her own. In 1890 John Doyle had gone to work for Mrs Haughton and, as her farm was quite a distance from his home, he lived in a lodge on the Haughtons' farm.

The following details of the story are compiled from reports in several different newspapers in 1891, including *The Wicklow Newsletter* and *The Wicklow People*.

It appears that while John was in the employment of Mrs Haughton, her eldest daughter Sarah Jane, who was 16 years old, formed an attachment with him. However, Mrs Haughton did not approve of her daughter's interest in John Doyle. Matters came to a head in April 1891.

Normally on a Sunday morning, John Doyle was given time off to go home to Aghowle to visit his family and would return later in the afternoon. On Sunday 12th April, John left as usual to go visit his family and Sarah Jane Haughton left to go to church as was her normal Sunday routine. But as the afternoon wore on, Sarah Jane had not returned from church and John Doyle had not returned from Aghowle. Mrs Haughton became concerned. Upon inquiry, Mrs Haughton was told it was believed that Sarah Jane had not gone to church, but had run off with John Doyle.

Mrs Haughton went to the police in Wicklow Town and reported that her daughter had been abducted. Newspaper coverage of the subsequent trial that followed gave details of the events as they transpired. The couple had left the farm on that Sunday and in the company of some other young people went to a football match in the vicinity of Bollinass, near Ashford. Later that day, they went to the home of Mrs Esther Murphy in Bollinass, who was a relative of Sarah Jane Haughton and Sarah Jane stayed the night here, while John Doyle went home to his family in Aghowle. The next day, John visited Sarah Jane in Mrs. Murphy's house and in the early evening John and Sarah Jane came back to John Doyle's family house in Aghowle. John's mother implored Sarah Jane to go home to her mother in Roscath but she refused to do so.

By this time, the police from Ashford had become aware that Sarah Jane

Haughton was in Aghowle. They came and arrested John Doyle on charges of abduction and they took Sarah Jane back to her mother. John Doyle was placed in Wicklow Gaol until the next court hearing, which was on the 29th May. Meanwhile, Mrs Haughton dispatched Sarah Jane into the service and care of the Rev. Ross of Bradford in England.

On 29th May, the court hearing took place in Wicklow where the details of the case were outlined, and John's defence solicitor put forward the case that John had committed no crime and that Sarah Jane had left with him of her own free will and wished to marry him. To illustrate this claim, a letter was produced, which had been written by Sarah Jane from where she now resided in Bradford, to John Doyle. This letter was reprinted by the newspapers covering the case (see below). At the conclusion of the hearing, John Doyle was released on bail and the case went forward to the next assizes.

At the trial, which was held on 23rd July, much detail regarding the case was covered and witnesses were called, including Sarah Jane's mother, John Doyle's mother, and Mrs. Esther Murphy of Bolinass. The newspaper also reprinted further correspondence from Sarah Jane in Bradford to John Doyle and a letter from the Rev. Ross to John Doyle – see below.

The outcome of the case was that the jury found John Doyle was innocent of the crime of abduction and it was to be noted that there was nothing against the character of Sarah Jane Haughton.

Letters reprinted by papers

This letter was reprinted by the *Wicklow Newsletter* Newspaper on 30th May 1891 as part of the coverage of the initial court hearing:

> *4 Ashley Crescent, Manningham,*
> *Bradford, 6th May*
> *My Dear Jack, –*
>
> *I write to you a few lines to let you know where I am. I am sorry not to have seen you before I went away, but I will not forget you. I am nearly always crying when I think of you having gone to jail.*
>
> *I hope you will not forget to write to me when you get mine. You must forgive me for not writing to you before now, but I could not help it. I have been very sick since I seen you. I hope you will not forget the promise you made to me and I will not forget mine to you, on that day we left home.*

I am sure what you told me is true, but if mother knows it and if she seen me, she would kill me for it.

I have thought of you coming over here: but it would be better, I think, to wait a week longer, until we see further.

If you would like me to come home as far as Dublin, I will in about a month. I think it would be better for me to come home to Dublin than for you to come here.

I hope you will forgive me for writing so bad. I am in a hurry to finish it. I hope you won't show it to anybody, for if mother would see it she would write to my mistress and I would be prevented writing again.

Write when you get this. I have no time to write more at present, but I am not forgetting to send you a kiss – I remain your dear friend.

Sarah Haughton.

The newspaper report also added the following:

Miss Haughton does not omit to fulfil the last-mentioned promise, for the letter, towards the termination, is embellished lavishly with the usual symbols – thirty-two crosses – that indicate the "soul felt flame"

In the *Wicklow Newsletter* coverage of John Doyle's trial on 23rd July 1891, it concluded its report by reprinting the following correspondence from Sarah Jane and her employer the Rev. Ross, to John Doyle.

Since her alleged abduction, Miss Haughton has been employed in the service of a clergyman in England and during her residence there the following correspondence took place, which might throw some additional light on her future intensions:

Manningham, Bradford, June 16, 1891.

Dear John,

I write to let you know how I am going on. I hope that you are in good health now. I never heard from mother since I left home. I am not contented at all. I am always thinking of you and when I am in trouble I always say that I wish I could see you: but mistress is always throwing you up in my face, but all they say won't differ me a bit; and mistress says so. Did you ever see Ellen Murphy since, tell her I was asking for her and her family? Where is Rosey now, a girl is only a fool to stay in Ireland, for a girl that knows her business has good wages. I am cooking for seven in family and it is a horrid job, for I don't quite understand all the things but mistress says that I am improving every day. Write soon and let me know when the assizes will be and tell me who the bails are and don't put anything you think or care about in the letter, for I am afraid that it would be opened by mistress, for the postman calls four times a day; the mistress always answears and gets the letters.

The letter you wrote me, the first I got and she wanted to know who it was from. I wouldn't tell her, but she found out from Mr. Miller. I hope you will be freed at the Assizes, I expect you will come to England then and it is as good a place to get on in as Ireland. Are you working yet or at home? I never heard anything from them at home since I left. I wrote to them the night I got your letter for the first and they did answear it, but they sent to mistress something for me, but she wouldn't tell much about them. I now conclude with love to you – I remain your sincere friend,

Sarah Jane Haughton.

"Love is kind and suffers long;

Love is meek and thinks no wrong:

Love, than death more strong;

Therefore give us love"

====================

To John Doyle

Aghowle

Ashford

Co Wicklow.

I am astonished that you have the audacity in daring to write again to Miss Haughton – and such a letter – after my communication to you from her a fortnight ago. I have to inform you that I have forwarded your letter to be dealt with in the proper way by the authorities and the same course will be taken with any further letters which you may be so unwise to send. Miss Haughton told me on June 18 of her own accord that she had solemnly made up her mind never to have anything more to do with you. She then requested me to write on her behalf and tell *you so. She has since conveyed the same joyful news to her mother and sister. There is no doubt that while the appeal of her own good sense and reason helped to bring about this determination, it was greatly helped on by the disgraceful way in which you caused her letter to you to be made a common laughingstock in the Court and then to be printed in the public newspapers. It all went to show matters and people up in their true light and it helped to open her eyes.*

Robert Ross

Vicar of St Marks Manningham

So, while John Doyle was found innocent of the charge against him and walked free from the trial, it would appear there were no winners at all in the whole affair. John had lost his employment and had spent time in Wicklow jail awaiting the initial hearing. Also, he apparently had lost the affections of his sweetheart, Sarah Jane.

Sarah Jane Haughton, who was only 16 years old, had been banished from her home and family into service in England and no doubt was heartbroken at her separation from John, whom she intended to marry. She must also have felt much betrayed, by having her personal correspondence to John shown in court and published in the newspapers. One imagines that John Doyle's solicitor might have advised on this course of action to help prove his innocence and avoid a jail sentence. Whether John was happy with the decision to do so, we do not know.

Mrs. Haughton, who had been widowed at a young age, was trying to run her farm and bring up her two daughters on her own. She must have suffered considerable stress and public humiliation, in her attempts to preserve the good name and character of her 16-year-old daughter, while trying to prevent her from entering into what she considered a very unsuitable marriage.

The family of John Doyle must also have suffered great distress and worry in the whole situation and as a labouring family with 7 children, ranging in age from 25 to 7 years, one wonders how they were able to meet the legal costs for such a case to prove their son's innocence.

One supposes that if John Doyle and Sarah Jane Haughton had been of the same social standing and religious beliefs when they met and formed an attachment, things might have turned out quite differently for them.

Eight years later, John went on to marry a girl from Saggart in Co Dublin, named Mary Mansfield and the couple began their married life in Aghowle (see the story of house no 7).

The 1901 Census shows that sometime between 1891 and 1901, Sarah Jane Haughton returned from England and at the time of the census she was living with the family of her mother's sister in county Wexford. The family were farming, and their residence was recorded as an 11-roomed house.

In the 1911 Census, Sarah Jane is recorded back living with her mother and younger sister, Mary Susanna, in the home of Mrs. Haughton's brother Matthew Moore, who lived at Moorshill near Arklow, the Moore family were farmers. Again, their farmhouse is recorded as an eleven-roomed house.

A death record for Sarah Jane Haughton shows she died in 1951, aged 76 years. She had remained a single woman all her life and her occupation was recorded as a farmer. She resided in the Woodenbridge area of Co. Wicklow, which would have been close to where she was living at the time of the 1911 census.

The Local Woods get Clogged

Earlier in this book, there is a folklore story reprinted from the Ashford Historical Journal, about the cobbler who could be heard up on Carrick Mountain mending the shoes of the little people. Back in the late 19th century if one was wandering through the local woods one might have thought there was some truth in this folk story, as you might have come across a group of men with strange accents, tapping away as they made wooden clogs.

During the Industrial Revolution in England, it became popular for workers to wear wooden clogs as they were often standing all day on cold and damp factory floors or in wet conditions down in the coal mines. Many of these clogs were made in Lancashire and the wood of the alder tree was found to be suitable for their manufacture.

During the late nineteenth century, cloggers from Lancashire came to make clogs on the spot in the Ballycullen and Ballymanus woods from the alder trees that grew there [ITCT/p.179]. At this time, Mr Tighe of Rosanna owned the plantation at Ballymanus, while the plantation at Ballycullen was part of the Glanmore Estate. I do not know if these cloggers lived where they worked in the woods, or if they found accommodation in the locality. I did not find any trace of them in the 1901 census records, but they may have returned to Lancashire by then.

The Supposed Case of Smallpox at Aghowle, Ashford

The above headline appeared in the Wicklow People Newspaper dated 2nd March, 1895, the article relating to a meeting of the Board of the Rathdrum Workhouse where the supposed case of smallpox at Aghowle came up for discussion and in particular, the manner in which the Workhouse had dealt with the case.

The background to the case was that a few weeks previously during a period of snow and frost, a man had called to the home of George Hatton of Aghowle (House No. 4) and Mr Hatton had taken him in and gave him shelter. Mr Hatton said the poor man was not very well in the head and the next morning he was not able to get up. The family let him remain for some days hoping he would recover. As his health did not improve, Mr Hatton consulted with a local member of the board of the Rathdrum Workhouse, who advised him to contact the workhouse doctor to come examine the man and certify him suitable for admission to the workhouse. When the doctor arrived on the Monday he said the man had typhoid and he thought

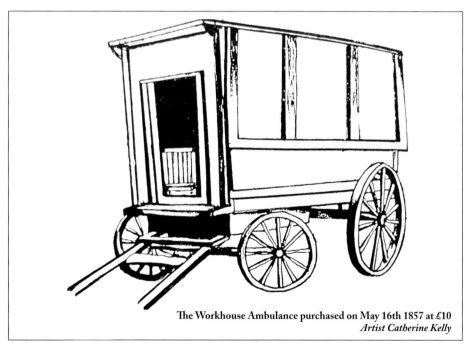

The Workhouse Ambulance purchased on May 16th 1857 at £10
Artist Catherine Kelly

The Rathdrum Workhouse Ambulance, for which George Hatton waited in vain for a week.
Illustration is taken from **From Shadow to Sunlight**
by kind permission of Kevin Byrne

the very ill man also had smallpox, and that no one was to go near him, except a workman in the Hatton household. The doctor left a sealed letter with Mr Hatton, and Mr Hatton was then waiting daily for a car from the workhouse to come collect the ill man, but it never arrived. By Thursday, he contacted the workhouse again, and on Friday a doctor was again sent to examine the man at Mr Hatton's house in Aghowle, but by that time the poor man had expired. The doctor that arrived then stated he thought the man had died from pneumonia.

Mr Hatton had come along to the workhouse board meeting to outline what had happened and to state that he thought the situation had not been handled correctly and that such an ill man should not have been left so long in his care. The board concluded that there had been a problem with the normal procedure being followed in this case, as there was a temporary doctor on duty.

Local Entertainment

The notice below appeared in the Wicklow People Newspaper on Saturday 24th September 1892, announcing an upcoming Sports Day in Ballycullen to be held on Monday 17th October. One imagines the date set for this event would probably have coincided with the completion of the harvest in the local farming community, and hopefully if all the crops were harvested and saved and the yearly rent, which fell due on 29th September, was paid to the landlord, then the tenants were free to enjoy a day of entertainment and sport before the winter set in.

Notice from Wicklow People Newspaper – Saturday September 24, 1892

BALLYCULLEN
(County Wicklow)
PONY, JENNET & DONKEY RACES,
And
ATHLETIC SPORTS
Monday 17th October, 1892
PROGRAMME OF EVENTS
Will be issued in a few days
Subscriptions will be received by
HUGH McDermott, Hon Sec.
Thos. Colquohoun

Chapter 7

20th Century - The Townland before the Free State

Tables are Turning

The first decade of the twentieth century heralded an era of change in the Aghowle valley - the tenant farmers were at last able to take the first steps towards land ownership. The newspaper article reprinted below relates to this very significant change in the lives of the local farming community. *Dublin Daily Express October 31st1903:*

> *THE SYNGE ESTATE*
> *On Wednesday evening a largely attended meeting of the tenants on the Synge estate was held at Ashford Co. Wicklow, to consider the offer of sale made by the landlord Mrs. Gardiner and terms on which they would agree to purchase their holdings. The chair was occupied by Mr George Manley, Ballycullen, who stated that the terms Mrs. Gardiner was willing to sell at were 6s in the £ to tenants who had never been in the Land Court, 4s in the £ on first term rents and 2s in the £ on second term rents. It was resolved to inform Mrs. Gardiner that the terms at which they were willing to purchase their holdings were 8s in the £ on first term rents and 6s in the pound on second term rents, with corresponding reductions in those cases which had never been in the Courts. A deputation was appointed to wait on Mrs Gardiner at Glanmore Castle and the meeting adjourned.*

The meeting, which was held on Wednesday 28th October was also covered in an article in the Wicklow People Newspaper dated 31st October 1903. This article listed some of the tenants who were in attendance. Among those listed were the following Aghowle tenants: Garrett Short (House No. 2), William McDermott (House No. 4), James Turner who held a farm in Aghowle but was living in Ballycullen, James Byrne (House No. 10), Simon Rutledge who was the leaseholder of House No. 7 in Aghowle but who resided in Wicklow town at that time, and Peter Mooney who was the leaseholder of House No. 9.

Also in attendance at this meeting in Ashford was my grandfather Patrick Connolly (House No. 8) - as we will shortly see, he would be back down again in the village of Ashford the following morning to get married in the local church!

For several centuries, most of the land in Ireland had been held by landlords and their tenants had never had the right to own the land upon which they lived and farmed. In many cases, they were given no more security than a one-year lease. Finally, after years of political struggle and bitter land wars, these tenant farmers were now being offered the chance to obtain the full rights of ownership to their own land.

While the Aghowle farmers would remain as tenants of the Glanmore estate for some time, they were now no longer just tenants at will, but were in the process of purchasing their own farms. They now knew that the work they put into building up their farms by reclaiming and improving their land would be for their own benefit and for that of the generations to come after them.

Wedding Bells, Arrivals and Departures
This first decade of the new century also brought changes in many of the farmhouses in the townland including births, marriages, deaths and emigration. Between 1900 and 1905, there were wedding celebrations in 5 of the 10 local farmhouses, and between 1900 and 1910 there were 15 babies born into the townland and 11 people died. While some of these deaths came at the end of long fulfilled lives, two of the deaths were younger people who died from consumption and two were young children who tragically died by fire. Three residents also emigrated during this decade - one to England and then on to India, one to America and one to New Zealand.

The new century had only just arrived when the first marriage took place. In March 1900 (in house no.5), the local saddler Edward Smith (who had been widowed for 12 years) married Rachel Edge of Moneystown (who was also widowed and a mother of two adult sons). Romance was to blossom a second time between these two families, as just over three months later, Edward Smith's only daughter Martha married Rachel's son, Thomas Edge. The younger happy couple also came to live in the Smith's farmhouse at Aghowle.

In the autumn of 1903, there was marriage in the air at Aghowle

Upper, this time in the Connolly farmhouse, (House No. 8). In 1898, my grandfather Patrick Connolly and his sisters had moved from Knockraheen (near Roundwood) to live and farm in Aghowle. The Connolly farm was situated just across the main Aghowle road from the Byrne farm (No. 10) and five years after the Connollys arrived, on 29th October 1903, Patrick married Annie Dempsey who was living on the Byrne farm, where she was housekeeping for her 4 elderly uncles.

It is likely that Patrick and Annie's wedding was a subdued occasion, as Patrick's sister Kate had passed away just a month earlier on the 26th September. Kate had been ill for several years and died from T.B. (or consumption as it was called at that time). Just a month after Patrick Connolly's marriage, his sister Jane married Thomas Byrne of Knockrath

This photograph, taken later in their lives, depicts Thomas Byrne seated and his wife Jane (nee Connolly Aghowle) on the right. Thomas and Jane were married in November 1903. Photograph courtesy of Thomas Byrne's grandson Tommy Byrne, Ballylug

and moved to live in Thomas's place in Knockrath, which was about 8 miles away. Sadly, Kate Connolly had not lived to see either her brother or her sister wed and in just over two months there had been a funeral and two weddings from the Connolly's farmhouse.

Two weeks after my grandfather Patrick Connolly married, there was another wedding - this time in the next farmhouse down the valley. Sarah Moran was the only child of William and Ann Moran, who lived in that farmhouse. She had originally married Andrew Cunniam in 1891, just a few weeks before her 18th birthday - but just 6 years later, Andrew tragically died from a throat infection that could easily be treated today by modern medicine. Sarah was left a widow at 24 with two small children. Five years later she remarried. Her new husband was Jeremiah Farrell from Ballycullen.

The two marriages from the Connolly farmhouse had taken place while the household was still in mourning, but the wedding of Sarah and Jeremiah was a much livelier celebration. In those days following the church ceremony, a celebration was held in the family home, with food, drink, music and much merrymaking. The celebrations were held in Sarah's farmhouse and stories remain yet about the boisterous behaviour of some of the local lads that night, including lowering a billy goat down the chimney into the kitchen full of wedding guests.

In the autumn of 1903, the little community of Aghowle Upper had witnessed three weddings and a funeral.

Less than two years later, in August 1905, there was another marriage in Aghowle. This time Patrick Connolly's youngest sister Ellen married Terence O'Reilly of Aghowle Lower (house no.3). Ellen had been working in Dublin for some time, but on trips home to her family in Aghowle, it seems romance blossomed between herself and Terence. The couple married in Dublin in August 1905 and then came to start their married life in O'Reilly's farmhouse in Aghowle Lower.

The Townland Witnesses a Terrible Tragedy
Just over a month after Ellen Connolly and Terence O'Reilly married, on the 28th of September 1905, the whole townland was devastated by the horrific deaths of Mary and John Doyle's two children, who perished when their cottage at Aghowle Upper burnt down. The details of this tragedy are covered in the story of House No. 7 - see section "A Fire Tragedy".

While one cannot possibly imagine how this horrific event must have been for the Doyle family, I feel it must also have greatly affected the families in the surrounding neighbourhood, when one considers what a small tightly knit community these families would have lived in at that time. At Aghowle Upper, there were 6 houses, Mary and John Doyle's house where the tragedy happened, stood on the brow of the hill, not far from the base of Carrick Mountain. Their cottage was the highest house in the valley at that time. The other 5 houses at Aghowle Upper lay scattered around beneath them, all less than half a mile away from the Doyle's home.

   John Doyle was a labourer and as the newspaper reported at that time, he was working for the local farmers in the area. The nearest house to theirs was John's family home, where his parents and siblings lived. John's father and brothers were, like John, agricultural labourers who would have worked in the surrounding neighbourhood. The remaining four local families were all farming families who spent their days living and working on their farms at Aghowle Upper. All these people lived within this small community, only travelling outside the valley to attend mass or church service each Sunday or to go to the local village or town to shop or sell their produce. For these people to witness John and Mary Doyle's cottage burn down and two of their children perish within it, must have been a very traumatic experience. The two houses that lay in the valley just below the Doyle's were where Jeremiah Farrell and Thomas Edge lived - these two men had tried in vain to enter the cottage and save the children. I feel that in the initial years following the fire, the memory of the event would have hung heavy over the valley and remained vividly in the memory of these local families who witnessed it.

Emigration
During this decade, there was also emigration from several of the local farmhouses. By this time, George Hatton (house no.4), was the only remaining member of the Hatton family on this side of the Atlantic. As covered in earlier accounts, over a 30-year period his brothers William, Edward and John and his sister Annie had all migrated to California. In 1903 George sold his house and farm at Aghowle Lower. While it is unclear what he did in the following years, but it is known that in 1909, George, who was by then a man of around 60 years of age, went to join the remaining members of his family now living in America. Sadly, George did not live very long to enjoy his retirement there, as he died in April 1911 in Monterey. As this grave stone indicates he is buried with his older brother Edward and younger brother John, in Monterey California.

Grave of the three Hatton brothers, Monterey California
GEORGE HATTON May 18, 1845 - Aug 26, 1911
JOHN HATTON Apr 8, 1862 - Apr 7, 1912
EDWARD HATTON May, 9 1842 – Oct 6, 1924
Photograph from www.findagrave.com

The 1901 census records for the Smith-Edge household at Aghowle Upper (House No. 5), show that Edward Smith's youngest son Samuel is still living in the family home at the time of the census but soon after this record was taken, Samuel emigrated to join his brother Frank in New Zealand.

Samuel married, settled and prospered in New Zealand and we will hear more about his brother Frank in the story of the next decade, when he made a return trip back to Aghowle.

Sometime around 1905 or 1906, Esther Shannon of Aghowle Lower migrated to England, where she found work in London. Here she met her future husband George Lawrence and they were married in 1908. Not long after they married, George's work took him to India, where the girl from the little farmhouse in Aghowle found herself living for several years with a young family.

1911: New Church opens at Parkmore, Moneystown

From a religious viewpoint, the townland of Aghowle was part of the Church of Ireland parish of Killiskey and the local Church of Ireland families living here attended Nun's Cross church, near Ashford. Their children went to school in Kilfea school near Nun's Cross, and later on to Nun's Cross school which opened in 1877.

Before 1864, the townland was part of the Roman Catholic parish of Wicklow Town, which included the Ashford and Glenealy districts. Then in 1864, Ashford became a separate parish. For the Roman Catholic families, the churches at Ashford and Glenealy were their local parish churches and the nearest school within their parish at that time was Ballylusk National School.

Ballylusk School was convenient for the families of Aghowle Lower - but for the families in the upper part of the townland, the school at Moneystown (belonging to the Roundwood/Glendalough parish) was closer and therefore these children attended Moneystown School. Up until 1911, the Catholic families of the townland went to mass in either Ashford or Glenealy. Ashford church was about 4 miles away and it was nearly 5 miles to Glenealy church, if one went by the road.

Back Row: _____, Tim Kenna, _____, _____, Tom Grimes
Second Row: Mary Rochford, Kate Rochford, Lill Rochford, Sue McManus, Mary Timmons
Back Row: _____, _____, Patsy Timmons, _____, _____

The opening of the church at Parkmore Moneystown 1911
Photograph from "A Pictorial History of Roundwood, County Wicklow, 1870-1970"
Courtesy of Joseph McNally

But of course, when the main way of travelling was mostly by foot, people used the shortest route, which was usually through fields and over hills. It was common practice for the Aghowle people to walk over Carrick to mass in Glenealy.

In 1911, they were given another option, as a new catholic church belonging to the Roundwood/Glendalough parish was built at Parkmore Moneystown. For those living in the upper end of the townland this new church offered a much shorter journey to Sunday mass. They now travelled a route through the fields of either Connolly's farm, or up the Raheen lane, (which was part of the O'Brien's farm, after 1914) and out onto the road between Slanelough crossroads and Parkmore. The journey this way to Sunday mass was only about a mile. While these families still considered themselves very much part of Ashford parish, they frequently used the church in Parkmore for Sunday mass. In time when bicycles and cars became more popular, the mass paths through the fields fell out of use, but the gate where the path came out on the road was known as the mass path gate for many decades afterwards.

The Old Tin Church
Moneystown.
Opened 1911.

Photo c.1922

Moneystown Church C.1922
Photograph from "A Pictorial History of Roundwood, County Wicklow, 1870-1970"
Courtesy of Joseph McNally

The weekly gathering of the rural community for Sunday mass would have been a major event in the lives of the local people and soon the new church at Parkmore became a very important focal point for the local community. As well as the religious obligation of attending mass, the social coming together of the neighbourhood was also very important.

This social gathering was not without its rituals. People walked by mass paths from many directions, joining in along the way with people from the surrounding districts. When they arrived at the church, the women and children would gather together, and the men would separate out into different groups. Those that arrived on horseback or in pony and traps had their own area to tie up their horses under the trees, where there was a water trough for the horses. As well as attending mass, another important part of the Sunday morning gathering at Parkmore was the purchasing of provisions in Kit Timmons's shop, situated across the road from the church.

Jack Murtagh of Moneystown, born in 1939, recalls the Sunday morning gatherings at Parkmore church from his younger days:

> *I remember the crowd that used to stand outside Park chapel before mass time, they all had their own stations. The week's gossip would be discussed and trashed out there, every Sunday morning. At the corner opposite the chapel a crowd of the older farming men stood including my father (Willie Murtagh), the 3 Aghowle men, Paddy Connolly, Bill Farrell and Miley O'Brien, then Tommy and Johnny Miley, Andy Mernagh, Rich Cullen, John Gallagher of the lane and Greg Cunniam, Larry Timmons, Jack Lawler and Charlie and Jim Lawler of Montiagh.*
> *A different group of men gathered at the side of the church and us younger lads used to gather under the cypress trees, we were the football crowd. I remember one morning there was great excitement. The evening before one of the farmers had been burning bushes and it had spread to the neighbouring farmer's ditch and burnt it and a bit of a row broke out between the farmers under the trees, the next morning before mass. We younger lads had to go over and separate them, there was peace restored that Sunday outside the church before mass and world war three was averted.*

1914-1918 World War 1: Three Local Casualties

In August 1914, the United Kingdom declared war on Germany and its allies, initiating what became known as the Great War and what we now refer to as World War I. At that time, many Irish men were already soldiers in the British army and many more enlisted during the War. When it concluded over 4 years later, it is estimated that over 35,000 Irish men had died.

Even the small townland of Aghowle was touched by this great loss of life - three men connected to the townland were among the war dead.

Harry Hearn

The first of these three men was Private Harry (Henry) Hearn, who was the stepson of William Henry Smith, who had been born and reared in House no. 5 in Aghowle. In 1898, William Smith married Ellen Hearn, a young widow with two small children - May (aged 10) and Harry (aged 9). William and his new family lived for a short while at Tiglin and then moved to Ballycullen. William's stepson, Harry Hearn, had a great desire to join the army and joined while still underage (several years prior to WW I). His mother was heartbroken and a local landlord, Wilfred Tighe, bought Harry out of the army. But young Harry was still searching for adventure and ran away and re-joined the army. Once again, Mr. Tighe bought him out and returned him to his grateful mother. But Harry was determined to be a soldier and as soon as he was of legal age, he joined the Kings Regiment (Liverpool). In August 1914, World War I broke out and Harry's regiment was sent to France. Just 3 weeks later, on the 20th

Harry Hearn, Born 1890, Died 20th Sept. 1914,
Killed in action in France
Listed on La Ferte-Sous-Jouarre Memorial
Photograph from "Ashford a Journey Through Time"
Courtesy of Sheila Clarke

September 1914, Harry was killed in action in France. Just over two weeks after Harry's death on 7th October, his sister May set sail for New Zealand as the bride of Frank Smith of Aghowle, her step father's younger brother (see the story of house no. 5). It is not known whether news of Harry's death had reached his family at Ballycullen before his sister May departed. But either way, within a few weeks, Harry's mother was to learn of the loss of her son Harry and to say goodbye to her daughter May as she headed to the far side of the world, knowing it was very unlikely she would ever see her daughter again.

John Shannon
- Born 02nd December 1876, Aghowle
  - In some publications of the lists of Irish men who died in the First World War, details state that John was the son of Thomas and Catherine Shannon of Aghowle Ashford, but record he was born in Sandycove, Dublin, which is incorrect. John was living in Sandycove before he joined the army and probably gave his address in Sandycove on joining and the records incorrectly indicate that he was also born in Sandycove.
- Died 09 September 1916
- Killed in action in Mons, Belgium

The second local casualty was John Shannon, who had been born to Catherine and Thomas Shannon of Aghowle Lower (House No. 2), on 2nd December, 1876. John's story is covered in the history of House No. 2 along with a copy of a poignant letter home to his parents from the army camp in Aldershot Hampshire before he went to the front.

Richard John Joseph Rutledge
- Born 1st July 1886 at Aghowle, Ashford, Co. Wicklow
- Died 13th October 1917
- Died in Belgium of wounds received

The third local man who died in the Great War is recorded as Private Richard John Joseph Rutledge, a member of the Black Watch Royal Highlanders. Richard died on 13th October 1917, from wounds received. He is buried in Dozinghem Military Cemetery in Belgium.

Richard was a member of the Rutledge family that lived in house no.7 at Aghowle. He was born in the Rutledge farmhouse on 1st July 1886 to Richard and Eliza Rutledge. A few years after Richard's birth, his family moved to the Ashford area. Richard's oldest sister Winifred was named as his next of kin on his army records. Winifred was born in the farmhouse in Aghowle on Christmas day 1880.

When I was a child, I recall that sometimes in early November, one of our protestant neighbours would call to the farmhouse selling poppies for Remembrance Day. My father would always buy a poppy and place it on the shelf of the Sacred Heart lamp in the kitchen, underneath the framed picture of the bearded Christ.

In this prominent place, the red paper poppy would remain throughout the year. As our family had no connection to the war dead, I am not sure if my father bought the poppy out of respect and politeness for our Protestant neighbours who called to the house selling them, or perhaps in remembrance of the local young men who had lost their lives in foreign lands. My father was born in 1907, so although he was just a child at the time of the First World War, perhaps the memories of the tragedies that were visited on the neighbouring families at that time remained with him still half a century later.

Easter Rising

Of course, while World War I was taking place on the international stage, there was the Easter Rising happening in Dublin in 1916. During the recent 1916 centenary year, there were many interesting Wicklow-related stories highlighted - but I am not aware of any direct Aghowle connections with the events that took place in Dublin during Easter week. While the small townland of Aghowle has been touched by several historical periods of turmoil over the years, this particular one seems to have passed it by.

Emigration 1914 – The Smith and Edge family leave for New Zealand.

As covered in the story of House No. 5, in early October 1914, Thomas and Martha Edge and their 4 young children left their farmhouse in Aghowle to migrate to New Zealand. Martha's brother Frank Smith, who had emigrated about 15 years earlier, had come home to Aghowle to visit and to escort Martha and her family back to New Zealand. While Frank was back in Ireland, he married May Hearn, the step daughter of his oldest brother. As mentioned above, May's brother Harry had died just three weeks after the start of the First World War and a few weeks before May and her new husband set sail for New Zealand.

Frank Storey kept a diary of his voyage home from New Zealand and his return voyage. See the story of House No. 5.

Ballylusk National School

School Days 1919

Following the spate of local marriages in the early 1900s, along with the arrival of the O'Brien family in 1914, there was by this time a new generation of children growing up in the townland. The Catholic children in the lower end of the townland went to Ballylusk School, while the Catholic children in the upper end went to Moneystown School.

The group photograph (overleaf), taken in May 1919, depicts four of the Aghowle children attending Moneystown school.

Nun's Cross School
Illustration reproduced from **A History of Nun's Cross School 1877-1977**,
by kind permission of Margaret Bloomer

Back Row: Larry Timmons, Bill Farrell, Murt Kenna, Charlie McManus, Tim Kenna, Willie
              Murtagh, Johnny Miley, Andy Timmons, Paddy Connolly, Paddy Bowen.
Third Row: Kate Kinsella, Lizzie Bowen, _____, Jimmy Timmons, Jack Storey, Paddy Storey,
              Mick Bowen, Bride Farrell, Kittie Timmons, Molly Storey, Jack Bowen,
Second Row: Maggie Lawlor, Molly Byrne, Maggie Byrne, Maggie Cunniam, Bride Timmons, Bride
              Miley, Maggie Murtagh, Lizzie Byrne, Bride Cunniam, Bride Mernagh, Nan Byrne.
Front Row: George Brinkley, Joe Brinkley, Jimmy Connolly, Martin Miley.

Included in the above photograph are 4 children from Aghowle
*Back row: 2nd from left - Bill Farrell, 9th from left - Paddy Connolly Next row: tallest girl
in centre - Bride Farrell
Front row: third boy from left - Jimmy Connolly, in his bare feet.
Photograph from "A Pictorial History of Roundwood, County Wicklow, 1870-1970",
courtesy of Joseph McNally*

The Smith children from House No. 5 would have attended the Church of
Ireland School at Nun's Cross. Before their departure to New Zealand, the
older Edge children would also have attended here and when the Bradshaw
family (House No. 4) arrived around 1918, they too attended Nun's Cross
School.

Reflections - Billy Smith Ballycullen (b.1944)
The Smith family that are living and farming in Ballycullen today have a
long connection with the townlands of Aghowle and Ballycullen. There is a
history of the Smith family farming at Ballycullen for generations stretching
back to the early 1800s. In 1870, one of the Ballycullen family, Edward
Smith, married and moved to farm in Aghowle (see the story of house

no.5 Aghowle Upper). Then Edward's oldest son, William, returned after his marriage to farm in Ballycullen, while Edward and his family remained farming in Aghowle for over 40 years. The descendants of Edward Smith are still farming at Ballycullen and the Smith family now also own several of the original small farms at Aghowle Lower.

In March 2016, I visited Billy Smith, great grandson of the above Edward, in the Smith's farmhouse at Ballycullen. Billy's knowledge of the locality and its people is unequalled and he can recall from memory the history of every farm and family in the area, going back through the generations. These recollections are often brought vividly to life with personal stories about individuals that he remembers from his own childhood, or stories passed on to him by his father and grandfather.

On a sunny March afternoon, we sat in the cosy farmhouse looking out across the farms of Aghowle Lower and Ballycullen that lie beneath Carrick Mountain, while Billy shared with me some of his vast knowledge of the local history.

Billy Smith Reflects on Local History

There is a cave up in Carrick, Bride Farrell used to tell me about being up there. The cave had an overhanging rock and there was a stone seat going around the inside of it. Bride Farrell and Molly Connolly [who were born in 1904 and 1905] *were young teenagers around the time of the War of Independence, when the local IRA/IRB men were training up on Carrick and the young girls used to go up to Carrick of a Sunday afternoon and pick up the empty cartridge cases among the rocks and from around the cave and bring them home with them. There was part of the rocks on Carrick used as a handball alley too, Dan Short and Jim Smith and the men of my father's generation, used to play handball up there.*

There was a castle in Ballycullen years ago, the site where it stood is known as Pluck's Walls. There was a roadway out of it that came down at Sheanes, it was a pebbled lane and it continued and came out somewhere in

Billy Smith, Ballycullen
Photograph courtesy of
Seamus Corcoran

Ballylusk. I used to be ploughing up there years ago and you would turn up some of the pebbles as you were ploughing. There was also said to be a tunnel running underground from the castle that came out in the middle of the field somewhere.

The field where the castle used to be, is near a lane called the Dairy Lane, it got that name from the time the farmland around there was owned by the Twiss family. On their farm was an area called the Rocky Pasture, it was a powerful place for summer grazing. The Twiss family kept a large herd of cows and did a lot of churning and butter making. They used to bring the cows down from the main farm and up the Dairy Lane to graze the Rocky Pasture.

There is a stream, or small river, that runs down through Aghowle and passes across Aghowle Lane and on through Ballycullen to meet the Vartry river, it is known locally as the Aghowle river. Where it passes across Aghowle Lane nowadays is covered over, but it used to be just an open river with a little foot bridge over it to one side, that had a railing and a bit of corrugated iron so you could walk over it at the side. I remember going in there with an ass and cart when I was a small lad and the ass wouldn't cross the water for me. I was rightly stuck, but Paddy Reilly that lived on the lane came along and he got the ass to cross through the water.

Ellen O'Reilly and her son Paddy, Aghowle Lane c. 1940
Photograph courtesy of Terry Timmons
Billy Smith recalls Paddy helping him get his ass and cart across through the river
on the lane

I remember that Dick Bradshaw who lived on the lane had machinery for hire and he used to get terrible hardship in the wet weather when the river would be high, trying to get the machines in and out through the water. One-night Bill Farrell of Aghowle was coming flying out along the lane in the black dark on his bike and there was an old ass asleep in the laneway, Bill very nearly got killed.

The river flows on through Ballycullen and many years ago, the locals dug a track and turned the river, diverting it into our ground and back around again for about 100 yards and that was enough to drive a mill to grind corn. The old shores were there in my memory, but the mill was gone, but my father remembered when he was a young lad, they used to be going down with ponies and traps to get their corn ground. At that time, Peter Timmons owned the mill.

My great grandfather was Edward Smith, who lived and farmed in Aghowle, about a mile and a half from here, he was a saddler by trade.

My grandfather William, Edward's son, married a children's nurse who was widowed young and had two children. They lived and farmed here in Ballycullen. After the rest of Edward's family went to New Zealand, he came back here to live out the last few years of his life with his son William's family. Although he was quite elderly at that time, he still carried on his trade from the yard here. My uncle Ned was handy with a needle too, so he was also called the Saddler. Edward's workshop here in the yard looked out over the haggard. The story goes that one day a neighbour was coming up the back field through the gap and picked up a bag of gold sovereigns near Edward's workshop. The man brought them in and told Edward to put them somewhere safe, so that he wouldn't lose them. Not long after that, Edward passed away and the sovereigns were never seen again.

My grandfather William was known as Crofton, he got this name because he used to have a pocket watch, back in the days before radios and televisions and he was very particular about having the right time. So, he used to check his watch was right 3 times a day, once by the Crofton's clock on their estate at Inchanappa, once by the bell from Nun's Cross Church and once by the horn from Deans saw mill, which blew every morning to call the workers to start work.

When my father got married here in the 1930s, Alec Carr who lived down the road and some of the local boys came around to the house to rise devilment at the wedding. They were horn blowing, with old horns of cows and rising a terrible racket. Alec Carr was just getting ready to give the horn another big blow, when my father snuck up on him and grabbed the horn off him and that put an end to that.

My father had a lorry back in the 1940s and used to carry stuff for people all over the countryside. He helped people move house and carried spuds and the like and at one time he drew headstones for a family called Stephens in Rathnew. Every week he went to Dublin with a load of rabbits to sell to the butchers' shops. At the time, a lot of people here were out lamping and hunting rabbits at night to make a few bob. On the day that my father was going to Dublin, the locals would be coming down here to the house at 7 o'clock in the morning, with asses and carts full of rabbits.

One day when he was in Dublin with a load of rabbits, he had an accident with the starting handle, while he was trying to start the lorry and damaged his eye, he was lucky he didn't lose his eye altogether. But that day he had to leave the lorry where it was on the street in Dublin and go to the hospital and when he went back to collect it, he found there was only the chassis left. It was during the wartime and people had come and stripped all the parts off it, he never got back on the road with the lorry after that.

My grandmother Ellen, had been a children's nurse before she got married and all her life she looked after all the sick in the area, those who had broken limbs, pneumonia, bad chests and everything else. She walked miles through the countryside to care for them and she was affectionately known by some of the locals as "The Doc".

Billy Smith Reflects on Local Families

I remember a lot of the families that used to live here, around Aghowle and Ballycullen. In Aghowle Lane there were 4 families, the Shorts, the Shannons, the Reillys and the Bradshaws. My grandfather and Dan Short were very great with one another and Dan would often be over here. Dan used to refer to his wife Mary as the polis [meaning the police].

Back in the 1940s, when the nylon stockings first came on the market, Dan had a problem pronouncing the word nylons, anyway, one day Dan was over here visiting and he said to my father "Be God the polis is after getting the lylons"

Dan Short was a big strong man, one time he walked over here to borrow a drill plough and he carried it back over his shoulders across the river and when he and the horse had finished his bit of ploughing, he carried it back over here again.

Dan Short and my father, also worked for a while on the forestry with horses and at one stage, Paddy Reilly of Aghowle Lane, worked with them too, at the time their wages was a fiver a week. Another local man that worked on the forestry was Alec Carr of Ballycullen. In those days, the men would bring their sandwiches for lunch with them in a little bag and they used to hang up the bags under a tree in the shade. Alec Carr's wife looked after him extremely well and always made him great sandwiches with big thick cuts of meat in them, these sandwiches were the envy of all the other men.

Also working with them on the forestry at the time, was a man called Kevin Reilly, who was always up to some mischief. So, one day when no one was looking, Kevin took the big slices of meat out of Alec's sandwiches and put them into Dan Short's bread.

When lunchtime came and they sat down to eat, Dan was surprised and delighted, with his lunch and said "Be God the Polis was queer and good to me today with the sandwiches", meanwhile Alec was sitting eating his two pieces of empty bread. When he got home he asked his wife why there was no meat for his sandwiches that day, but she replied "my dear I put lovely thick slices of meat in them this morning". Then Alec realised what had happened and rightly suspected Kevin Reilly. The next morning when Kevin arrived for work he found Alec was waiting for him, with a hatchet in his hand.

Reilly's house in Aghowle lane was a lovely little well-kept house. As a young lad, I had tea and apple tart in there many times, at that time Mrs Reilly [Ellen] was an old woman and lived in the upper room.

Years ago, my grandfather and old Ter Reilly, used walk over Carrick mountain into Glenealy and on to Killmacurragh estate to cut timber for the day and then walk back home again in the evening. They would always carry their guns with them, in case they came across any rabbits along the way. Those men were made of iron.

In the days before machinery was used, my grandfather and Charlie Shannon of Aghowle, mowed a two-and-a-half-acre field here below the house, in one day, with two scythes and that was considered to be some achievement, I often heard the old people talking about it.

At one time, Charlie Shannon had his eye on one of the Sheane girls of Ballycullen, this was when Tom Sheane was only a little lad and the sister used to bring Tom for a walk in along Aghowle Lane. But Charlie Shannon used to be trying to get the sister on her own, so he would say to Tom "go down the field there and bring me up the three cows I want to count them". and Tom would happily disappear off for a while, to carry out this important job.

Bradshaws also lived and farmed in the lane. After Dick got married he got farm machinery and went out for hire doing work for all the local farmers. Back in Dick's parent's day, before Dick was married, there used to be house dances sometimes over in Bradshaws. Dick's sisters were known as very fine women with many admirers and my uncle Ned used to go to the house dances over there. Ned used to tell the story that old Mrs Bradshaw used to say to him "you are very welcome to my home, but you are not welcome to my daughters."

In my time, the families that lived further up in the Aghowle townland were Turners, O'Brien's, Farrells, Connollys and the Rocher Doyle.

Turners land was in Aghowle, but their house was across the road in Ballycullen. They were two old brothers, Dinny and Johnny, as a boy I can remember old Dinny Turner coming in to my grandfather in the yard, with a nail coming up through his shoe and my grandfather put the shoe on a last and fixed it for him.

There used to be a gathering up in Sheanes in Ballycullen of a Sunday night, the two old Turner brothers used to go there and some of the other locals would gather there too. Often, someone would be telling ghost stories and the two old brothers would be afraid of their lives coming back out of it at night. Sometimes some of the lads would be waiting for them along the way, hiding in the wood by Twiss's and they would strike up a melodeon in the dark as the men were passing to frighten them.

There was a man called Jimmy Nolan, working for Bairds and he was some character. One particular winter's night, when the Turners were making their way home from Sheanes, he took the mare out and tied sacks to her feet so she wouldn't make any noise on the road. Then he got up on her back holding a broom with a white sheet on top of it, that covered him up and headed over to where the Turners would be passing, sure they nearly lost their lives with the fright of it.

I remember picking potatoes up in Farrells of Aghowle when I was a young fellow, we would be down in the field working away and old Sarah Farrell would come out to the yard and call "shoo hoo" down across the fields for us to come up to dinner. She would have bacon, cabbage and spuds ready and the big fire going. She was a lovely old lady, when I was a young lad she would have a sixpence wrapped up in a bit of newspaper and she'd hang around and slip it to me, when no one was looking.

Sarah Farrell and her daughter Nan, used to rear turkeys, they would keep one for themselves for their Christmas dinner and try and sell the rest to make a few bob for Christmas. One year, old Jer Farrell, along with Sarah and Nan, brought their turkeys in the pony and cart to the turkey market in Wicklow Town. Jer went off and had a few pints of porter, while Sarah and Nan spent the day trying to sell the turkeys in the market. At the end of the day, the women were very surprised and a bit annoyed, when Jer reappeared delighted with himself, as he was after buying them a goose for the Christmas dinner.

Billy Smith's grandparents: William Smith born in Aghowle in 1871, and his wife Ellen, known as "The Doc"

My grandfather, William Smith, was born in 1871, in the next farmhouse down the valley from Farrells' farmhouse, there was just a small field between the two houses. Just two years after my grandfather's birth, Sarah Farrell [whose maiden name was Moran] was born in the house across the field. Sarah and my grandfather William, would have grown up together and they remained very good friends all their lives. When my grandfather died in 1952, Sarah was then almost 80 years of age, but she made her way down to his wake here in Ballycullen. When she got as far as the garden gate here, she became too upset at having to say goodbye to her dear old friend and wasn't able to come in, so she turned around and went back up home again.

I remember the old O'Briens, Ellen and Mick, they used to go down to shop in Ashford in a pony and trap and on their way back up, Ellen would stop and give us in cakes.

I can remember too, going to the threshing up in Connolly's yard, in those days every farmer up along the valley would get the corn cut with a reaper and binder and draw it in to the yard or haggard and put it into a big stack. Then the threshing mill would come along, it would start at Ballycullen crossroads and working its way along and go in Aghowle lane, the farms in there were small so it would only be a couple of hours in each place There would be 10 or 12 lads working at the threshing, when we were lumps of lads we were sent along to help pitch sheaves, it was a great holiday for us. Then if you were moved up to cutting the sheaves you would be made up, unless there were thistles in them, then no one wanted to do the job.

There was a story about one day, when they were doing the threshing in a local farmer's place. In the evening time when the men were leaving, one of them spotted the wheel of a horse's dray lying in the ditch covered up in briars. He whispered to his companion "I will come back for that tonight" but he didn't realise the owner overheard him. So later that evening, the owner tied a rope to the dray wheel and hid at the other side of the ditch. Sure enough, the man stole back to get the wheel and started to try and pull it out of the ditch. But try as he might he couldn't get it to move at all, so he cursed and said, "Well what the devil can be holding this thing" and from the other side of the ditch the farmer's voice answered back "I am". He let go quick enough of the wheel then and ran away.

Further up along in Aghowle, up the back lane opposite Connollys, was where the Rocher Doyle lived. I remember one time when I was young, I was going to Darcy's forge in Moneystown with my grandfather, with the donkey and cart and he stopped to talk to the

Rocher Doyle, where he was thatching a piggery for Lar Timmons in Parkmore. I remember the Rocher was a big tall man with a pointy chin.

Billy Smith Reflects on People and Places around Ballycullen

There is a place called The Banshee's Bed, down along by Paddy's Hill, just below our house here. There was a black gate on the left-hand side of the road and below it on the right was the Banshees Bed. I don't know why it was called that, but something must have happened there years ago, when we were young lads cycling home late at night, we would pedal like hell passing up there.

My father and grandfather used to keep bees. Paddy Kearney of Moneystown was a great man for the bees, he used to come here to help my father.

I remember Paddy came here one day to give us a hand when I was a young lad. Paddy had tied up his flighty pony under the tree in the yard. Then, he and I, went about emptying out a hive of bees on to a big white sheet on the ground. When we got the bee hive onto the sheet, we waited till they settled and then Paddy tied up the corners of it and put the sheet full of bees into the cart. Then away he went up the road home for Moneystown, with the mad pony and the big hive of bees tied up in the white sheet and he sitting with his feet dangling over the edge of the cart and his wooden leg flying along. It's a great pity that no one was there to record the scene with a photograph.

Mr and Mrs Manley used to live down the road from here. They had no family, so some of the lads from here would go down to help them out. When old Manley wanted something done, he would come up as far as the Dairy Lane and whistle until someone up here in the yard heard him and then some of the lads from here would go down and give him a hand.

Eventually the old Manly couple sold up and moved down to Sweetmount. Mr Manley's brother-in-law used to live with them there and he did some bits of work about the yard. One day my father was passing their place and the old man was sitting out relaxing in the sun, so my father stopped to inquire how he was getting on. He said "sure things are grand, the brother in law does the few bits of jobs for me and I give him a pound a week and then he gives my wife a pound a week for looking after him and sure the one pound does the whole year around"

Another family that lived around here for generations was the Cunniams of Ballycullen. I was friendly with Greg Cunniam, he went to Ballylusk school and he used to say he was the only boy there with a real leather satchel. Greg kept this leather school bag all his lifetime and it became his filing cabinet. In it he had photographs including football teams he played with and tug-o-war teams he pulled with and many bits and pieces of correspondence. At one time Greg and his father decided to buy another farm over in the townland of Knockafrumpa and eventually Greg moved over to there. But when they bought the farm in Knockafrumpa, they needed money to stock it, so they applied to the ACC bank for a loan of £100

The bank wrote back looking for references from the parish priest in Roundwood and the sergeant in Ashford and the devil and all. The Cunniams got all the pieces for them and sent them in. So anyway, in time the bank replied to their application and said they couldn't give them the £100, but if they would lodge the deeds of the new farm with the bank, they would consider offering them £50. But Greg said "well we bought the farm ourselves without their help and we are not going to give them the deeds of it now. We will carry on ourselves without them"

Greg farmed the place all his life and cared for his parents and his older sisters at the end of their days and eventually was there living on his own. Then after he got broken into a few times, he decided it was time to sell up the farm. He did well enough and got a very good price for it at the time. A short while later when I was over visiting him, he told me he had a visitor a few days earlier. A knock had come to the door and it was a representative from the ACC bank, who had heard about the sale of his farm and had come out to offer him advise on how to invest his money.

Greg said, he sat the man down at the fireplace and went to the leather school bag and produced his original rejection letter from the ACC and handed it to the official. After the man had read the letter, Greg said to him "years ago, when I wanted the loan of a small bit of money off your bank to get started, you rejected me. Well, we got along well enough without you and now that I do have a bit of money, here you come along looking for me to give my money to you".

Chapter 8

1920-1930 – A Free State

Black and Tans in the Valley

While collecting the oral history of the locality, I came across several references relating to the period of the War of Independence and the presence of the infamous Black and Tans in the townland and the surrounding areas.

In the Ashford Historical Journal no. 2 1992, there is an article written by Andy Kavanagh Snr. recounting his memories of the Black and Tans in the Ashford area. In the first section of the article, Mr Kavanagh recounted as follows two separate incidents that took place near the Catholic church in Ashford village:

> At the time, we had the Black and Tans in the country, Ashford had a pipe band. Some of the instruments were kept in the home of the Fitzpatrick's (the gate lodge opposite the R.C. church), including the band's banner which was a lovely piece of work. For some reason, which I don't know, the Tans made a raid on the Fitzpatrick's home, took the banner and some of the kilts that the bandsmen wore and burned them outside the house.
>
> At that time, we had a local volunteer force here. For some reason or other they felled some of the big lime trees across the road. That was at Rosanna Gardens where John Synnott is living now. The felling took place on a Saturday night. I remember that when we came out of mass the following morning we were greeted by a unit of the Tans which was waiting outside. They rounded up most of the young men who were at mass, brought them down to Tighes's Avenue, gave them crosscuts and hatchets and gave them orders to get stuck in and clear the road. The tables were surely turned on that occasion!

Catherine Power (nee O'Brien), who grew up in Aghowle at the same time as myself, was able to supply me with some of the O'Briens' oral family history that had a personal connection to the above story. Catherine's grandfather, Mick O'Brien was one of the young men marched off after mass in Ashford by the Black and Tans. Catherine's grandmother Ellen O'Brien, witnessed her husband and the other young men being taken away at gunpoint from the church, but she did not know why they had been taken away or where they were going to.

Ellen returned home to their farmhouse in Aghowle to look after her young children. As the hours dragged by and there was no sign of her husband returning, Ellen became very concerned and feared that he had been shot by the Black and Tans. She sat wondering how she would be able to survive as a young widow with a houseful of small children to provide for. Luckily her fears were unfounded, and Mick returned home safely in the afternoon, when all the wood had been cut up and the road cleared.

Around this time, there were groups of local military volunteers meeting up in secret to carry out training. From local oral accounts, I have been told that some of these volunteers used Carrick Mountain for such purposes. At that time, it was common for the young people of the area to go up to Carrick on a Sunday afternoon to socialise. In 1920, my aunt Molly Connolly was about 15 years old and her friend Bride Farrell was a year older. Bride used to tell of how she and Molly would collect the spent cartridges that were lying around the rocks on Carrick where the volunteers had been practicing and bring them home as souvenirs.

Bride Farrell, aged 91, in her garden in Gloucestershire England.
When my mother and I visited Bride here in 1995, she still fondly remembered her childhood in Aghowle and her Sunday afternoons spent on Carrick.

Bride Farrell's family farm lay in the Aghowle valley beneath Carrick and I have been told by Bride's son, (Johnny Kenneally), that his grandfather Jer Farrell used to go up in the evening time under the cover of darkness, across the fields of his farm, to bring bread to the volunteers who were hiding out among the rocks.

From my own memory, I can recall my father's account of the Black and Tans visiting our farmhouse. My father would have been about 13 or 14 years old at that time (1920-21) and he recalled the uniformed men coming calling at the farmhouse and demanding bread and milk from his mother. While she was perhaps not that enthusiastic in providing them with the requested provisions, she felt she had no choice but to do so. Before they left they also took a good look around the house and farmyard and went in and searched around the turf shed.

I received the following story from Joan O'Brien Sweeney, a daughter of Peg O'Brien. Peg grew up in Aghowle, (house no.5). The O'Brien's farmhouse was about half a mile from Connolly's house, but it is not known whether this story of the Black and Tans refers to the same day that they had called to Connolly's farmhouse.

Reflections: Joan O'Brien Sweeney

I remember my mother's brother, Uncle Larry O' Brien, telling me that when he was a small child his parents went to town and left some of the children in the care of my mother, Peg O'Brien, for a few hours. I'm not sure of the exact year but my mother was born in 1914 so she would have been about 6 or 7 years old. Some neighbours came and told her that the Black and Tans were coming up the road and to hide quickly.

She took the younger children and ran to the field where the hay had been saved and led them under the haystack. They stayed there for a long time until everything was quiet again and it was almost dark. When her parents came home they told her it was a bad place to hide as the Black and Tans usually burnt all the hay.

Peg O'Brien with her daughter Joan, outside their home in Co. Cork
When Peg was a young girl in Aghowle she hid her younger brothers and sisters under a hay rick when the Black and Tans came.
Photograph courtesy of the O'Brien family

Schooling around Aghowle in the 1920s

Ballylusk National School: mid -1920s
Second row from front L-R: Second child is Julia Byrne of Ballycullen. Eighth is Paddy
O'Reilly, Aghowle.
Third row from front: Last child on the right is Greg Cunniam, Ballycullen
Back Row L-R : First - Liz O'Reilly, Aghowle; Second - Miss Giffney;
Third - Rose Doyle Ballycullen:, Fourth - Jinny O'Reilly, Aghowle

Of the children in the above photograph:

- Julia Byrne's reflections are recorded in "Reflections: Julia Byrne Reflects on Aghowle and Ballycullen 1920s-1940s"

- Greg Cunniam is featured in section "Reflections - Billy Smith Ballycullen (b.1944)"

- Rose Doyle's older brother and sister perished in the Aghowle cottage fire in 1905

Moneystown School c.1927

Top Row:
Jimmy Storey, Billy Kenna, Paddy Cullen, Mick Timmons, Billy Timmons, Joe Brinkley, Billy Timmons, Johnny Kearney, Ned Kenna.
Second Row:
Mrs. Timmons, Nellie O'Brien, Nellie Byrne (Tomriland), May Bolger, May Fitzpatrick, Lil Bolger, Lucy Kenna, Bride Lawlor, Maisie Timmons, Eileen Kenna, Sheila O'Brien, Molly Byrne.
Third Row:
Nellie Byrne, Rosie Timmons, Agnes Kearney, Annie Bolger, Bridie Kenna, Lizzie Fitzpatrick. Fanny Fitzpatnck, Birdie Byrne. Eileen Fitzpatrick, Kathleen Timmons, Larry O'Brien, Maura O'Brien, Mrs Redmond.
Front Row:
Tommy Kenna, Mick Bolger, Charlie Lawlor, Kevin O'Brien, Mike Kenna, Paddy Farrell, Mat Farrell, Jim Lawlor, Jim Timmons, Mike Kenna.

Pictured in this school photograph taken in 1927 are five members of the O'Brien family of Aghowle: Nell, Sheila, Larry, Maura (Mary) and Kevin
Photograph from "A Pictorial History of Roundwood, County Wicklow, 1870-1970"
Courtesy of Joseph McNally

Also pictured is Jimmy Storey, first left in back row. Jimmy and his brother Dinny were to go missing during the Second World War - see section "World War 2 and The Emergency".

Larry O'Brien, also in the above picture (3rd row), wrote a poem for the centenary of the Moneystown School in 1987. This poem can be found in the Poetry Appendix (see poem " The Old School At Moneystown").

The old school at Moneystown
Photograph courtesy of the O'Brien family

Friendly Fire at Aghowle Upper

As the country was recovering from civil war and the memory of the Black
and Tans was still very present in the minds of the local people, a shooting
incident occurred at Aghowle Upper. But on this occasion, it was nothing
to do with civil unrest but rather a case of friendly fire.

At the time, Miley O Brien and Patsy Connolly (my father) were young
lads in search of some adventure. While they had watched their fathers and
some of the other men of the locality going out rabbit hunting, they were
still considered too young to be allowed handle a gun by themselves - but
Patsy and Miley thought different.

One evening, they both sneaked out with their fathers hunting guns and
headed to Connolly's Rock field to try their hand at some rabbit shooting.
To add to the adventure, they had even managed to get a few cigarette
butts to have an illicit smoke as well. The Rock field was chosen because
of the likelihood of finding rabbits there and the presence of many furze
bushes to act as cover. The two lads decided the best plan was to spread out
a bit and see if they could locate some prey.

Patsy hadn't gone very far when he decided to light up his cigarette butt, so he sat down in the shelter of a clump of bushes to have a smoke. Meanwhile Miley was stealing along quietly, looking for potential rabbits, when he noticed some rabbit like activity in the bushes, so he took aim and fired. Unfortunately, Miley's rabbit turned out to be Patsy's leg!

Much commotion followed, and Patsy was brought to the hospital in Wicklow Town, where the wound was attended to and where he spent 6 weeks lying in a hospital bed. Conditions in the hospital at the time were quite basic and he often jokingly said he would have fared better in the nearby Wicklow Gaol.

Luckily, the wound healed quite well and he was left with just two consequences of the adventure. One was that he had a lifelong dislike of guns and he only allowed visitors who had been out hunting to enter the house if they left their gun emptied of cartridges outside the front door. The second consequence was that while the wound healed, some pellets of shot remained embedded in the flesh. In the following decades, every so often a gunshot pellet would work its way out through the flesh, to sit like a little ball bearing under the skin on his leg. When this happened, he would nick the skin with the blade of his penknife and remove the pellet, which he would keep as another souvenir from his youthful adventure.

While I think Patsy never held or fired a gun again, Miley, like many of the local men, went on to enjoy hunting - but for the rest of his life he kept his sights solely restricted to birds and rabbits!

Local Farming – Haymaking

In the days of traditional farming, hay was a very important source of fodder for the farm animals. Much depended on the saving of the hay each summer in order that there would be sufficient fodder to keep the animals fed over the winter months. In those times, the meadows would be cut by hand using a scythe. Nowadays, when machinery can cut acres of silage in an hour, it is hard to imagine how slow and labour intensive this work must have been for the farmers.

In Billy Smith's recollections of the local farming community, he recalled how his grandfather William Crofton Smith (b.1871-d.1952) and Charlie Shannon of Aghowle (b.1875-d.1962) managed to cut a two-and-a-half-acre meadow with scythes in just one day. This was regarded as such a great achievement that it was spoken of by their neighbours for many years after.

Haymaking in Aghowle c. 1930
Standing L-R, Ter O'Reilly, Jimmy Connolly, William Smith Senior (Crofton)
Seated L-R, Miley O'Brien, Bill Smith, Patsy Connolly
Photograph courtesy of Terry Timmons

As the picture above (taken around 1930) depicts, the farmers in the townland were by then using horse power for hay making. The photograph also illustrates how the local farmers came together and worked as a team to save their hay. It is not known on which farm they were working on that particular day, but members of the Connolly, O'Brien, Smith and O'Reilly families had all joined together to get the hay saved.

On most of the farms in Aghowle, the horse was still used in the mowing of the meadow and the saving of the hay up until around 1960. Several of the childhood recollections featured in this book from the 1940s and 50s recall the excitement of being carried on top of the cocks of hay as they were sligged by the horse from the meadow down to the farmyard.

By the 1960s, the presence of tractors on some of the farms made haymaking less labour intensive and the hay cocks were brought by tractor and buck rake down to the barn. As the photograph overleaf (taken in the summer of 1967 at haymaking time in Connollys' Top Field) shows, the tractor was now in use. Two of the young men from the earlier haymaking photograph c.1930 are also depicted here. Miley O'Brien and Patsy Connolly are still haymaking about 37 years later and the young lad in the white shirt, Terry Timmons, is a grandson of Ter Reilly depicted in the earlier photograph.

Aghowle 1967
Haymaking in Connolly's Top Field, with Carrick in the background
L-R: Mary Connolly, Ann Connolly, Bill Farrell, Terry Timmons, Miley O'Brien,
Patsy Connolly (on tractor) and Jock the Dog.

Around 1970, the last two remaining farms became very high tech and got a man with a baler to bale their hay, but a few years later saw the demise of the last remaining working farmyard in Aghowle.

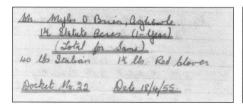

Three entries copied from the seed record book of Haskins merchants in Wicklow town.
These copies are reproduced by kind permission of John Power and would have been
initially recorded by his late father George Power.

The Seed Record Book entries above document the complex grass seed mix used by the Aghowle farmers during the 1950s.

138

Chapter 9

1930-1940:
Changes in the Landscape

Carrick gains a Forest
The lands beneath Carrick in the valley of Aghowle had remained mostly
unchanged for centuries. It had consisted entirely of a community of small
farms, farmhouses and farm labourers' dwellings. While the number of
dwellings dwindled from 25 in 1841 to just 9 houses by the 1930s, still the
overall patchwork of little fields, ditches and farms had remained almost
the same as it had always been.

As we have already seen, in the early decades of the twentieth century
the local tenants were in the process of buying out their farms from the
local landlord at Glanmore, but for some of these tenants they had not the
means or the desire to do so and these tenants were anxious to sell on the
interest in their holdings. Around 1920, a neighbouring landlord, Captain
Tighe of Rosanna, bought out some of the lands on the Aghowle side of
Carrick Mountain. Tighe's estate already included several other townlands
at the base of Carrick on the Glenealy side of the hill.

In the 1930s, as part of a government programme undertaken by
the Department of Lands to increase afforestation in the country, the
government began acquiring land to plant as state forestry. As part of
this initiative, they acquired from Mr Tighe's estate part of his lands
surrounding Carrick Mountain, including approximately 100 acres of land
at Aghowle.

For the first time in centuries, the local landscape changed from the
pattern of irregular little enclosed fields to a uniform forest plantation.
While this was a major change for the local farming community, it bought
the prospect of much needed employment to those living in the surrounding
areas. At that time, farmland could not provide sufficient employment for
all the local men and many of them had to move to Dublin, England or
further afield to make a living. But the introduction of the forestry industry
into the county meant many men could now find employment locally and
remain at home.

Even for the local farming community, the initial planting of the trees provided extra income. My own father, as he watched the plantation across from our farm grow and mature, used to recall how he had drawn those trees as small saplings to the workers who were planting the slopes of Carrick Mountain. These little saplings used to arrive by the lorry load and were left across from our house, in Bill Farrell's Bog field.

Here they were sprinkled regularly with water from Farrell's bog to keep them alive until they were planted. My father got 30 shillings a week for drawing the saplings by horse and cart up to the forestry workers who were planting beneath Carrick Mountain. At that time, a steady income of 30 shillings a week to help in the running of the farm was a godsend.

Miley O'Brien from a neighbouring farm got employment planting the trees and as Miley had seven younger siblings, his income was also much needed in their household. My father used to recall the harsh conditions the forestry workers had to endure, at that time. These men came from many miles around, in a time when the only means of transport was by bicycle. Their start time was 8 o'clock and on winter mornings the men would have to cycle miles in the darkness from the surrounding hills, often in poor weather conditions. My father spoke of seeing them cycle as far as they could up the hillside, then throwing their bikes down and running up the slopes to the foot of Carrick for their 8 o'clock start. At the time, there was a particularly strict foreman, who stood with his stopwatch in hand and his whistle, and if a man was even one minute late arriving, he was docked a half day's pay.

Over the next couple of decades, the Department of Lands acquired more of the local farmland beneath Carrick and the plantation expanded in phases. As the trees that were planted began to grow up over the farm land, the landscape changed. But beneath the forest many of the original little field boundaries and ditches remained and can still be identified at the base level of the trees today, as can the remains of some of the dwellings that existed on this farmland. In my childhood, my father and the other local farmers would often refer to sections of the forest by the names of the former families that had farmed there, such as "over there by Mooney's ditch", "go in by the Rocher Doyle's gate", or "the forestry men are working up there above Relish's place today" (which was in fact Rutledge's place but pronounced locally as Relish). The forestry workers planted trees in the area around the burnt-out ruins of the house where the two Doyle children had perished in 1905, but even today there are some stone remains of their cottage and fowl shed beneath the trees.

At the time of the initial phase of planting, one house in that area was still occupied. This was the home of Mick The Rocher Doyle (house no.9). Mick was a bachelor and his family had been tenants in the house since around the late 1880s. As covered in the story of house no.9, by agreement with the forestry authorities Mick was allowed to live out his days in his cottage - he remained living there until the late 1950s. By that time the trees had grown up around his house and from the roadway you would not have known that there was an occupied cottage hidden beneath the trees. After his passing, the forestry authorities took possession of the property and it was then used by the forestry workers as a place to shelter in, brew up a cup of tea and sometimes to stable a horse in. The house was always known to the forestry workers as "the Rocher's house". In recent decades, the house has fallen into ruins and a large laurel tree has grown over the remains of the walls.

The Tobacco Plantation of Aghowle

In the early decades of the 20th century, tobacco farming was carried out in some areas of Ireland. Locally, two Aghowle men thought they might get in on the act. My father, Patsy Connolly and his next-door neighbour and lifelong friend, Bill Farrell, decided to try their hand at growing tobacco. A small quantity of tobacco plants were obtained from Patsy's brother-in-law, Joe Murray, who lived in Dublin and was a man with many useful connections.

They chose Connolly's Turnip Field for the planting site, as turnips and mangolds did well here, so they thought maybe the tobacco plants would flourish too. The plants did survive and grew well, but the problem arrived after harvesting, when the plants need to be dried out. This would usually have been carried out in a specialised drying house, but Patsy and Bill had to improvise and set up a drying rack made of wooden poles in the calf shed at the top of Connolly's yard. The shed was empty over the summertime, it had a large wide door that could be left open in warm weather to create a breeze and it was hoped that the sun beating down on the corrugated tin roof would create a good warm drying environment.

But it turned out to be a cool wet summer. The leaves never dried but turned damp and mouldy and the vision of the Tobacco Plantation faded. I don't think that they got as much as a pipe full of finished product from their labours.

It is likely the two men did not actually plan to get into commercial tobacco farming, but rather had visions of growing enough plants to become self-sufficient for their own tobacco needs. Both men smoked pipes and were very heavy users of plug tobacco and their weekly bill for this at Timmons shop in Moneystown probably contributed greatly to the shop's profits.

Ann Connolly in Connolly's farmyard c.1958
Shed in background was the shed that was used for drying the tobacco plants
Also in the background is a black three-legged pot, which would have been used at that time
for cooking over the open fire

In hindsight, it is probably just as well the venture failed, as a ready supply of free tobacco might have further hastened both men's demise. Bill died aged 69 from throat cancer and my father (who lived to 87) spent many of his later years invalided from emphysema, having damaged his lungs from a lifetime of pipe smoking.

A New House

Another notable change to take place in the townland during the 1930s was the building of a new dwelling house. Previously, the last known house to be erected in the townland was in 1887, when a dwelling was built in one day for the evicted Carey family. As this particular dwelling does not appear in the 1901 census, it would seem to imply that it was of a temporary nature. Of the more permanent houses in Aghowle, the previously most recently built one was possibly House No. 5 which appears to have been built in the early 1860s, or perhaps House No. 9 which may have been built in the 1860s or 1870s.

Home at Aghowle Upper which was built in the 1930s by Wicklow County Council.
It was the home of Bill Lee and his family until the 1970s.

But then in the 1930s, the County Council built a new house in Aghowle, known at the time as a council cottage or labourer's cottage. This cottage was built for a man named Bill Lee who was employed by the County Council to upkeep the roads from Ballycullen to Parkmore. Bill Lee and his family lived here until the 1970s. The house was built by local brothers, Andy and Billy Timmons.

Lee's cottage was the first permanent house to be built in the townland for about 50 years and it would be approximately another 40 years before the next new house was built.

Local Farming - Sheep Rearing and Shearing

There is a long history of sheep farming in the Wicklow hills and sheep rearing would have been a very important part of farming in the local Aghowle area. The following information is taken from *www.wicklow sheep.com*:

> *Origin of the Breed*
> *The date of origin of the Wicklow Mountain sheep can only be guessed at, but there is concrete evidence to show that in the middle of the fifteenth century, there existed in the Wicklow Mountains a valuable breed of fine woolled sheep.*
>
> *The breed was distinct in appearance and character from any breed in existence on the island. At this time the Wicklow Mountain Sheep were contributing very materially to the reputation of Irish woollens, not only in the spun-wool markets of Holland and the manufactured-woollen markets of Flanders, but also in the markets for both these commodities in England.*
>
> *The flourishing condition in which the Wicklow Mountain Sheep existed in the 18th century is indicated by the fact that in 1793 the Flannel Hall in Rathdrum was built by Earl Fitzwilliam at a cost of £3,500, to serve as a mart for the sale of produce of Wicklow Mountain Wool.*

The Griffith's Land Valuation records [AAI/GVR] from the 1850s show that as well as paying yearly rent for their farm holding, the local tenant farmers in Aghowle also paid a yearly sum for the grazing rights on Carrick Mountain. The sum charged for the grazing on Carrick appears to have been calculated as a percentage of the acreage of farm land the individual farmer was leasing. Some of those that were leasing only a few acres held no grazing rights, as they probably had no need of it. In 1854, the following 13 farmers from the townland had grazing rights on Carrick:

Charles Edge	Ephraim Faulkner	Matthew Carey
Robert Moran	Laurence Rutledge	Edward Hatton
Sarah Moran	Laurence Toole	Catherine Reilly
Jeremiah Moran	Nicholas Ward	Esther Shannon
Patrick Short		

All of the above families, except the Faulkners, were tenants at will i.e. their lease was renewed yearly, whilst the Faulkner family held a lease for several life times. When the Faulkner family were selling the interest in their farm in 1901, the sale notice in the local newspaper stated that the sale of the 25-acre farm included the liberty rights for 25 sheep on the hill [Carrick] and also turf liberty.

In the past when wool was a much-valued commodity, the income for the farmer from the yearly shearing of his flock was a significant contributor to the farm economy. Hence, shearing time was a big event in the farming year. Back in the time before the lands around Carrick were planted with trees, the local farmers would probably have all gone together at shearing time to bring down all the sheep from the hillside and then separate out and take home their own flock for shearing.

My mother recalled that when she came to live in Aghowle in 1951, the local farmers still used, at shearing time, to block a portion of the river that ran through Bill Farrell's farm. This was done so that they could wash the wool in preparation for shearing by running the sheep through the river and into a wooden sheep pen at the other side where they were kept until the wool dried out. Although this was extra work for the farmers, the money paid for washed wool was higher than unwashed. Later on, when wool prices began to drop, the practice of washing the wool stopped.

Sheep shearing at Aghowle, May 1938
L-R Back: Patsy Connolly, his father Patrick, his sister Molly Murray (nee Connolly) and
neighbour Dan Short?
Front: William (Crofton) Smith and Molly's three sons Paddy, George and Tom.

As mentioned earlier in this book, there is a sheep fold (that is a stone sheep pen), marked at Aghowle Upper, on the late 19th century Ordnance Survey map. This pen may have been used at shearing time in days gone by, when the farmers were separating their sheep.

Up until the mid-twentieth century, most of the shearing here was done by hand, usually by the farmers themselves. Sometimes they would hire in the help of someone in the locality who was very skilled at the job. After electricity arrived in the townland in 1955, electric shearing machines started to be used and this greatly reduced the time taken to shear a flock of sheep.

The photograph (previous page), taken on Connollys' farm in May 1938, belongs to the days of the hand shearers. It captures my father Patsy Connolly and one of the neighbours, William (Crofton) Smith of Ballycullen, hard at work hand shearing in Connollys' Bank field.

At that time, when the shearing was finished the local farmers would have drawn the fleeces by horse and cart into Rathdrum, where Vincent Pierce was the local wool merchant. These farmers continued to sell their wool to Pierce's, the wool merchants in Rathdrum into the 1970s.

Butchering Lambs

While every farm would have kept some sheep for breeding and selling, there was no tradition by the farming families here of slaughtering any of their sheep for use as a source of meat for themselves. This was probably due to the fact that the animal was more valuable to the farmer as a wool source and for breeding. Also in the days before electrification, the meat would not have kept for long, unlike the cured bacon from the pig.

But there was one local farmer who became an expert at butchering lambs. In the 1930s and 40s, Captain Tighe owned considerable lands in Aghowle and many of the other townlands around Carrick mountain and he used some of these lands to produce lamb for market. He employed William Smith Senior (Crofton) to butcher these lambs for him at Smith's farm in Ballycullen. William became very skilled at this job and he went on to train Mark Kavanagh, of Kavanaghs' butchers in Ashford, in how to slaughter and dress the lamb.

The above information was received from Billy Smith of Ballycullen in September 2016.

Local Farming - Dairy and Butter Making

While some of the farmers in the surrounding townlands kept large herds of cows and sent milk to the creamery or co-op, the Aghowle farmers only kept a few cows to produce enough milk for household use, butter making and perhaps to rear a few calves. Fancy milking parlours and milking machines never made their way to any of the Aghowle farmyards. Instead the farmer milked his few cows by hand into a tin bucket while sitting on a little three-legged milking stool.

On all of the farms here, there was a very strong tradition of butter making and this was carried out not just for the family use but also on a commercial basis, where the extra money it brought in went towards the running of the farmhouse.

My father used to tell us of how his mother Annie Connolly (b. 1869, d. 1937) used make butter and each week she would carry 8 or 10 pounds of butter on her back as she walked over Carrick to sell it in the village of Glenealy. She sold her butter to the local shops and sometimes at the train station, where it was bought by arrangement and sent on by train to the butter market in Dublin. With the money that she got for the butter, she bought the groceries she needed for the house and carried them home again, walking back over Carrick. Sometimes my father would take the butter with him on Sunday mornings, when he and the other neighbours walked to mass in Glenealy and then the local people of the village would buy the butter from him on the way to mass.

Some of the farmhouses had a separate "dairy" where the milk was stored and the butter made. The dairy was usually a small cool room, which was kept meticulously clean and situated in or near the farmhouse. In the census returns taken at the start of the 20th century, four of the 8 farmhouses have recorded a dairy as one of their farm out-buildings. These farmhouses belonged to Shannons, Byrnes, Connollys and the house occupied by the Hatton family in 1901, later occupied by the McDermott family in the 1911 census and later still by the Bradshaw family. Of the remaining farms, it is remembered that in the O'Brien farmyard, there was a separate building beside the farmhouse, known as the dairy and people recall Nancy O'Brien making butter there during the 1940s.

Also in Farrell's farmyard, there was a small stone building known as the dairy.

Into the 1950s, the Aghowle women were still making butter to sell to the local shops but by the early 1960s, although butter was still made in every house, it was mostly just for personal use. Local people recall the following women who lived in the farmhouses in Aghowle Lane, making butter: Mary Short, Tess James, Kate O'Reilly and Florrie Bradshaw. Elsewhere in

Farrells' Dairy
Small building on left hand side was the dairy on Farrell's farm up until the 1950s.
The building has been retained by the current owner.
Photograph courtesy of the owner Seamus Corcoran.

the townland, the butter makers remembered were Nancy O'Brien and her mother Ellen O'Brien, Bridget O'Brien, Nan Cunniam and her mother Sarah Farrell and my own mother May Connolly.

In the late 1930s, the Irish Folklore Commission carried out a schools' project, where they asked school children to record the folklore, skills and traditions of their locality. One of the copybooks submitted from Moneystown National School belonged to Nancy O'Brien of Aghowle. In her copybook, Nancy had recorded[2] a detailed description of how her mother, Ellen O'Brien used to make butter (see overleaf).

Ellen O'Brien's granddaughter, Catherine, told me this interesting story about her grandmother's butter. Ellen O'Brien had a crooked little finger and the knuckle on this finger was raised up. Usually when the butter maker had her butter shaped into pound slabs she would draw the wooden paddle along the surface of the slab to leave a corrugated design on the top. When Ellen O'Brien did this movement, her crooked little finger left an extra distinctive mark along the edge of the pound of butter. As the O'Brien's butter was known to be of a very high quality and much sought after, the customers in the local shops would search through the different slaps of butter seeking out those bearing the mark of Ellen's little finger.

2   Nancy's detailed account of butter making on the O'Brien farm in the 1930s is part of the Schools' Collection, in the National Folklore Collection of Ireland

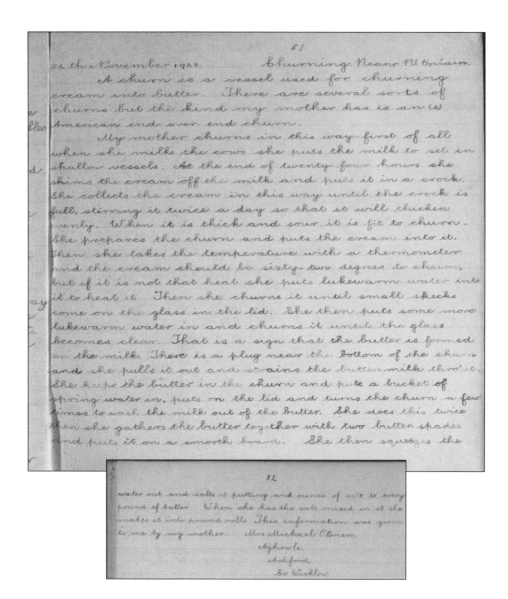

The Schools' Collection, Volume 0918, Page 081 [NFC/SC/MS]

As well as writing in detail of her mother's method of making butter, Nancy O'Brien must have also paid great attention to learning her mother's skill, as several of the people I spoke with during my research remembered that when Nancy had grown into a young woman and was running the O'Brien household, her homemade butter was exceptional.

One of the by-products of butter making was buttermilk, which was the liquid remaining in the churn when the butter had formed. This liquid

24th November 1938   Churning. Neanc Ni Briain

A churn is a vessel used to churn cream into butter. There are several sorts of churns, but the kind my mother has is an American end over end churn.

My mother churns in this way-first of all when she milks the cows she puts the milk to set in shallow vessels. At the end of twenty -four hours she skims the cream off the milk and puts it in a crock. She collects the cream in this way until the crock is full, stirring it twice a day so that it thickens evenly. When it is thick and sour, it is fit to churn. She prepares the churn and puts the cream into it. Then she takes the temperature with a thermometer and the cream should be sixty-two degrees to churn but if it is not that heat she puts lukewarm water into it to heat it.

Then she churns it until small specks come on the glass in the lid. She then puts some more lukewarm water in and churns it until the glass becomes clear. That is a sign that the butter is formed on the milk. There is a plug near the bottom of the churn and she pulls it out and strains the buttermilk thru' it. She keeps the butter in the churn and puts a bucket of spring water in, puts on the lid and turns the churn a few times to wash the milk out of the butter. She does this twice, then she gathers the butter together with two butter spades and puts it on a smooth board. She then squeezes the water out and salts it, putting an ounce of salt to every pound of butter. When she has the salt mixed into it she makes it into pound rolls.

This information was given to me by my mother -
Mrs Michael O'Brien
Aghowle
Ashford
Co. Wicklow.

was used when making soda bread and some people also liked to drink it with their meals. My mother recalled that on butter making day in our farmhouse, Tom Sheane who worked on our farm, would have a path worn to the kitchen door to check if she had finished making the butter, as he relished the taste of a big mug of buttermilk straight from the churn.

While my sisters and I did not like the taste of buttermilk, we did become fond of buttermilk for another reason. At one time, when we were children, there was a man from Wicklow Town passing by our farm and he got chatting to my father, as many people did. The man inquired if we ever had any fresh buttermilk, as he loved the taste of it. My father told him he was in luck as it was churning day and sent him in to my mother, who filled up two large bottles of fresh buttermilk for him. He was delighted and offered to pay, but of course my mother refused to take any payment. She told him if he wanted some more and was passing again to just drop in. It transpired that this man worked for the mineral bottling company in Wicklow town. A few weeks later he dropped by again, this time with two large bottles of mineral for my sisters and me. Now, this was in the days when a bottle of mineral was a real and rare treat and was only ever seen in our house at Christmas time or for a very special occasion. Thus, started a very happy arrangement for us and the man from Wicklow Town, as every so often he would appear with the two large bottles of mineral for us and my mother would fill up fresh buttermilk for him into the empty mineral bottles from his last visit.

Reflections: Julia Byrne Reflects on Aghowle and Ballycullen 1920s-1940s

Julia Byrne was born on 01 December 1921 in the townland of Ballycullen, where she lived until she married Nicholas Byrne in July 1947. She then lived for about a year in Ballylusk, before moving to live at Parkmore, Moneystown. Julia's family home at Ballycullen was situated beside the main road close to Ballycullen crossroads.

In September 2015, I visited Julia in her house at Parkmore, where she shared with me some of her very vivid memories of the local communities of Aghowle and Ballycullen during the 1920s, 30s and 40s. She had very clear recollections of the local people who used to pass by her home going about their daily routines of farming and shopping, or gathering to socialize at the nearby crossroads.

Sadly, Julia passed away just a few months after my visit in September 2015, but I wish to thank her family for their very kind permission to include Julia's reflections in this book.

My father was John Byrne, he was born in the place they call the Rock at Ballylusk [Ballylusk quarry]. These two brothers, Daniel and Andrew Byrne, came up from Craanford in Wexford years ago, one of Daniel's sons got married to one of the Cullen's over there, the other man married someone belonging to the Dowlings. They were my father's people. I think there was a bit of land attached to their place, but my father also used to go over to Scotland to cut timber.

My father married Bridget Kavanagh of Ballyknocken. Her father, Patrick Kavanagh, was a postman, he got a certificate from the King of England for non-broken service, having never missed a day until he retired. My father went to Ballylusk school and I went there myself too.

Julia Byrne pictured outside her home in Parkmore
Photo courtesy of the Byrne family

I can remember a lot of the families that lived in Aghowle when I was growing up and living in Ballycullen. Dan and Mary Short used to be going up and down to Ashford in a pony and trap, Mary kept the house and little garden lovely. It was a small little farmhouse and had a huge open fire. Dan in his youth was a tall smart looking man. They adopted a little boy called Joey. Dan Short had a sister called Kate that married Joe Doyle. At first Joe and Kate Doyle used live in a little old house near Reilly's lane, but then they moved down to Ballylusk. Joe Doyle was a man of many witty sayings and people often used to quote "As Joe Doyle would say …."

The Shannon family lived in beside the Shorts in Aghowle lane. They had a nice little farmhouse as well, with roses outside. I was very young when I used to be in there, so I don't remember too much about it, but I do remember getting bread and jam there. In those days when you went on a message to a neighbour's house they would always bring you in and bring you up to the fire and give you a big slice of freshly made bread and jam. I remember that I was always brought up to the fire in Mrs. Smiths of Ballycullen as well.

Charlie Shannon was a bit lame, his sister Kathleen used to live there sometimes too. She had married a man named Mr. James and sometimes she and some of her children, came back there to stay with Charlie. I remember Kathleen going up and down the road on a bicycle, it would be laden down with bags of shopping. She used to dress very well in a black suit and she wore make up when none of the other local women around here did. She was very friendly and would always hop off the bike and say hello when she was passing. Sometimes when we were very young she would give us sweets. Later on, Kathleen's daughter Tess James stayed living there with her uncle, Charlie Shannon and she used to do some dressmaking. I can remember the sewing machine sitting in the kitchen, she used to do a good lot of dressmaking for me. She was very good at doing alterations as well.

I remember the Reilly's house in Aghowle Lane as well, it was a lovely comfortable homely house, with a little garden at the front. At the side of the house was a path that went up towards Carrick, you had to cross a few fields at the top of the path and you were in on the rocks on Carrick. Mrs. Reilly [Ellen b. 1870 – d. 1949] would always bring you in for tea. On a Sunday in the summertime when a few of us would go up to Carrick, she would be out talking to us and give us bread and jam and tell us to call in for tea on the way back.

Ellen Reilly's husband Ter, used to work on the roads, years and years ago, we used to hear his heavy workman's boots passing our house early in the morning, about half past seven, when he was on the way to work. I must say the roads were kept very well in those days.

I remember the Reilly girls, Ellen and Ter's daughters, we used to see them pass the house when they would be walking up from Ashford on their time off. They would get the bus from Dublin down to Ashford and there was no other way up than walk in those days. We would be playing around outside and they would give us sweets, I remember Kitty Reilly, she was always dressed up lovely.

Kitty O'Reilly in the fields above her house in Aghowle c.1925
Julia Byrne recalled Kitty was always very well dressed.

At Halloween, everyone dressed up and went around the houses, when we went to the Reilly's house, I remember that Mrs. Reilly always had a big pot of colcannon for us. It might be a cold old showery night, but we would always still dress up and go out and the big bowl of colcannon and a dollop of farmer's butter was lovely and would keep us going.

We would call to all the houses, there would be a big crowd of us, Tom Sheane always came with us and he played the mouth organ in every house. Now we wouldn't be looking for anything when we were going around. We would end up at Joe Cunniam's up on Ballycullen Hill and as a great concession, we were allowed to have tea in the parlour, we would stay there for ages and ages. I remember a big tall fire and a lovely tea and we would be singing and dancing and they would be delighted with us. I was about 10 or 12 at that time, we dressed up in old clothes and wore a mask and you would have your head covered. It was lovely back then, you could just call into every house, you didn't have to make an appointment, you just dropped in.

I remember the Bradshaw family too, that lived in Aghowle lane. Bradshaw's had a nice farmhouse, a bit bigger than the other cottages in the lane. They had a lovely orchard and would give us apples, they were a very nice family. There was also a Bradshaw family in Ballycullen opposite Bairds, they were called the Baily Bradshaws, I don't know if they were related to Dick Bradshaw's family in Aghowle.

I remember we would go up to Bradshaw's for milk, there was a little gate going in and a lovely garden and well-kept hedges. Then there was another gate you could go around to the farm. I remember one day myself and Kitty Carr was coming out through the garden past the lovely roses and I went to pick one of them and old Mrs. Bradshaw started coming up after us, so we had to run away without the lovely roses.

There used to be a little shop in Bairds of Ballycullen. There was a little addition to the house, it was very small, I remember Mrs. Baird serving in it. You tapped on a long narrow window and it opened inward, there were shelves on each side. She practically had everything there you would want in the line of groceries and the bread car called there, so she had fresh bread too, she didn't have fresh meat, but she did have rashers. I remember the fresh bread was really lovely.

There were shelves of everything and sometimes she would have to go in the back for to get some things. It was there when I was a little girl of about seven or eight years of age, going up for messages and it was there for a long time after that as well.

Everyone around Ballycullen and Aghowle used to deal there, it was great. Otherwise they would have to walk to Ashford or Moneystown. But back then everyone walked everywhere, and they would never complain. People used to go off walking to Wicklow or Ashford and do a heavy shop and carry it home and think nothing of it.

Julia remembers some of the people further up the townland of Aghowle:

Old Mr. and Mrs. O'Brien [Ellen and Michael] used to go up and down to Ashford in a pony and trap, or pony and cart, I can't remember which now. There were a lot of the O'Brien children, I think most of them went off to work as soon as they finished school. People reared big families in those days and then they had to go away to make a living. I was very friendly with Lar O'Brien, he was a great reader and so was I, we used to swap books with one another when we used to gather in my sister Bridie's house, in the evening time. Then when these people went off to England you used to miss them terrible.

I also remember Nan Cunniam and her mother Sarah Farrell, going down to Ashford in the pony and cart to shop. In those days, they would be bringing back a ten-stone bag of flour.

SHOPPING IN ASHFORD, 1932
(Reproduced by kind permission of Nancy Manning)

1932

		£	s.	d.
May 11th	10 St Flour		16	0
	1 cwt Pollard		8	8
	1 cwt Maize		8	8
	½ St Sugar		1	11
	½ lb Tea		1	2
	2 pkt Jelly			6
	2 Loaves			9
23rd	1 cwt Pollard		8	8
31st	1 cwt Pollard		8	8
	1 cwt Clarendo		8	8
	10 st Flour		16	0
June 25th	10 st Flour		16	0
	1 cwt Pollard		8	8
	4 st Indian Meal		4	6
	3½ lb Sugar			10
	½ lb Tea	1		0
	2 lb Bread soda			6
	2 Loaves			9

Transcription of a receipt from a shop in Ashford for goods purchase by the O'Brien family of Aghowle during May and June 1932, This record is reproduced from the Ashford Historical Journal 1993, by kind permission of Sheila Clarke.

Julia Byrne recalls the Aghowle families going down to Ashford to purchase a 10-stone bag of flour and this receipt shows that the O'Brien family appear to have used a 10 stone bag of flour approximately about every 3 weeks.

In Upper Aghowle as well as the O'Briens, Farrells and Connollys I remember another little woman who lived in a small thatched farmhouse up the back lane [this was Kate Dempsey 1873 – 1935] *she did a bit of farming and used to always be dressed all in black.*

During the recession times in the 1930s and 1940s, times were hard, and people had to make do with very little. But back then most people did have their own milk, eggs, butter, potatoes and cabbage. Also, some of them kept a pig and when they killed that, they could live off it for a while. Of course, rabbits at that time kept many a family alive. You were never stuck if you had a couple of rabbits, terrible skinning them and getting them ready though. You could roast them, stew them and then you had rabbit soup too. Or they were lovely boiled with a bit of cabbage as well. But I hated the skinning of them and of course you had no running water in the house in those days. We did have the river going down near the crossroads, so we could get the water there and we used to keep a bath under the eaves to collect water, that was the slop water. But we used to go to Kelly's spring well for drinking water.

I remember we kept goats for milk, I can still remember the smell of the goat's milk, which I didn't like, but it was very pure. They talk of goat's cheese now as been a great thing all together, but I still keep thinking of the smell of the goat's milk. I remember my father used to go over to milk the goat and we would use that milk in our tea. Everyone at the time kept goats, you had to keep them tethered so they wouldn't ramble, or put a bell on them so you would hear them if they were getting away.

My sister Bridie got married around 1936 and after she married, herself and her husband Dermot lived in a little house belonging to Charlie Shannon in Aghowle. It was very warm and cosy, later on they moved to a house in Glenealy. In the first house in Aghowle there were some sheds in the yard and Dermot put up a punch bag in one of them, I remember Dick Bradshaw and some of the others used to come over to it. A crowd of locals used to gather in their house too in the evenings, I remember all the Sheanes used to come down. Bridie and Dermot had an old record player, so we would put a record on and sit listening to it. I remember they used always want to hear "Oh Mama" at that particular time that was a popular song. We would sit around the fire and listen to the music and talk. Then around half past eleven everyone would head home.

In those days in nearly every house there would be a card game too, even our house in Ballycullen would always have a crowd in playing cards. The Bradshaw family that lived in Ballycullen, had men working for them, so those workmen used to come over to play cards in our house, I remember some of the Kellys used to be there too. You would make them a cup a tea, it was no big deal, just a cup of tea and maybe a bit of currant bread. In every house you went in to, there would be a cake of bread standing cooling on the kitchen dresser. You would make the bread in the pan over the fire and when it was cooked you put it on the dresser to cool, rather than wrap it up in a tea towel. Back then you would be always offered a bit of homemade bread when you went into houses.

Gatherings at Ballycullen Crossroads:

There used to be always someone gathered at Ballycullen crossroads. When we were children and teenagers, we had a great time down there. All we had to do was look down from our house and see was there someone down at the crossroads. Often there would be a fire there too. There was a place as you turned up to go up Ballycullen Hill, on the right-hand side there, where they used to light a fire. In the winter, it was lit to keep warm and in the summer to keep the midges away.

People used to gather there to chat, play cards and play music. Of course, Tom Sheane would be there with the mouth organ, he would take it out for any occasion. It was a great old time, nobody had anything, but we were all together and no one was any different to anyone else.

I remember the big snow of 1947, my sister Bridie had moved down to Coolnakilly near Glenealy at the time and I was staying there with her, so I wasn't too badly off. But during the big snow someone died in one of the houses up on Ballycullen Hill, I think it was one of the Meads and the hearse couldn't get up there through the snow drifts, so they had to carry the coffin down as far as Ballycullen crossroads to meet the hearse.

Later on that year, on the second of July 1947 I married Nicholas Byrne and we lived for about a year over in Ballylusk and then we moved up to live in the townland of Parkmore Moneystown.

Even after Julia married and moved to Parkmore, she remained a very regular presence in the townlands of Aghowle and Ballycullen as she used to travel back to visit her family home and later as her father became elderly she would make the trip daily to visit and help care for him.

Initially Julia made this trip by bicycle, but later got a Mobylette (a moped by French manufacturer Motobécane), which made her return journey up the valley considerably easier. At that time, there were very few cars on the rural roads and the Mobylette had a very distinctive hum that carried quite a distance. I recall in the summer-time when we would be out on the farm with my father, the sound of the Mobylette would drift up through the fields to where we were working. Then my father would lift his head, look down across the valley, smile and say *"Ah, here comes Julia on her bee in the bottle"*.

Liz O'Reilly and Tom Sheane, at Aghowle, C. Late 1920s
Julia Byrne recalled Tom Sheane often played the mouth organ at Ballycullen crossroads.
Photograph courtesy of Terry Timmons

Chapter 10

1940-1950:
World at War Again

World War II and The Emergency
When Britain went to war in 1939, Ireland was a free independent state and therefore the country could remain neutral. But that does not mean that the country was not greatly affected by what was happening on the world stage. As well as food shortages and rationing, many of our people ended up going to war as part of the British Army. Some Irish people had chosen to join the British army as a career opportunity, but many others found themselves involved in the war without wishing to be there. The need for soldiers was so great that Britain had to bring in conscription in October 1939. Initially this was just for young men, but as the war progressed, they had to include conscription for older men and single women.

During the 1920s and 30s, employment prospects in Ireland were very poor and many young men and women had to head to England to seek employment. Then when the war broke out and conscription was introduced, many of these Irish people found themselves part of the British army. Amongst them were people with connections in and around Aghowle.

Jinny (Jane) O'Reilly was born in House No.3 Aghowle Lower in February 1911 and later went to England to find work. During the Second World War, Jinny enlisted in the Royal Air Force and is pictured here in her RAF uniform. She later married a fellow officer, James Croft in 1947.

Jinny O'Reilly of Aghowle in her RAF uniform
Courtesy of Terry Timmons

In 1934, Bride Farrell of Aghowle had married John Kenneally from Co. Cork. John was in the Irish army and had been a body guard for Éamon De Valera. John left the army after he married and after a few years, he and Bride moved to England where they settled. When conscription came into force, John had to join the British army. Given his Irish military background, this was probably a difficult time for him. Bride's family and close neighbours in Aghowle were very anxious for his welfare during the war years. John did survive the war, but sustained some injuries that restricted his employment opportunities when the war was over.

Another two men who were in the thoughts of the local community during the war years were the Storey brothers of Moneystown, Dinny and Jimmy. The O'Brien, Farrell and Connolly families of Aghowle knew the Storey brothers very well, since they had all gone to school together in Moneystown. Also, when Jimmy Storey had finished school, he had worked for several years on Loughlins' farm at Slanelough, which bordered the farmland at Aghowle Upper.

The Storey brothers, like many others, had gone to England to find employment and when the war started they found themselves part of the British army. During the war years, they were missing and presumed dead. Here, their cousin Jack Murtagh of Moneystown recalls the anxiety of their family at that time:

Jimmy Storey of Moneystown who was missing during the Second World War, but returned safely.
Photograph courtesy of the O'Brien family

> *We were related to the Storeys of Moneystown, my grandmother was a Storey. Two of my father's first cousins, Jimmy and Dinny Storey went to England and they were there at the time of the Second World War and they were conscripted and were sent to Burma, fighting the Japs.*

I remember during the war, when I would be up in Storey's farmhouse when the parents were saying the rosary at night and they would always pray for them. There was no communication at that time and they thought their two sons were dead.

Anyway, when the war was over Dinny and Jimmy returned, they had been prisoners of war and they had stories of eating grasshoppers and snails and everything to survive. Sometimes when they would be back home, there would be a houseful up in Storey's and Dinny would come down here to sleep on our settlebed. I was only a young lad at the time and they probably thought I wasn't listening, but I used hear Dinny telling my father all about the war and the torture and how they managed to survive it.

Jack Murtagh, July 2016

Rationing and Compulsory Tillage

One of the implications for Ireland of the Second World War was that many essential goods became rationed. The people of the farming communities were better off during this time than some of the other Irish citizens as they had their own produce such as butter, eggs, potatoes and vegetables. Some farmers grew wheat and had it ground into flour so they could make their own bread. This bread was coarse and dark in colour, but when flour and bread rationing came in, they were grateful for what they had. Of course, the farming families still needed essentials like tea, sugar, paraffin etc. and had to make do with their allotted amount.

I was told the following story by the late John Timmons of Parkmore about an Aghowle man called Jer Farrell, who found it hard to understand why he could not get goods in the local shop during the war time, even when he had the cash in his hand to pay for them.

Jer went to Kit Timmons shop at Parkmore Moneystown, to get some paraffin oil for the lamp. Kit told him that there was no oil, as the war was on and when it would come in, he would have to share it out among everyone, according to their allotted ration. Jer was not well pleased with this reply, but said "Damn it then man, give me a pound of candles instead". But Kit replied he did not have any candles either. Jer asked "Are you saying now that you have no candles either?" and Kit replied "Yes, I'm telling you I have no candles, sure don't you know there is a war on". To which Jer replied "Well holy God, are you telling me now that they are out there fighting the war with candles?"

Another effect of the war and the food shortages was that the Irish government passed a law that required farmers to use a certain portion of their land for tillage.

At that time, Group Captain Tighe of Rosanna owned some land at Aghowle. He had sold a portion of his land to the Ministry of Lands for forest plantation but he still retained a sizable portion for agricultural use. To meet his requirement for the compulsory tillage, he tilled this land at Aghowle and planted crops in it.

Here Billy Smith of Ballycullen recalls his father's role in this project:

> *In my time, the Tighe family of Rosanna owned some of the land in Aghowle going up towards Carrick Mountain. In the 1940s, during the war time, there was a compulsory tillage order which meant that Captain Tighe had to plough and sow this land up in Aghowle. In the spring time, he had stables for the horses down near Slanelough crossroads. My father used to look after these horses for him and he also ploughed a lot of the land for him, up under Carrick Mountain, with four horses under a two-furrow plough. Then in the autumn my father used to collect men and women from around the Rathnew area, in a horse drawn wagon belonging to the Tighe family and bring them up to Aghowle to pick the potatoes for Captain Tighe. Later, Tighe sold this land to the State Forest and it too was planted with trees.*

Turf Cutting

Up until the early 1960s, all the local families cut and saved turf as the main fuel source for the house. Many of the Aghowle farmers had turbary rights on the nearby Moneystown and Parkmore bogs. The families that did not have rights on these bogs usually rented a turf bank on a yearly basis. In the days when these families were tenant farmers, their turbary rights would have been allotted by their landlord. Records show that Glanmore estate held turf banks at Tiglin, but it is not known if these banks were allotted to their Aghowle tenants or if they were given turf banks elsewhere. In section "The Moran Family Who Never Forgot Their Townland", there is a reference to two of the Aghowle tenants taking a case to the local petty courts, regarding the use of a turf bank.

Reflections: Michael Graham on Turf Cutting in the 1940s

Michael Graham, or Mick as he is known locally, was born in Clara Beg North, near Clara Vale in 1926. He lived there until 1958 when he married Maura Timmons and moved to live in Moneystown.

In September 2016, I visited Mick in his home at Moneystown where he shared with me some of his memories from his earlier years and reflections on a way of life that has now disappeared. During our conversation, Mick recalled cutting turf on Moneystown bog in the mid-1940s, alongside some of the families from Aghowle.

When I was a young lad working for Johnny Miley of Parkmore, I remember cutting turf on Moneystown bog. It would have been around the mid-1940s. There was up to 50 going to the bog at the time, they all had rights to cut turf there. Most of the families in Aghowle were there, I remember the O'Briens, the Farrells, the Rocher Doyle and Dan Short. Then there was the Byrnes of Garryduff, the Lawlers of Montiagh, Tommy and Johnny Miley, Behans, Bill Bohan, Black Jimmy, Greg Cunniam and a good few others too. I was there with a big flattened tar drum and the mare fastened to it.

At that time, they had started to tar the road around Rathdrum and if you went to the lads who were working there with the horse and car, they would give you the empty tar drums. For the price of 6 pence, they would put the roller over it and flatten it into a sheet. People used to buy them to make sheds and everything. Johnny Miley

Making hand turf on Park bog c.1937
Jack Lawlor (Montiagh), John Kearney (Moneystown), James Lawlor (Montiagh),
James Lawlor (Moneystown)
Photo is reproduced from
"A Pictorial History of Roundwood, County Wicklow, 1870-1970",
by kind permission of Joseph McNally

would throw up the turf and I would spread them on the tar drum and go off across the bog and tip up the drum and let them slide off onto the ground. Then they would be left there to dry. The farmers always cut the turf before they sowed the turnips, because the June fly used to eat the turnips when they would be coming up.

You see, back then there would be great excitement on the Sunday morning outside the chapel gate. They would be all lined up an hour before mass and all the talk and the planning would be about going to the bog the next day, they used all go on the one day.

They would cut the top off the turf bank and they used to leave a little dam, then if you could get down to the bottom without breaking the dam you could get to the real good turf that was like coal. You could hop it and kick it and it wouldn't break, it was terrific. Sometimes they would come on a big lump of deal and then they would try and take that up without breaking the dam.

When they had the turf cut, then the farmers would stay at home for a while and sow the turnips. Then they would get back to the bog to get the turf stucked up for drying, before the turnip thinning started. After the turnip thinning it was back to the bog for bringing home the turf.

You always knew when the last of the turf was drawn out of the bog, because they used to leave the big lumps of deal to draw out last. They used to saw up the pieces of deal for firing, it made powerful firing. When you saw the Montiagh men drawing the load of deal down Park, or the Aghowle men drawing a load of deal over by Slanelough, you'd say "there's the turf finished now, they are drawing home the deal".

Mick also shared some of his memories of the Aghowle families:

As I was living over in Moneystown I often only saw the Aghowle people at mass, the Farrells, O'Briens and Connollys used to come to mass in Moneystown and sometimes the Shorts and Tess James as well.

At one time, I kept a few sheep on Dick Bradshaw's ground in Aghowle. I remember they broke out one night and got up out onto Carrick Mountain. Dick's wife was a lovely woman and like all the farmers' wives, she was a hard worker too. I remember when I had the sheep down there, she would be up on the brows under Carrick with a horse and dray, spreading out manure on their fields.

We were somehow related to the family of the Rocher Doyle that lived in Aghowle. At one time, we had the receipt here for the funeral of Mick the Rocher's father [This was Henry Doyle]. *He was buried in Kilcommon graveyard outside Rathdrum and the receipt from Woulohan's of Rathdrum for the whole funeral was for £6–10.*

Local Farming - Harvest Time and Threshing

Back in the 19th century, the local farmers would have brought their corn to be milled at Cunniams mill in Ballycullen. In the Griffith's Valuation Field Book records [NAI/VOB/BC], taken in April 1842, it was recorded that the mill at Ballycullen was capable of grinding 10 barrels of corn per day and that it was in use for two months of the year. The mill was in the field below Smith's farm in Ballycullen and Bill Smith Senior (1903-1972) recalled seeing the local farmers bringing their corn to be milled there when he was a boy. At that time, the mill was owned by Peter Timmons.

Every farmer in the townland used to sow some corn. Those who had small farms might have only planted just an acre or two of oats to see them through the year, while the farmers with larger holdings would plant considerably more. In past centuries, the people of the valley would have had to thresh their corn by hand, which was a very laborious task. After the invention of the steam engine, the threshing mill emerged, making the operation a lot easier. The early mobile threshing mills were operated by horse power and later on by tractor power. At one time, some of the more prosperous farmers invested in their own stationary threshing machine, which was operated by horses. In my research, I was given accounts of two such machines that had operated in the locality and also some information on local corn stacks.

Information supplied by Dick Mahon in October 2015. He is now living in Laragh East but he grew up on the Mahon's family farm at Ballycullen:

Hand and Horse threshing of Corn.

Before they had threshing engines, the farmers used to thresh the corn with a flail. It had two bent sticks, with a metal bit and a leather strap in the middle. They used this to beat the corn off the stalks. Some of the better off farmers had a horse thresher. This was a machine set up with a long wooden beam on it and as the horse would walk around in a circle it would beat the corn out. I never saw it in operation myself, but I do remember seeing the machine above in Bolton's farm in Ballycullen.

Corn Stacks

I remember there were stone corn stacks in many of the farms around Aghowle and Ballycullen when I was young in the 1940s and 50s. They were not in use at that time. We had them on our own farm in Ballycullen. There were 4 standing granite stones with a flat stone on top of each one and they would put a piece of timber over them, this kept the rats out of the rick. In the past, they were used when they brought the corn in from the fields before it was threshed, it stopped the rats getting up into the rick and eating the corn.

Information obtained from Jack Murtagh, Moneystown, June 2016.

There was a horse threshing machine up in Storey's of Moneystown, it was a revolving threshing machine operated by horses and there are the remains of it still in the ground up there on Storeys.

Threshing Time in Aghowle

The Threshing was a major event during the farming year and much depended on having a good harvest, so there was a great coming together of all the local community to get the job done. Although the work involved long dusty days and strenuous labour, it was usually carried out with a sense of comradery and high spirits.

Local people who still remember threshing time in the valley, recalled how the threshing mill would start at Ballycullen crossroads and work its way up the valley through the farms of Ballycullen and then in along Aghowle Lane and proceeding up through Upper Aghowle to Slanelough crossroads. Usually, all the farmers between these two crossroads worked together at threshing time. As well as the men coming together to work as a team, the farm women also worked together at harvest time. In the little two and three roomed cottages, the woman of the house, with the help of her neighbours would prepare, cook and serve a large dinner to 10 or 15 men and usually all this was achieved from a few big cooking pots sitting on top of a turf fire.

In the late 1930s and during the 1940s, the local farmers felt a certain pride in the fact that the big threshing mill that arrived at their haggard gate on threshing day belonged to one of their own. Miley O'Brien of Aghowle had set himself up in business with his own threshing machine. Although he was still a young man in his twenties and the oldest of 8 children, Miley had managed to buy a threshing engine and a Fordson tractor. Each autumn he went out for hire, working his way through many of the townlands in south east Wicklow. He used to say the local terrain suited his work, as the corn down near the coastal areas would be ready for harvesting a good three weeks before the corn up around the hilly districts of Trooperstown and Clara Vale.

Miley O'Brien with his sister Sheila and mother Ellen, Aghowle
During the 1930s and 40s Miley owned a threshing mill
Photo courtesy of the O'Brien family

Miley kept a detailed log of all the farms he went to and the fee charged for their threshing and his daughter Catherine still has this log book today. This record book shows that Miley threshed in more than 30 townlands from coastal areas around Brittas Bay, through Ashford and Rathnew, up through Ballycullen, Aghowle and on through the Moneystown and Trooperstown districts, usually finishing up in the Clara Vale area. He also took in townlands around Rathdrum such as Newbawn and Balleece. At that time, the farmers planted mostly oats and maybe a little wheat, but over time barley became more popular as it gave a good yield and the farmers got a better price for it.

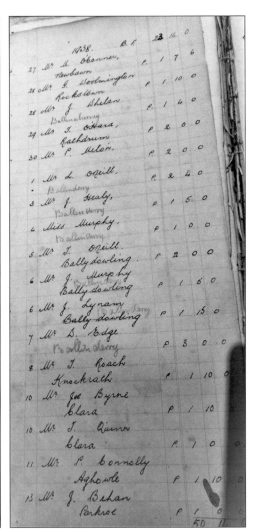

2 Pages from Miley O'Brien's threshing log book
by kind permission of his daughter Catherine
Page on left: 1947 - records threshing dates for 30 different farmers,
including his neighbours in Aghowle
Page on right: 1938 - records threshing dates for farmers in 10 different townlands

Stories from the Threshing Time

Although threshing time was a great coming together of the local community, I also heard some stories of segregation based on class and religion. I did not hear of any such stories relating to the Aghowle townland, but I was told accounts of such happenings in some of the other townlands in the district. It seems it was common practice in some farmhouses for the labourers to be sent to the kitchen for their dinner, while the farmers were seated in the parlour. Of course, this practice could only happen in houses that had the luxury of owning two such rooms.

At one time, there was also the practice in some of the protestant farmhouses of separating the workers according to their religion. As time went on, this was met with disapproval among the local community. But the practice persisted on one particular farm, where the woman of the house would stand in the doorway as the men came in for their dinner and direct the Protestant workers into the parlour, where a superior meal was served. The Catholic workers were sent to the kitchen. But one year, the situation came to a head. The woman of the house was directing the men into their separate rooms, as was her custom and she proceeded to direct her own farm labourer, who was a Protestant man, into the parlour. But the man stood in the doorway and faced his employer and said, "*I will not sit down to eat my dinner in this house today, until the good neighbours who have turned up here to help us with our harvest, can sit down in whichever room they want, no matter what church they go to on a Sunday*". All the Protestant men who were already in the parlour stood and said he was right and that they agreed with him. The woman stepped back out of the doorway and the segregation at threshing time ended.

It was customary on threshing day for the family to go to great lengths to provide a substantial meal for the workers in the middle of the day, as well as some tea breaks and perhaps a few bottles of stout in the evening time. But of course, there were always stories of the exceptional farmer who was less than generous in looking after the workers. It was noted that it was commonly the very farmers who had sufficient means to provide a good meal for the men that were known to dish up a rather inferior offering.

If the dinner offered was not up to the men's expectations, there was sometimes a witty comment or two made to highlight the fact. Various such stories still survive in the local area. Several of these stories are attributed to a witty man named Joe Doyle who used to assist Miley O'Brien on his threshing engine. One such story related to a day where the men were sitting down to their dinner in a particular house, which was well known for serving poor food. This day, Joe had been presented with a plate that contained a piece of extremely fat greasy bacon, which wobbled in a glutinous mass when he tried to put his fork into it. Joe was heard to address the piece of meat in a loud clear voice "*Ah honey, you needn't be sitting there shivering and quaking on the plate, for I have no intention at all of attempting to try and eat you.*"

Another story relates to a house where the family kept a live-in work man. It was common knowledge that the woman of the house was not very generous when it came to providing this man with his meals. On the day of the threshing, she was anxious to create a good impression for all the men who had come to help and she made a great show of dishing up their dinners on her brand-new dinner plates she had just bought in Wicklow Town. The men at the table noted that she had given her own workman a rather small portion compared to their own. She then asked her diners what they thought of her lovely new plates, which depicted a pattern of a big sailing ship. From the bottom end of the table her workman was heard to say, "*The new plates are grand ma'am and the ship sure is fine, but the cargo on mine is damned light!*"

The Big Snow of 1947

The local people are no strangers to heavy snowfalls during the winter months - often one could leave the village of Ashford with just a few snowflakes on the ground, but by the time you travelled uphill to Ballycullen crossroads there could be a light blanket of snow covering the landscape and by the time you reached Slanelough crossroads at the top of Aghowle, the road may be impassable.

The Big Snow 1947
This wall of snow, 14 feet high, was pictured on the road from Aghowle to Moneystown.
It is recalled that 45 Council workers had spent two days clearing the road.
Then on evening of the second day, another heavy snow-storm undid their work
Photo is reproduced from
"A Pictorial History of Roundwood, County Wicklow, 1870-1970",
by kind permission of Joseph McNally

But the snow storm of 1947 was unlike anything the local people had ever witnessed, even those in the valley who had survived more than 80 winters. It started on Sunday 26th January with what everyone thought was a normal winter snowfall that would be gone in a few days - but little did people realise that for the next 6 weeks, the locality was to lie buried in snow and some areas would be beneath 12-foot snow drifts.

The following 6 weeks saw continuous arctic temperatures and intermittent heavy snow falls throughout the country. National newspapers carried reports of transport routes blocked, animals dead in the fields and people running out of food supplies. The County Councils and Corporations worked tirelessly to try and keep main roads open and food supplies moving.

The Wicklow Mountains were particularly badly affected and articles in the national papers made references to the plight of the cut off areas of Roundwood and Moneystown and reported that some of these snow bound people had received no bread supplies for weeks.

Each week, the Wicklow People newspaper carried reports on the situation in the County, including the Council's efforts at clearing the road networks and reports of isolated communities in the

CORRESPONDENCE

SERIOUS PLIGHT OF MONEYSTOWN INHABITANTS.

At a meeting held in the club rooms, Moneystown, on the 18th inst., I was directed to forward to you for publication in "The Wicklow People" some facts concerning the serious plight of the inhabitants in this district.

It is now over three weeks since the snowstorm started and since then Moneystown and the surrounding townlands are isolated. During that period no motor car, lorry, bread van or commercial van has been able to enter this area on account of the state of the roads. Only for the enterprise and organising ability of the young men there would be no bread in the area. Farmers kindly lent horses and sacks to go to Annamoe (three miles away) to meet the bread vans and brought the vital bread here. Now, other supplies are failing and the people are really perturbed about them. One shopkeeper who tried to obtain flour was informed by letter that it would be sent to the nearest town. But then, how is it to be brought here when roads are impassable? There are several roads leading to Moneystown, one from Rathdrum; one from Ashford one from Roundwood and one from Annamoe, but not one of them is open to traffic. Attempts were made by a lorry and bread vans to reach here, but all were fruitless. The people are asking how long will this state of affairs last, and what is going to happen if the roads are not immediately opened to traffic? From the newspaper, it is seen that other places which were snow-bound are now being served by every kind of vehicle, while Moneystown is being treated as a cinderella.

It is to be hoped that the authorities responsible will, without delay, have the roads cleared, so that the residents can do their business.

Desmond Fitzgerald,
Moneystown, Roundwood.

Letter written on behalf of the People of Moneystown during the 1947 snow

mountainous areas of the county. Printed here is a letter written on behalf of the people of Moneystown that was printed in the Wicklow People newspaper 22nd February:

A few weeks into this extraordinary snow fall, there was a tragic loss of life in the nearby hills. A local man named Jack Kelly, who was from the townland of Montiagh but staying at the time in Roundhill near

Clara Vale, came on horseback to Kit Timmons's shop in Parkmore Moneystown to get some provisions. He made it safely to the shop and got the supplies but on his return journey through the hills which were covered in very large snow drifts, some misfortunate accident occurred, and he never reached home. The details of the tragedy were reported on in the local Wicklow People newspaper on Saturday 15th February as follows:

The death record for John (known locally as Jack) Kelly states that he died on 12th February from cardiac arrest due to prolonged exposure to cold. Jack was from the townland of Montiagh, not far from Aghowle Upper. All the local families knew Jack and his family very well. As news of his death spread around the Moneystown area, everyone was shocked and saddened at the loss of his life.

SNOWSTORM TRAGEDY.

Mr. John Kelly, married man, living at Roundhill, between Moneystown and Clara Vale, a lonely, mountainous countryside, lost his life in the snow blizzard, his body not having been found until Thursday morning.

On Saturday Mr. Kelly rode from his home on horse back across the snow to shop at Mr. Christopher Timmins' premises at Parkmore, Moneystown, and on his return homewards was seen by neighbours. From that moment he was not seen afterwards. Two men living with him believed he might have gone to relatives in another part of the district, and it was not till Wednesday, when the two households could contact each other, that it was ascertained that he had not gone there, and that consequently he was lost.

Search was made for him all Wednesday, and his hat was found at a spot a good deal off the track which he should have followed to reach home. Then came the finding of the body buried in the snow-drift.

Guards and neighbours came together to fetch the body to his house, and the coroner was communicated with, also the priest and doctor.

The following report from the *Irish Times* Newspaper dated 11th March 1947, shows that the Moneystown and Roundwood districts were still quite isolated even six weeks after the start of the snow storm:

> *Early yesterday evening a bulldozer which a gang had working near Calary, reached Roundwood, but the passage cut would not make the road available to vehicular traffic.*
>
> *In view of the reports of distress received from the district of Glasnamullen, a gang was switched over to deal with this by-road immediately. Two gangs from Roundwood are going through three miles to Lough Dan, where they hope to arrive today. Another gang from Roundwood was switched over to work towards Glencree. The men in the Moneystown area reached the village yesterday and another gang working from the Rathdrum area has reached the upper end of Glenmalure.*

1970s – Aghowle Lower: Shannon's abandoned farmyard.
Photograph courtesy of Ed Ryan.

2017 – Aghowle Lower: The ivy-clad remains of the gable end of O'Reilly's farmhouse.

2017 – The Aghowle River at Aghowle Lane.
The river now flows under the laneway but it used to flow across the lane
and there was a small makeshift footbridge to one side.

2017 - Carrick Mountain, Aghowle Lower: The Handball Rock.
This has recently come back into view after the surrounding forest trees were removed.
Photograph by Róisín Beirne.

C. 1980 - The Back Road at Aghowle Upper:
Patsy Connolly and Ali.
Ali was the pet dog that replaced
Patsy's last working sheepdog.

Late 1980s - Patsy Connolly with Roy,
his last pet sheepdog.

Late 1960s – May Connolly and daughters (L–R: Margaret, Ann, Mary) outside the Connolly farmhouse. The whitewashed stone buildings in the background were part of the extensive farm buildings that were removed after the sale of the house and farm in 1971.

View of Glanmore, the farm buildings and stables, Ashford Co. Wicklow. (c.1825–1830) Artist: John Synge. By kind permission of Sheila Clarke.

2017 – The entrance from the Back Road at Aghowle Upper into the Coillte forest.
This led to the house where Mick the Rocher Doyle lived until the late 1950s.

Late 1970s – Aghowle. The last remaining farmyard and farmhouse (O'Brien's) is in the right foreground and what was previously Farrell's farmhouse is in the left foreground.
The three white bungalows in the background were all built in the 1970s.
Photograph courtesy of Seamus Corcoran.

2017 – View of Carrick Mountain from Ballycullen.
Fields on right are part of the townland of Aghowle.

2017 – View from bottom of Carrick Mountain, with the townland of Aghowle in the foreground.
This is taken from nearly the same spot as the Late 1970s colour photo of Aghowle and shows the change in the
landscape over 40 years.
Photograph by Róisín Beirne.

C.1955 – Short's farmhouse: Standing: Dan Short with his gun; Seated: Joey Reilly, girl unknown.
Photograph courtesy of Tommy Byrne.

1990s – Aghowle Upper: Farrell's farmyard, which has been retained and preserved by the current owner.
The small building on the left was used as a dairy until the late 1950s.
Photograph courtesy of Seamus Corcoran.

The county engineer also said that there was still about 110 miles of road throughout County Wicklow blocked and on the previous day some of the gangs who went out discovered the roads they had cleared the previous weekend were blocked again with two feet of snow.

The Big Snow in Aghowle

I was born 12 years after the Big Snow of 47, so it was still very much part of the stories recounted around the fireside during my childhood. Some of my memories of my father's retelling of that winter are as follows:

Living in the Connolly farmhouse in 1947 were my father (known to the family as Patsy and to others as Paddy), his brother Jimmy and their aged father Patrick, who was in his late 80s and in failing health. All the roads were blocked with snow drifts and as my father and Jimmy were watching their father grow weaker each day as he sat in his chair by the fireside, they became very fearful that he might die. They prayed he would not pass away during the snow storm, as there might be no way of getting his body buried until the roads were cleared again.

At the start, the snow storm did not cause any great concern, as everyone thought it would be like other snow falls and that it would be all over in a few days. At the time, my father had his flock of sheep in the Bushy Field, which was at the top edge of the farm adjoining Bradshaws' farm in Slanelough. Some days after the first fall of snow, there was another heavier snow fall during the night time and this time it was accompanied by high winds, causing the snow to form large drifts. In the morning time, my father's neighbour Peter Bradshaw who was farming at Slanelough, came down to the farmhouse to tell him that the snow had drifted heavily in the Bushy Field and he could see no sign of my father's flock of sheep. Peter and my father set out for the Bushy Field armed with two shovels and Peter's sheep dog. At first, they could find no trace at all of the sheep until the dog located them down in the far corner, under a very large snow drift. The dog kept digging down with his paws until he would locate the sheep and then the two men dug them out with the shovels. While there were a few casualties, most of the flock were saved. When retelling this story my father always credited the kindness and assistance of his good neighbour Peter Bradshaw and the amazing work of Peter's dog in having saved his flock of sheep.

As the letter from the people of Moneystown to the Wicklow People newspaper highlighted, one of the main concerns during the snowfall was that the bread vans were not getting to deliver bread to the isolated areas.

While the farm families were perhaps in a better situation than some other people as they had access to milk and potatoes, they would have still relied on bread and flour deliveries. The people of Aghowle would have normally bought bread at least once a week from Fitzpatrick's bread van that delivered bread from Wicklow Town. In between times they would have made their own bread and also bought extra supplies from Kit Timmons's shop in Moneystown. Then when the big snow fell, the bread deliveries stopped.

In Connolly's farmhouse this was initially not a problem, as they had part of a large sack of flour stored in the settle bed beside the fireplace. Neither my father nor his brother Jimmy were talented in the art of bread making but they used the flour to make large, thick pancakes which they cooked on a frying pan over the open fire. For the first few weeks of the snowfall, they used this flour every day to make pancakes - especially for their elderly father who was in poor health and also for their neighbour, Mick the Rocher Doyle. Mick lived nearby in his house at the edge of the woods. He lived alone and was in his seventies. After the first few days of the snowfall, he had no food left in the house and since everywhere was snow bound, he had no way of getting any. So my father and Jimmy went across the snow drifts each day to bring him pancakes and milk. But as time passed and the roads remained blocked, there were still no supplies getting through and the flour began to run out.

My father knew he would have to try and get flour or bread somehow and the best option was to try and make it down to the village of Ashford, which was about 4 miles away. Because of the continuous frost and the snow drifts, the way down was treacherous. In places, the drifts were so high it was not possible to make out where the road should be. My father and his horse set out on the journey, both very nervous of the strange landscape and slippery surface. With much difficulty, they did manage to reach the village safely. To recover from the journey, my father went into Synnotts' bar for a bottle of stout and to hear the local news, as they had been living in isolation for weeks. As well as running the local bar, the Synnott family also had a grocery shop attached to their premises. While he was having his drink and chatting to the Ashford men, John Synnott, who owned the business, came to him to ask how he and all his neighbours up in the hills were faring in the harsh conditions. My father told him no supplies were getting through and that they had run out of flour and that he had come down to the village in the hope of getting some supplies. John told him to come around to the back of the premises when he had finished his drink, which my father did.

There John was waiting for him with a sack half full of loaves of bread and pieces of cake. He apologised that much of it was not very fresh, as they had not had any deliveries for some days, but my father said he was most grateful for everything in the sack. Then John said, *"Paddy my good man, God speed you safely up the valley, now get up on that horse and get out of here as quickly as you can, for if the housewives of Ballinalea knew what you have in that sack, they would lynch both you and I"*. He explained that the local women were beating a path to his door every day looking for more bread, but he said there will be a delivery here again in a few days and they can get some more, while God only knows when you poor people up in the hills will get anything, not until those roads are cleared or the snow thaws.

John Synnott of Ashford who gave vital bread supplies to the Aghowle people during the Big Snow
Photograph from "A Pictorial History of Ashford, Co. Wicklow, 1860s-1960s", courtesy of Sheila Clarke

Luckily my father and his horse made it safely home, unlike poor Jack Kelly who perished while on a similar errand. The supplies from Synnotts' were distributed among the neighbours and kept them going until the Aghowle road was eventually cleared. My father and the local neighbours never forgot the kindness of John Synnott during the Big Snow and they often recounted the story around the fireside and it was also often retold over a glass of stout in Synnotts' pub in Ashford.

As it transpired, my grandfather did survive the Big Snow and he rallied through the springtime and into the summer. One day in July of that year, he walked using his hand stick from the kitchen door across the yard to look over the farmyard gate at the flock of sheep that had survived the Big Snow. He then turned and died peacefully in the warmth of the summer sun.

In the local houses at the time, keeping humans and stock alive were the main concern – but in one of the neighbouring houses, a young man was also occupied with a concern of the heart. Larry O'Brien had by this time been working in England for some years and had met the love of his life, Ivy Snape. Larry had proposed to Ivy and when she accepted, he headed straight home to Aghowle to share the good news with his parents. But while he was at home, the Big Snow fell, and he became snowbound. There were of course no telephones in the area at the time (it would be nearly three decades later before the first telephone would arrive in the townland), and postal deliveries were disrupted. So as days started to head towards weeks Larry had no way of letting Ivy know why he had not returned and meanwhile Ivy was sitting in England fearful that her fairy-tale romance was shattered. The wonderful man she wanted to spend her life with must have changed his mind and was not going to return to marry her.

As soon as the roads were passable and transport began to operate again, Larry quickly made his way to Ashford and on to Dublin to catch the ferryboat to England. When he eventually got back to Ivy, he could explain all and while he was delayed because of the artic conditions, it was not a case of pre-marriage cold feet. Within a few months, Larry and Ivy were married.

By St. Patrick's Day, the snow had finally thawed. The roads were clear again and the local community began to return to normal living. Luckily for the farmers, the summer that followed was a good one.

Many farmers had lost stock during the extreme weather conditions and my mother told me that even the farmers who managed to keep their stock housed and fed with whatever fodder they had during this period also suffered losses. These animals were so weak and compromised after this long period under shelter with reduced rations, that when they were put out to grass and began eating normally again, it was too much for their weakened bodies and they died in the fields.

In the weeks after the Big Snow, there were notices placed in the newspapers that the government would give interest free loans to farmers to purchase more animals if they had suffered loss of stock during this period.

While from time to time since 1947, there have been some winters with heavy snow falls in the Wicklow hills, thankfully none have been anything remotely as bad as the Big Snow of 1947. The memory of those harsh conditions was still vivid among the local community when I was a child and I recall that as winter began to set in, my mother would stock up the top shelf of the kitchen press with extra flour, tinned food and dried goods. If the weatherman forecast snowfalls for the Wicklow area, my father would half-jokingly say to us, "*Think we had better bring the shovel in tonight*". For he still had vivid memories of the Big Snow, just over a decade ago, when they had to shovel their way out through snow drifts that reached half way up the farmhouse windows.

Larry O'Brien and Ivy Snape, on their wedding day in 1947
Photo courtesy of the O'Brien family

Chapter 11

1950-1960:
Changing Times in the Farmhouses

1955: Let There be Light

In November 1955, there were two new arrivals into Connollys' farmhouse. One was my sister Mary, who was born on 15th November of that year - the second was the "Electric Light".

My mother recalled that when she gave birth to her daughter Mary in the Prague Nursing Home in Wicklow Town in November 1955, she was looking forward to taking home her baby to a new illuminated world. While she was away giving birth, the electric light (as it was always referred to) had reached Aghowle Upper and the farmhouse had been connected. There had been much preparation for, and anticipation of, the arrival of the electricity to the locality. When it was announced that the electricity was coming up the valley, each household had to decide if they wanted to sign up for the supply. Some of the older people were quite reluctant to commit to getting this strange new technology into their homes. Initially, Sarah Farrell said she had survived quite well for more than eighty years without it and did not see the need of it now, but eventually she was persuaded to sign up. When the supply was connected, she was terrified of switching it on, as she felt sure she would be immediately electrocuted - but in time she got used to it and enjoyed its benefits for her remaining years.

Not every house signed up for the supply at the initial stages. Some did not see the need for it and some of the houses were a distance in from the main road and the cost of running separate supply lines in to them would have been too expensive. My mother recalled how great it was that dark November in 1955 to have this new bright source of light throughout the farmhouse and especially about the farmyard and farm buildings when they were milking and feeding the animals on the dark winter evenings. But what she remembered with greatest joy was the electric iron. Up until that time she had to do the ironing with a heavy box iron, heated by putting burning coals from the fire into its centre.

With this new technology, some other changes took place about the local farms. The old battery radios were replaced with plug-in electric radios and infra-red lamps were bought and used to supply heat for new born piglets, day old chicks or a donny (weak) newborn lamb. But if one compares our use of electricity in the home nowadays with these farmhouses in the late 1950s and into the 1960s, one would find a vast difference. There were 7 farmhouses in the townland at the time of the electrification and with one exception, none of these houses ever, during their remaining years as farmhouses, owned a fridge, electric fire, electric cooker, electric kettle or a washing machine. Nor did they use the electricity to pump water into the farmhouse - instead they continued to carry water by bucket from nearby spring wells or streams. The women of the house continued to wash the clothes by hand in tin baths, bathed their children in tin baths in front of the fire, and they mostly continued to cook and bake over the open turf fires.

Local Farming – The role of women on the farm

In the past, farming would have been perceived as a very male occupation and at that time there were very few employment options for females,

Late 1940s
Ellen O'Reilly minding her grandchild in her farmyard at Aghowle
Photograph courtesy of Terry Timmons.

especially after they married. But it is perhaps often overlooked that women played a very significant role in the running of these traditional farms. Many farmers married farmers' daughters, who were well skilled in all aspects of farming. While these farmers' wives often reared very large families, sometimes in small two and three roomed houses, they usually also did a sizable share of the farm work. I noted from my research that, in the 19th century, when the local farmers were all tenants and leasing their farms from a landlord, the lease would have been normally held in the farmer's name, but if he died first, the lease transferred to his wife, even if they already had adult sons living and working on the farm. In the early 19th century, the farmer's wife was sometimes recorded as "the widow of", but later on, her own full name appears as the lease holder.

The records for the Moran farm and farmhouse (no. 6) in Aghowle [VOI/CB/AU] show that Sarah Moran (who was the widow of Simon Moran) remained the leaseholder for approximately 30 years after her husband's death, until 1882. I estimate she would have been near 90 years old before she passed the lease on to her son William, who was by then over 60 years of age, married and working on the family farm. The records also show that Sarah Moran's daughter Winifred married into the neighbouring Rutledge farm (no.7) and was left widowed with seven children. Winifred also remained the leaseholder for about 30 years after her own husband's death, although her oldest son was by then married with a family of his own and living with his widowed mother.

On farm No. 10, Kate Dempsey had come to care for her 4 aged uncles. Andrew, the last of these uncles, lived well into his 80s and I assume by this time, his ability to farm would have been greatly diminished. It was probably Kate who was running the farm for him in his later years. When he died, he left Kate the farm and house and she continued to farm there for her remaining years until she died in 1935. On farm no. 2, Charlie Shannon also lived into his 80s, but was quite invalided by that time. Again, it was his niece, Tess James, who cared for him and helped run his farm. Just beside the Shannons' farm was the O'Reilly's farm (no. 3) and when Paddy O'Reilly died at the age of 35 in 1952, his widow Kate was left with two very young children. But she stayed on working the farm and reared her sons.

On these farms in the 20th century, people I spoke with remembered the women taking a very active role in helping to run the farms. In each house, the women made and sold butter, reared fowl and sold eggs. Also, in several houses the women reared turkeys for the Christmas market. They would also have reared pigs and helped cure the bacon. I recall Nancy O'Brien, (farm no.5,) telling me that when she was still living at home on the O'Brien farm, she would rear and fatten a pig and when the pig was ready for market, she would walk it 8 miles into Wicklow town to sell it. These women also helped tend and feed the livestock and in many cases, milk the cows. They would have worked alongside their husbands, planting and picking potatoes, thinning turnips, making hay and stucking and stacking oats and often helping out on the bog, saving turf.

A gathering of women outside O'Brien's farmhouse Aghowle in the late 1930s.
Second from left: Ellen O'Brien, fourth from left at front: Ellen's youngest daughter Nancy
Photograph courtesy of the O'Brien Family

From the stories told me during my research, I have formed a picture of a very active workforce of women on the farms here in the valley. I include in this group our own mother, May Connolly – she and our father ran the farm very much as a team and she was a great role model for my sisters and I. Johnny Kenneally, who spent his boyhood summers on the neighbouring farm (no. 6), recalled that the first time he met my mother in the early 1950s, she was on her hands and knees in the field thinning a drill of turnips.

Reflections: May Connolly Reflects on Farming in Aghowle in the 1950s

In August 1951, my mother, May Connolly, came as a young 21-year-old bride to live and farm in Aghowle. She had grown up about 3 miles away in the townland of Ballinastraw and was the oldest of 6 children in the Pierce family, who farmed in Ballinastraw.

Like many other children who were from farming families at that time, when May reached 14 years of age, her school days finished and she began working fulltime on the family farm. By the time she got married 7 years

1957, Connolly's farmyard Aghowle
L–R Back, May and Patsy Connolly
L–R Front, Mary Connolly, Ann Connolly, Patsy's nephew Joe Murray

later, she was very skilled in all aspects of farming. As well as everyday housekeeping, she had experience in butter making, jam making, bacon curing, rearing all kinds of fowl, tending animals and helping sow and harvest the crops.

She recalled that while she was still a young girl of 15 or 16, she would set out before daybreak to walk cattle with her father to the fair in Roundwood some 8 miles away. Often, they would have to stand all day on the fair green trying to negotiate a good price for the animals. If trade was bad and there was no sale by the end of the day, she, her father and the animals would then have to turn around and face the long road back home again. So, although she was still a young woman when she arrived in Aghowle, she was arriving very skilled for her new role as a farmer's wife. The following are some of her remembrances of farm life in Aghowle in the 1950s, as she recounted them to me in 2012 when she was 83 years old.

Neighbours

The neighbours in Aghowle were all very good, they always came together and helped one another out. When I came here first, I remember Farrells were the nearest neighbours. Bill Farrell and my husband Patsy, were the same age and were lifelong friends. Bill's parents were still alive then, his mother, Sarah Farrell, was a lovely old woman and very kind to me when I moved here. His father, Jerry Farrell, was a small little man with glasses and smoked a pipe. Bill's half-sister, Nan Cunniam, also lived with them, she used to bring eggs and butter to Wicklow to sell every week. She was sometimes a little bit cross, but I think the poor woman suffered a great deal with pains.

Butter Making and Fowl Rearing

I used to make about 10 lbs of butter a week and sell it either in Ashford, or to Pierce's in Rathdrum. You would put the milk into a bucket, or crock and cover it and leave it to sit in the cool, down in the parlour, for about 3 days until it started to curdle. Then you would put it in the dash churn and churn it until it turned into butter. The length of time this took depended on the strength of your butter cream. You would then wash the butter in spring water. I always liked to use the water from the spring in Farrell's bog, as for some reason, I thought it made better butter than the water from our own spring well.

We also used to sell eggs every week to the local shops. You would wrap up the butter and eggs well and put them in a little box on the back of the bike. I remember I would get a shilling a pound for the butter. The money was a godsend, when times were hard and money scarce. You would be able to get a box of groceries in return for the butter and eggs, so you would never go hungry during the week.

We used to rear turkeys as well. We would bring them down to the market in Ashford to sell. You brought them down in a pony and cart and sold them from that. Then the money from the turkeys bought the new clothes for Christmas. The turkey mated in April and sat on the eggs for a month. When I was a young girl living at home in Ballinastraw, one of my jobs was to take the turkey hen in a box on the back of the bike, up to a place in Ballygannon above Rathdrum, to mate her with the turkey cock.

I used to keep ducks and geese in Aghowle. The ducks would only live near somewhere there was water to swim in. Our ducks used to go to Bill Farrell's bog to swim. Then you would have a hell of a job getting them home to put them in their house in the evening time. The last ducks and geese we had in Aghowle were 10 ducks and 7 geese and the foxes ate them all one night. We gave up on them after that.

Killing Pigs

In those days the farmers killed their own pigs. Like nearly everything that took place about the farm in Aghowle, the three local farmers would come together to help one another out. So, Miley O'Brien and Bill Farrell, would be there on hand when we were killing our pig and Patsy would go help them when it was their turn.

The pig had to be fasting 24 hours and I had to have a big pot of water boiling on the open fire. I won't go in to the actual killing, but the 3 men carried out the boiling water to where the pig was tied up in the back haggard. When he was killed, the hot water was poured over the pig and he had to be skinned very quickly after killing and the meat rubbed with salt peter. Then the meat was put in brine. After three weeks, it was turned. It was kept in a box in the corner of the parlour, where it was cool.

Each farmer killed a pig for themselves. It was said that you couldn't kill a pig unless there was an r in the month and we would usually kill one each April and November.

When the meat was cured and dried out, it was hung from hooks in the chimney to smoke it. It hung there for 3 weeks and then it was taken down and put into boxes. It you wanted a rasher for your tea, you would just cut a slice off the side of bacon and put it in the frying pan. All the farmers used to make their own black and white puddings. You used the gut of the pig to put it in, after you washed it out, you then added breadcrumbs, flake meal, salt, pepper and onions, along with various parts of the pig chopped up. The black pudding was made with the blood of the pig, I would have to go out and catch the pig's blood while it was still warm. We used to smoke the pudding, and this kept it longer.

Salting Herrings

In November when the herrings came in to the sea around Wicklow, men used to drive around selling them from the back of a van. We would buy a couple of dozen and we would salt them in a crock and then smoke them up the chimney. Then for weeks you could have a fried herring for your supper. They were very tasty but salty. You would have a fierce thirst on you after eating them.

Jam Making

I always made our own jam. Often, I would make 7 or 8 different kinds of jam each year, mostly from the fruit we had ourselves, or that you got from neighbours. We had our own gooseberries and blackcurrants. We also had rhubarb, so I would make rhubarb and ginger jam. Raspberries and blackberries grew along the ditches up the back road and down towards Farrells. O'Briens, or some of the other neighbours, would give you some apples in the autumn and you'd make apple and blackberry jam, or apple jelly and sometimes I would make crab apple jelly too, if there was a good crop on the tree over on Lawlers' ditch.

The only fruit I would usually have to buy for making jam were strawberries from Synnotts' in Ashford. Occasionally some of the local children would go up on Carrick to pick fraughans to make a few bob for themselves, so I would buy the fraughans off them to make jam. I remember when I was about 13 or 14 going picking fraughans myself in Ballinastraw wood, with my mother and sister Peggie. At that time, during the war, the dealers in Rathdrum bought the fraughans and paid a good price for them. My mother bought me my first ever new coat with the money we got from the fraughan picking that year.

Some years if fruit was plentiful, I would make 8 or 10 pounds of each kind of jam. That was put up in the press to last you until the next summer, but of course that often didn't happen. You would give a pot here and there, as a gift to people calling to the house, that didn't make their own jam, then Patsy's relations from Dublin always liked to take a pot of homemade jam back with them and if you were going visiting a house, it was nice to be able to bring a jar of jam with you, as a little gift.

Card Games and Bread Making

There used to be card games in the houses in the evening time. Maybe 6 or 7 neighbours would gather in. Around here they used to play cards in Lawlers, Farrells and O'Briens and our own place. Sometimes they might be playing until 1 or 2 o'clock in the morning, during the evening I would make them a cup of tea and give them a bit of homemade current cake. In those days, you did all the cooking and bread making on the open fire. I used to make bread in the 3-legged pot. You would build up the coals of the fire into the shape of the pot and then put your pot with your bread in it, on top of the coals and put the lid on it and let it bake. When we got the gas cooker it was a lot easier to make the bread and do the cooking, but then, some said the bread didn't taste as good out of the gas oven as the stuff made in the 3-legged pot.

Hand shearing in Connolly's farmyard Aghowle 1956
L-R: May Connolly, a member of the Gallagher family of Slanelough, Patsy Connolly
Children: Ann and Mary Connolly

Shearing Time

They used to block up the river in Farrells and make up a sheep pen beside it and run all the sheep through the river to wash the wool before shearing. At one time the farmers used to shear their own sheep, using a hand shears or clippers, which was very slow work.

Sometimes they would get in a man for hire, then later on the electric clippers came in and it was much faster. Some could shear 100 sheep in a day and others could do only 30. Tom Cowman of Parkmore was a good man to shear sheep.

Tramps

When I came to Aghowle at first, there used to be still some tramps passing through the townland. They would come to the house looking for a bit to eat, they would have a mug that they would hand in at the kitchen door and you'd give them a mug of tea and a bit of bread and butter. At first, I was a little afraid of them, as I wasn't used to them. In Ballinastraw, we lived in a bit from the road, so they didn't come to our house. But I took my cue from the older people, like Sarah Farrell, she was always very kind to them. As times improved, the tramps and beggars disappeared from the roads.

Shopping

For small shopping, Timmons shop in Park was very handy, then for bigger shopping I used to go to Ashford on the bike. I would get 2 big bags of shopping and put them on the handlebars and maybe a box on the back carrier as well and then you would have to wheel the bike up nearly all the way from Ashford, as it was all up hill.

At one time, there were some sellers used to come around to the house too, which was very handy: Brady's had a travelling shop that sold food and animal feed and Fitzpatricks' of Wicklow used to come twice a week with fresh baked bread.

Later on, McNulty's grocery of Ashford would come with a van. You would give them a shopping list on a Friday evening and they would bring you the shopping back the following Friday, so you would have to know a week in advance what you might be going to run short of.

At onetime Tom Dowling, who had a butcher's shop in Wicklow town, used to come around in a van every Thursday. If I wanted fresh meat, I used to put a sheet of newspaper with a stone on top of it, on the farmyard wall facing the road and Tom would know to stop and call in. He was a good butcher and always had very good quality meat, but the locals used to call him "the calf" because if you asked him for a nice bit of beef he would always say "I have a lovely bit of young calf here for you" no matter what age the animal was that the meat had come from.

Then sometimes traders used to come around to the houses selling clothes. These were proper traders selling new suits and blankets and stuff, but were a good deal cheaper than the shops. Patsy and some of the other locals would buy their work clothes from Cheap Jack at the fair in Rathdrum. About every third month the fair in Rathdrum would be a big fair day, so as well as all the livestock there would be a lot of traders selling clothes, farm tools, galvanised buckets, pots and pans, tin baths and the likes.

Favourite Times on the Farm

I always liked the early summertime on the farm, when all the crops were sown and the stock went out to grass. We usually put the cattle that were in the houses over winter, out to grass around the first day of May. On that day, I would go around and bless them all with holy water. We used to also make a little May alter in the house with the flowers that came out in the fields and ditches at May time.

Threshing time was a nice time too, by then you would have the hay saved and in the barn and threshing day was always a great day on the farm. There would be a lot of work in the kitchen getting the dinner ready for a big crowd of men. There was usually bacon, or corned beef, with cabbage and turnips and potatoes and if the apples had ripened, you would make a few apple tarts as well. You would have to do all the cooking on the open fire, but the neighbouring women would come and give you a hand. You would give the men a tea in the evening time and they would usually have a few bottles of stout at the end of the threshing.

Reflections: Dick Mahon Reflects on the 1940s and 50s in Aghowle

The Mahon family lived and farmed in the townland of Ballycullen - their farmhouse looked across the Aghowle valley towards Carrick Mountain and the family were very much part of the farming community of both Aghowle and Ballycullen.

Prior to 1933, Sarah Davis had been living with her aunt Sarah Gregory on her farm in Ballycullen. In 1933, John Mahon from Laragh East married

Sarah Davis and the couple began their married life farming at Ballycullen where they went on to have 5 children.

Their first-born child was Richard who was born on 03rd May 1934. As Richard grew up, he became known as Dick to his family and friends. He first attended school in Nun's Cross School and then attended the Technical School in Wicklow town. When he had completed his training in the Technical School around 1950, he went to work for the three farmers at Aghowle Upper: Miley O'Brien, Bill Farrell and Paddy Connolly, working two days a week on each farm. After a while Dick moved on to a better position and another local man from Ballycullen named Tom Sheane took up the position with the three farmers.

On the 14th October 2015, I visited Dick in his home at Laragh East where he shared with me some of his memories of the townlands of Aghowle and Ballycullen during the 1940s and 1950s and his memories of his days working on the three farms in Aghowle Upper.

Dick Mahon in his kitchen at Laragh East, October 2015

I remember the Shannons, their house was a low little farmhouse, the inside was typical of the farmhouses of the time, a big dresser, table and chairs and stools beside the fireside.

Charlie Shannon used to go around on two sticks because at one time he had a fall off a horse and cart. I think he may have broken his leg in the accident. His sister Kate James lived there too at one stage and Kate's daughter Tess James remained there looking after Charlie. Then as he got older she took over looking after the cattle for him as well. I remember Charlie used to have a saying or phrase when he was going to tell you something he would say "looked oh aye"

I used to be over ploughing in Shannons, Charlie had a bay mare and my father had a horse, most of the farmers around us at the time were one horse farmers. As a young lad, I would go over to plough for Charlie and then when we were ploughing at home, we would go over and borrow Charlie's bay mare and we would have a pair to do our own ploughing with.

I recall one day I was ploughing over in Shannons. It was a real warm day and I used to like to drink milk, so I asked Charlie for a drink of milk from the jug on the dresser. I took a big long drink out of it and God hadn't it gone off. Charlie had a cow he was trying to let go dry and was only milking her every three days. Well I couldn't drink milk for years after that.

Another day when I was ploughing over there with the two horses, I was taking up a furrow and I came to a place where I knew there was a stone and Charlie came out on the two sticks and was looking at the ploughing. He told me to drive on the horses a bit and I said to him there was a stone there, but Charlie hit the horse on the hoof to go on anyway and broke the nose of the plough. So, he went off inside with himself after that and left me to do the ploughing.

Next door to the Shannons were Dan and Mary Short. Dan used to work in the woods with his horse, dragging out the timber. He did his bit of farming on his farm as well as the forestry work. Mary Short used to say: "be hell a man"

When I was going to school, I remember Ter Reilly used to be working on the roads. His wife, Mrs Reilly in my memory was a woman who was kind of bent over with arthritis and she always wore a white apron.

Their son Paddy used to work along with Jimmy Connolly, in Laragh House. It is gone now. It was burnt down. Paddy Reilly would cycle from Aghowle Lane to Laragh House every day to work, which was some cycle.

Paddy O'Reilly and his sister Molly,
with the bicycle used for his daily commute from Aghowle to Laragh House
Photograph courtesy of Terry Timmons

I heard a story once that Ter Reilly carried a big sack of flour home from Glenealy, walking over Carrick Mountain.

I remember working on the farms up in Aghowle. Paddy Connolly was very easy going. If you didn't do something right, he would never say so. He would just say "it will do damn fine". I remember we would be ploughing with the two horses up in the crossroads field or the one above it and then we would come down to the house for the dinner. There would be bacon and cabbage and Paddy would empty the big pot of potatoes out onto the table. Connolly's used to kill their own pigs and cure the bacon, I remember doing it along with them and you used to have to rub it with this big block of coarse salt.

Jimmy Connolly had a head of hair like a furze bush, he never put a comb through it and Paddy's hair wasn't as bushy. Jimmy worked in Laragh House, trapping rabbits. He also worked trapping rabbits for my uncle Hugh Mahon in Laragh. During the war, Jimmy used to be out all the time hunting the rabbits and he would sell them to the dealer Dinny Cullen who came around every week. When Jimmy was younger, he was out on the road with his three dogs. He had a collie, a greyhound and a terrier. The greyhound got hit by a lorry and he picked the dog up in his arms, but the dog was in such pain that he bit through Jimmy's lip. He was brought to Wicklow hospital for treatment, but he was marked for life. When I was working in Connollys they had a cow that used to graze the long acre, that was the grass verges at the side of the roads. This cow would head off every morning down the road and by milking time in the evening she might have gone down past O'Brien's Lane. At the time, Paddy had this dog. He was a bit bad tempered but a great herding dog. All Paddy had to do was say to the dog "go down and get the cow for milking" and off he would go on his own and bring the cow back.

I remember Mick the Rocher Doyle lived up near Connollys in a little house at the way into the wood. I was in the house once with Paddy Connolly when we were looking for sheep that had gone missing. I remember by that time Mick was an old man with a pipe, sitting on a stool at the fireplace.

In my time the farms coming down Aghowle on the right-hand side were, Farrells, O'Briens, Mullens and Turners. Turners' house was on the left side of the road and in Ballycullen, but their land was across the road and in Aghowle. I never heard about the Careys that were evicted, but I think there were ruins called Carey's walls in Egan's Wood.

Miley O'Brien was grand to work with, but if something went wrong for him you might want to get out of the way, there could be spanners flying. Miley's father, old Mick O' Brien, was a grand old fellow. I would say in the evening time, I better be going home now and he'd say: "well if you are going home, you better go, I won't detain yea".

Miley had a trashing mill and the first tractor in the locality. The tractor was a Fordson. Then he got an International 1020. I never saw one of those tractors since, even at rallies.

The first tractor I drove myself was with Miley O Brien. We were collecting turnips on the Raheen and you had to keep moving on the tractor as you threw the turnips in. So, Miley got fed up jumping up and down to move it on and told me to do it. The tractor had very heavy pedals so would keep cutting out, but eventually I got the hang of it. When Miley got the first tractor in the area he went up to do some work for Paddy Connolly. Paddy used to be very particular about his gates. He used to make these grand pole gates by splitting down pieces of wood with an axe and using an auger. They were about six or seven-foot-wide and were suitable for the horse and cart to get through. But when Miley came in with the new tractor, it was wider and it broke the gates. Paddy, who wasn't one for getting annoyed just put his hands up to his face and said "Well, I am going to have to go and widen all me gates now for this fellow and his new tractor".

Miley was also the first man around to get the tilly lamp. It gave out a great light. I recall he also had a Cossor battery radio. It had 3 batteries in it and the batteries would need to be charged up every week, so Miley would have to go to Ashford to have them charged. He kept a few spare ones so he could rotate them. When Miley got the radio they all thought it was a great thing, so then Paddy Connolly had to get one too. He got a Murphy Radio. When the electricity came, Miley gave me the Cossor Radio. It was hard on batteries, but had a great sound from it.

O'Briens had a little dairy off the farmhouse where Nancy made butter. She was very good at butter making, very thorough and clean. You had to take great care making the butter. If the milk was left in a house where the turf fire smoked, it would taint the butter. She had a milk separator and she would separate the cream out from the milk after milking, then she would save the cream in an earthenware jar, which had a black glaze on the inside.

On butter making day if I was there working around the yard, Nancy would come out with two white enamel buckets and say: "Dick will you go up to the spring well at the top of the lane and get me two buckets of water to wash the butter" Then in a little while, out she would come again and ask me to go for two more buckets of water.

I remember cutting turf with Miley O Brien in Mernagh's bog, I would go along with the ass and cart. One of the times we were on the bog, Liz Timmons (nee Reilly) of Parkmore was there too cutting her turf. It was a wet bog and I remember there was a big pond of water and Liz's children, Terry and Jane, were little ones playing about.

They used to come in beside where I was working and throw sods of turf into the pond of water to splash me. So, I ran after them. They of course avoided the pond, but I went into it up to me waist and got drowned through.

I remember hearing that when Jer and Sarah Farrell got married [1903], the wedding celebrations were in the farmhouse, as was the custom at that time and some of the local lads came up the roof at the back of the house and put a puckan, that's a male goat, down the chimney into the kitchen. The house would have been thatched at the time and the ground at the back of the house came well up the walls, so it was probably easy enough to get the goat up to the chimney and all the farmhouses back then had the big wide chimneys.

When my father and mother got married, the wedding celebrations were up in the house in Ballycullen. There was dancing and music in the house and I believe some of the local lads were up to high jinks that night too. My mother used to play the melodeon and sometimes there would be house dances in our place.

There was a path from Aghowle to Ballycullen. It was down past where the lane went up to O'Briens' Raheen. It ran up there on the left and brought you out near our place [Mahon's] but you could continue on through a long strip of wood and come out on the Upper Ballycullen road near Mahoney's. I remember myself and my sister used to go up through the wood to Timmons shop in Moneystown.

My father used to smoke a pipe, so on a Saturday night he would send us to the shop for two ounces of tobacco, the Wicklow People Newspaper and a loaf of bread, or whatever else might be needed. On the way, we used to go into Mrs Mahoney. She was an old woman with grey hair and a sack apron. You couldn't see the inside of the house for smoke from the turf fire and all your clothes and everything would smell of smoke after you had been in there.

She might want some small messages from the shop, a quarter of tea or something. She used to give us bread and jam, or maybe a sixpence – the one with the greyhound on it and we would be delighted, as then we could get a couple of bars of chocolate in the shop. There was another house up there called Meades. It had a thatched roof. When we were children, as we were passing we used to always ask Jimmy Meade what time it was. For Jimmy had this watch that he kept wrapped up in a load of rags in his pocket and it used to take him ages to unwrap all the rags and we got great amusement out of watching this.

Local Farming - Sheep Dipping

In my childhood, there were several dipping baths, or dip troughs as they were called, around the Aghowle area. There was a large one across from O'Briens' farmyard, which belonged to Billy Timmons. It was used by Miley O'Brien, Billy Timmons and Richard Hatton of Ballycullen and sometimes the Smiths of Ballycullen. There was a smaller one at Connollys which the Farrells and Connollys used and there was another one in Slanelough belonging to Larry Timmons of Parkmore. In the later decades of the 20th century, when the original Aghowle farmyards fell into disuse, some of the people who rented the lands at Aghowle used to bring their sheep to be dipped at Larry Timmons's dip trough at Slanelough.

William Smith of Ballycullen with his daughter Olive driving sheep to be dipped c.1950s

Dick Mahon October 2015
Sheep Dipping
   Most farmers had a small dipping trough themselves, but around the area there were larger licensed baths, that the farmers brought their sheep to be dipped. The dipping inspector would come to these baths and certify that your sheep had been dipped. We used to bring our sheep to Joe Byrne's in Moneystown for inspection, as he had a licensed bath. Then often the farmers would give them an extra dipping as well in their own place.

Chapter 12

1960 – Early 70s: Arrivals and Departures

Tarring the Road

Up until 1964, the main road up through Aghowle going towards Moneystown was still not tarred. It consisted of hard packed stones and gravel. The council employed Bill Lee, who lived in a council cottage in Aghowle, to maintain this road. In his reflections from the late 1940s, George Murray recalled Bill sitting by the roadside breaking the stones which he would use to repair this stretch of roadway.

In 1964, another piece of modernisation arrived in the townland, with the announcement that the Council was going to surface the road from Aghowle to Moneystown with tarmacadam. This was just before I started going to school in Moneystown and to a young child the surfacing of the road was an exciting event. I still recall that the council men kept some of their machinery for this operation on the grass area outside our farmyard and also some machines were kept in the cart shed at the bottom of the farmyard.

I think the weather at the time must have been quite wet, because I can recall there seemed to be a lot of days when our kitchen was full of council workers dressed in dripping oilskins, drinking tea around the fireside.

The operation itself brought much excitement. There was the smell of the tar heating up in a big machine and the activity of all the men as they spread out the chippings into the freshly poured tar. The big rolling machine that flattened them down into the tar vibrated so much that it made the delph on our kitchen dresser rattle and shake.

When the work was completed, everyone agreed that the new flat, smooth, dust free surface was a great improvement. Most of the traffic using the road at that time would have been people walking or cycling. There were few cars but on Mondays there was increased traffic as farmers from further up the hills travelled by tractor and trailer or by van down to the livestock sales in Ashford.

One of the cars that did travel this newly surfaced road was a source of great entertainment for us children. A neighbour down the road in Ballycullen, named Hugh Mahon, was very talented as a mechanic and was always fixing up cars. At one time, he had a three-wheeled bubble car and sometimes he would drive the car over to Timmons shop in Moneystown to get some messages. When we heard the sound of the car coming up Aghowle, we would run out to see it pass by and as we knew it would be returning in about half an hour, we would wait on the roadside to witness this amazing sight coming back again. As it turned out, the tarring of the Aghowle road was well timed, as it was around this time that there began to be a lot more traffic using this road, with timber men and timber lorries coming and going to the forestry at Aghowle.

Road Maintenance in Past Times

A notice appearing in the Wicklow-Newsletter newspaper, in November 1866, shows how almost a century earlier, the County Council used to upkeep these very same roads by contracting out their maintenance to local residents, on a three-yearly contract:

"to keep in repair for three years, the 630 perches of road between the cross roads at Ballycullen and the three roads at the Giant's Grave, at 4d per perch.

Applicants, Michael Timmons and Gregory Cunniam" (both were men from the townland of Ballycullen)

The Forestry around Aghowle Matures

When the Forestry had originally planted the lands at Aghowle and around Carrick Mountain around 1930, they then left the trees to grow and mature and there were not many workers employed in the woods during this phase. But by the 1960s, the trees had grown and had reached the stage where they needed to be thinned out so that the remaining trees could reach maturity.

This thinning out work was contracted out to non-Forestry employees. During this phase, there was a lot more activity around the townland as there was the daily coming and going of the men who worked with horses felling the trees and dragging out the timber. These men worked long hours, often in mucky and wet conditions. During this time the large timber lorries that came to load the timber and draw it away became a frequent sight on the Aghowle road.

The men who came to fell the timber were usually from the surrounding Wicklow locality, but I do remember at one time there were a couple of men from another county who came to fell timber here. They had a caravan which they parked in our front haggard and they slept and ate there and worked very long hours in the woods. My father used to let some of the timbermen graze their horses on our farm and he also became friendly with the men that drove the timber lorries. Often when these men had finished loading the lorries, they would be wet and tired, so he would invite them in to the farmhouse for a cup of tea before they started off on their journey.

Reflections: Billy Crean Reflects on the Aghowle Forestry

Billy Crean was born in March 1944 and when he was a young lad of about 20 years of age, he went to work for Irish Forestry Products. This work was based in the state forests which had been planted a few decades earlier. One of the locations that Billy worked in during the 1960s was the forestry that had been planted in and around the townland of Aghowle.

In September 2016, I met with Billy and he shared with me some of his memories of working in this area.

In the early 1960s when I was a young lad of about 18 or 20 I was working for Irish Forestry Products thinning out the trees in the woods up at Aghowle. I had a horse for sligging out the timber and I employed my cousin Johnny Byrne, known as Flintstone and sometimes my brother and one or two others as well.

There was a forestry man overseeing the project at that time. Then another forestry man came along and marked, with a white mark, the trees they wanted us to fall. Generally they were taking out every third line of trees. Then after we fell them, another forestry employee, Tom Quinn of Mount Alto, came along and painted the butts that we left behind, so they didn't get diseased.

Our job was to fall the trees and then slig them down and out to the roadway, we did this with the horse and a slig chain. Then we had to cut them into lengths. The big ones went for pulping to the Clondalkin Paper Mills; the other lengths went to a place in Maghermore.

We needed to get grazing for Bob, the horse, so we came to an arrangement with two of the local farmers in Aghowle regarding payment. Making a living out of falling the timber was difficult and money was tight, so Paddy Connolly and Miley O'Brien gave us the grazing for free and in return we used to go down and give them a hand on the farm when they needed it. We usually grazed the horse in Connollys, but if grass was getting tight there, we would move down to O'Brien's for a while. Then when there was hay making or an extra hand needed around the farmyard for something, myself and the lads would help out. I remember making hay in Connollys and May Connolly coming up to the hay field in the afternoon with sandwiches and a big pot of tea, sitting in a nest of hay in a bucket. After the O'Briens and Connollys sold their farms, we still got grazing for the horses in Aghowle, but we then had to pay cash for it.

In the bad weather, we needed to keep the horse inside somewhere and at that time there was an empty little stone house in the wood, where the Rocher Doyle had lived, so we kept Bob in the upper room of the Rocher's house. Then at the weekends, we used to have to go up and give him a bit of hay and take him down for a drink to the little stream on the back road beside the wood. At the time, I was going out with Marie, who is my wife now and our Sunday outing was to go up to Aghowle to feed and water the horse. After a while when I got myself set up I got a second horse, I got him from Paddy Smith of Killiskey.

I remember one time when we were working at the timber up there I ended up in Wicklow hospital. At the time, we were working in the section of wood on past Aghowle, around Ballymanus and the horse we had was a young flighty one that was just broken in. This particular day there was a bit of snow on the ground and we were just stopped working, making ourselves a cup of tea around 10 o'clock. The next thing, a big stag deer came tearing down through the wood and frightened the flighty horse. We had tied the horse to a tree, but he dropped the winkers and got off and he took flying off through the woods.

So, when we had finished our drop of tea, we set off in the wagon to look for him. He had gone down and out onto the road and was grazing at the bottom of the by-road that went up towards Ballinakill. So, I caught him by the mane and brought him around to the back of the wagon and I went to get a bit of rope to tie him up. But he decided to take off again and he still had the heavy slig chain attached to him. The chain went over my boot and somehow got caught around it and knocked me to the ground. Then when he took off he sligged me on my back behind him. The Ballinakill road at that time wasn't tarred, it was just stones and gravel. The lads jumped into the wagon after us. But as the little road was narrow they couldn't get past the horse. They *were shouting and roaring and Matt Carthy who lived in a house up along the road heard them. So, he came out to see what all the commotion was and as he saw the horse sligging me up the road, he figured out what the situation was. Matt got a pitchfork and stuck it up to stop the horse. The horse went sideways and got caught against a big stone pillar of a gate going into the field opposite Carthy's house. The collar broke and left me lying on the ground.*

The lads got me into the back of the wagon and brought me into Wicklow, Dr. Liston was attending up in Wicklow hospital. He put me lying on my stomach and checked me over. He said I was very lucky there was nothing broken, but my back was very badly cut and torn. He cleaned and dressed it and told me I had to stay in the hospital lying on my stomach for a few days. But I thought I would recover better at home, so the next day I got someone to bring me in my clothes and I went home, but I was very sore for a long time afterwards.

Around that time, as well as working drawing out the timber, we used to sell logs for firing around the area. One of the places we delivered them to, was to the houses in Aghowle Lane. Dan and Mary Short and Tess James lived in there around that time. We had a pick-up truck and the road in to the houses there was in a terrible bad state with pot holes. Anyway, at that time I was starting to get involved with trying to get things done in the local community. After talking to a few people, we managed to get the council to drain, widen and tar the road in along to the houses in Aghowle Lane and this was a great improvement for the people who lived along the lane.

Reflections: Jack Murtagh Reflects on The Aghowle Forestry
Jack Murtagh was born in August 1937 in Moneystown North, in the little farm house where his father had been born in 1910 and where his grandfather had been born in 1855. In the 1960s and 70s Jack worked for the Department of Lands, who managed the State Forests at the time. During that time, one of the jobs he was given was the making of the new roads through the forestry plantation around the Aghowle area.

In June 2016, I visited Jack in his home in Moneystown North where he shared with me his memories of his time working in the woods around Aghowle.

When they planted the land around Carrick there were no roads as such put in, there was ride lines from A to B for people or horses to walk through and there was still some little lanes and pathways around from the time it had been farmland and farmhouses. As the first planting of trees were ready for thinning out, they needed to put in roadways through the trees for the men to slig out the timber and for lorries to get in to pick it up. The original roads were only made about 8-foot-wide, big enough for horses or a small lorry to come in and collect the timber, it was all hand loaded at that time. But as time went on the men started using tractors to draw out the timber and there were big 30 tonne lorries collecting it, with a winch for loading it. This meant they needed to widen the roads to 22 foot for the new machinery. So, surveyors and road engineers came and mapped out where these roads were to be made. As it was very steep going up towards Carrick, they had to do a 1 in 10 gradient. Then you ended up with roads that were not straight, but had twists and bends on them. My job was to make these roads with a bulldozer, upgrading the little raggedy tracks and 8-foot roads, to 22-foot roads. The early roads were made using stones not gravel. I made all the roads through the woods there around Aghowle and up to Carrick.

Jack Murtagh in his kitchen in Moneystown North, June 2016

I made the road in by the Rocher Doyle's house, where you went in from the back lane there up from Connolly's land. The line of that road was different from the little pathway the Rocher would have come in through the trees to his little house. The Rocher's house was empty at that stage – sometimes the forestry men used it to shelter in and make a cup of tea.

Further up along the wood around Ballymanus there was another abandoned little cottage. It was called Shannons' the new roads were made around it. there were 5 cross roads near the gable end of that house. I used to sometimes use it for shelter. There was a well beside it that never went dry, where I used to get a drop of water for my tea and go in and shelter in the house when I was working up around there. The Holy well [Lady's Well] that they have opened up again in recent years, was up near there at that time. There was nothing around it or anything. It was just a drop of water coming out of the ground, at that time.

Later on, I also did some work making the road into the woods that were planted on the other side of the Aghowle road, down past Miley O'Brien's place. It had been formerly Ashley Brown's ground and bordered Lawlers of Ballycullen. The forestry ground there ran up the top, to where Boltons used to live.

I remember Dan Short of Aghowle – he used to work for the forestry. He had a horse and car and when they were making the stone roads through the forests, Dan was the main man. He drew the stones to the men that made the 8-foot roads. He used to deliver the stakes, wire and fencing to the men as well.

The Magic of Mushrooms

As a child one of the many things I loved about summertime was the prospect of going out through the damp fields in the early morning, looking for mushrooms. For this pleasure, I had to wait until near the end of the summer and hope that there had been a spell of good warm dry weather, broken by a day or two of heavy rain around the end of July. This was the type of weather most favourable for the magical appearance of mushrooms in the fields behind our farmhouse. They seemed to prefer land that was kept solely for sheep grazing and only fertilised by the sheep themselves or a little farmyard manure.

I loved the excitement of getting up early before breakfast, taking a bowl or saucepan from the kitchen and heading up to the bank field through grass that was still damp and glistening with the early morning dew. At that time of the year, the grass would be high, often hiding from view the little white clumps - but from experience we knew the most likely locations to search for them. We had to go early in case the slugs got there before us or the sheep trampled the delicate domes as they wandered about grazing through the field.

There was something wonderful about finding these perfectly formed snowy caps, where nothing had existed the previous day and gently plucking them out of the soil. I can still smell their wonderful fresh earthy aroma.

Of course, there were mornings when you could search the whole field but find that the magic had not happened overnight - but that made the days when you did find them even more special. Then we would run home to cook them on the pan with a bit of butter or perhaps some lard that the rashers had been cooked in and they tasted simply sublime.

Sometimes if we had not woken up early enough to go check for the mushrooms, our father would walk through the fields while he was out bringing in the cows for milking. If he found some mushrooms he would take off the cloth cap that he permanently wore about the farm and place the mushrooms inside it. Then, when he was coming back through the farmyard, he would awaken us by knocking on our bedroom window and handing in the cap, telling us to go down to the kitchen and get Mammy to put them on the frying pan. When he came in for breakfast a short while later, we all sat down to feast on the cap full of mushrooms that had been growing in the field behind the farmhouse less than half an hour earlier.

My father told us that when he was a boy, our grandmother used to make mushroom ketchup in the summers when mushrooms were plentiful. While he couldn't remember exactly how she made it, it involved cooking the mushrooms in a solution of vinegar and bottling them. Then this was used over the winter months when fresh vegetables were in short supply, to add to stews or to spice up cold meats.

He also told me that the year I was born had been a long hot summer and that the good weather had broken with a big thunderstorm just before my arrival. At that time, women were beginning to move away from home births in favour of hospital deliveries and a midwife named Nurse Leonard had set up a nursing home in Wicklow town for this purpose, in which I was born.

The day after my birth, my father came to visit and Nurse Leonard asked him if any mushrooms had appeared yet in the fields around his farm, as she loved the taste of the fresh field mushrooms. My father told her that after the hot summer and recent rain the fields were white with them and promised to bring some in to her when he came back to collect my mother and the new baby. On the morning when he was coming to collect us, he went to the Crossroads field at Slanelough (in which our bungalow now stands) and filled a galvanised bucket full of beautiful fresh mushrooms. Nurse Leonard was so delighted that a good part of the bill for my delivery was paid for with mushrooms from the Crossroads Field.

In my childhood on our farm, the Bank field, the Top field and sometimes the Crossroads field were the best places to find mushrooms, while on Farrells' farm it was the Bog field. Up on Brownes' land and on O'Briens' farm, they usually grew on the Field over the New Ditch, the Long Field and the Green Cart Road field on the Raheen. Larry Timmons's School House Field at Slanelough crossroads was also a good location for mushrooms.

It is rare now to find any field mushrooms. Many people believe this is because of the use of artificial fertilisers and more intensive farming. But on rare occasions, in fields that are mostly used for sheep grazing, an odd one still pops up to remind us of what a real mushroom should taste like.

Local Farming - Sheep Dogs
On any livestock farm, a good dog is said to do the work of at least an extra man, if not two. For the sheep farmer, his sheep dog is an essential member of the team as well as a loyal and trusted friend. I noticed whilst researching for this book that in many of the photographs of local farming families, their sheep dog is very often included in the family group.

Catherine O'Brien outside their farmhouse door feeding Shep (left) and Jess (right) c.1961
Catherine recalls she used to ride around on Shep's back
Photograph courtesy of the O'Brien Family

In Wicklow, the local collie dog is valued for his sheep herding instinct, his intelligence and his good temperament. Since 1865, it has been law that the owner of a dog must hold a licence and as some of these dog licence registers have in recent years been made available through on-line websites, [FMP/IDLR], we actually have a very comprehensive record of the dogs that lived in the townland from 1866 to 1912. These registers tell how many dogs each farmer kept, along with the breed and colour and sex of the dog. Alas, it does not give us the names of the individual dogs.

In the first year of the registration of the Aghowle area in 1866, we see most of the farms kept just one sheep dog. These dogs are described in a variety of colours from black and white, to grey, yellow and red. The Shannon's farm appears to only have had a black and white terrier and the O'Reillys had a black and white cur dog. The only person to register 2 sheep dogs was John Faulkner.

Ann Connolly outside the farmhouse with Jock the sheepdog, C.1957

As the dog was registered by its owner, these dog licence records give a very good account of who was living in the townland at a particular time. They also indicate when a farmer died, as his widow or son would then be recorded as the new licensee of the dog - it seems that whoever was the named lease holder for the land was the person responsible for licensing the dogs. By 1910, nearly half of the farmers had two collie sheep dogs, in a variety of colours.

The Last Working Sheep Dog on Connolly's Farm

In the early 1960s, my father's sheepdog Jess was accidentally killed by a passing car outside our farm gate. As well as my father being extremely upset at the death of his dog, this also left him without a sheepdog on the farm. At the time, our neighbour Brendan Timmons of Parkmore had a young dog he had just finished training, so my father bought this dog from Brendan and decided to name the dog Bren after his trainer. Bren was a large, placid, black and white collie, who was very intelligent and had a gentle nature. From the start, he showed great intuition and skill for herding sheep. He was a little less suited for herding cattle, as some of the bossier cows got the better of his gentle temperament.

Late 1960s, Connolly's farmyard
Back L-R: Mr Convery and Beth Murray visiting from Dublin, May and Patsy Connolly
Front L-R: Mary, Margaret, Bren the sheepdog, Ann Connolly and Jock the sheepdog

At this time, my father was still driving his sheep on foot down to the sheep sales in Ashford. After the first few trips down to the sales with his new sheep dog, my father marvelled at Bren's herding ability. The route from our farm down to Ashford was about 4 miles and held many potential trouble spots when driving a flock of sheep. There were numerous lanes and side roads, where the sheep at the front could divert from the main road and lead the rest of the flock astray. But my father noted that once Bren had accompanied him a couple of times on this journey he seemed to have memorised where all these potential dangers lay. As they neared a lane or side road, Bren silently crept along in the ditch to get in front of the flock, or sometimes he hopped over the ditch into a field and out again when he had passed the flock. He would then run ahead and guard the potential danger spot and only when all the sheep were safely past would he drop back to walk with my father until they neared the next laneway or road. My father used to say he could nearly let Bren out on his own to drive the sheep down to Ashford.

My father, like most farmers, had a great love of and affinity with all the animals on the farm but he had a particular fondness for both cats and dogs and it is difficult to find any photograph of him whether out on the farm or inside the house that does not have either a cat or a dog beside him. But over the last eight years of his farming life, he formed a very special bond with Bren the sheep dog. When he sold the farm in 1971 and the family moved to live in the bungalow at Slanelough crossroads, naturally Bren made the move too. My father then set up a market gardening business in the field beside the new house. Here he spent most of his days digging and tending to the vegetable plots, with his beloved dog following him around the vegetable patches or dozing nearby in the ditch. Often, they were joined by my father's cat that would look to be picked up and petted. Sometimes she would climb up on my father's shoulder and drape herself there while he continued working.

After several years, my father's health failed, and he had to give up his market gardening and pursue a more sedentary life sitting relaxing in the garden or inside by the fireside. No matter where he was, faithful Bren would always be by his side. I imagine sometimes they both sat and dreamed of past days herding sheep in the fields around the farm. Also on days when my parents took the car out to go shop or visit neighbours, Bren would always be waiting to hop in and sit in state on the back seat. For a collie sheep dog, he lived a long life. But as he was approaching his 18th year, he had become deaf and blind and arthritic. He spent his days lying in the sunshine at the back door and his evenings stretched in front of the fire. My father would have to tap him gently to let him know it was bedtime and he would hobble out after my father to his cosy bed in the shed.

But my father knew that the poor dog's quality of life was dwindling away. One day when the vet from Wicklow Town was passing, he dropped in for a chat and my father asked if he could do anything for the dog. The vet looked at my father and said: "*I think you know, Paddy, the best thing you can do for your dog at this stage is to bring him in to the surgery and we will let him go for his final sleep*". My father reluctantly agreed to bring the dog in to the vet on the following Friday.

On the Friday morning, it was with a very heavy heart he went to let Bren out for his last wander around the yard. But when he opened the shed door, he saw that Bren, the ever intuitive and kind dog, had done his master one last act of service and had gently passed away in his sleep. My father said he was never as happy about anything as he was to find Bren curled up dead in his own bed. In return, my father had his last act of service to do for his dog. He dug a grave for him in the field beside the house and laid him to rest in the land where he herded sheep in his youth and where he wandered at my father's side in his retirement.

Having had one or another dog beside him for all his life, my father was not going to live out the rest of his years without a four-legged companion, so Bren was succeeded by two non-working pet dogs. Ali was a beautiful Shetland Sheep Dog that survived until 1986 (and he was followed by Roy (until 2002), a small black and white Border Collie.

Roy, bless him, wasn't the most intelligent dog ever but he was very loving and a good guard dog, wary of strangers. His judgement of people's character could also be of value – when my future husband-to-be, Brian, would come to visit Aghowle, Roy would happily go off for a walk with him. My father reckoned that if Roy trusted him, then maybe he was suitable enough to be courting his youngest daughter!

The Last Bicycle Post and the Man with the Van

Up until the latter half of the 1960s, the postal service to our locality was still delivered from Ashford Village by bicycle. The post man was Jim McCabe, known to many as Lal McCabe and to us children as Mr. McCabe. In those days, when there were no telephones in the area and for most of the people their only means of transport was walking or cycling, the postman was a central part of the community. For as well as delivering the post throughout the area, he also carried the local news throughout the parish. As he called to each house, or met the people going about their daily routine on the farm, he stopped and chatted, picking up and passing on the local news. He would be the first to know when a new baby had arrived, or the funeral arrangements of someone further down the valley that had passed away. He would know if a sick animal had recovered, or what price someone had got for their stock at the local fair.

Jim McCabe was postman in the Ashford area for 49 years and while he had worked several routes, in his later years his postal route included the townlands of Ballycullen, Aghowle and Slanelough and part of Parkmore. This was a difficult route for an older man, as he had to cycle up rising hills nearly all the way from Ashford village on his big black bicycle. Not only was the route all uphill, it also took him up and down numerous laneways to houses. He also had to cross the stream to deliver post into Aghowle Lane, which sometimes in winter would be in flood. Often by the time he reached our house near the top of Aghowle, it would be approaching 4pm. He had, of course, stopped for a rest and a cup of tea in a few houses along the way. As he was related to Dan Short, that would have been one of his stops.

In the afternoons when I would come in home from school it was quite common to see the big black bike resting against the wall outside our farmhouse. In the winter, Jim might be having a cup of tea by the fireside as he warmed himself and in the summer, he would be sitting at our kitchen table drinking his tea, with his heavy tunic unbuttoned and his postman's hat sitting beside him on the table. My sister Mary recalls, if there was an important horse race on, such as the Grand National, that Jim would have it timed to arrive at our house before the race started. Then he would sit drinking his tea and listening to the race on the big wireless that sat in the kitchen window.

Ashford Postman Retires
To mark his retirement after 49 years as postman, Mr. Jim McCabe, Ashford, is here seen
being presented with a clock and wallet of notes, by Miss Lily Hender, Postmistress, on
behalf of the people of Ashford. Also in the picture is Sergeant John Duignan, Ashford.
Photograph reproduced from "A Pictorial History of Ashford, Co. Wicklow, 1860s-1960s"
By kind permission of Sheila Clarke

In the last year or so of his service, Jim found the route more difficult and sometimes in the depths of winter, darkness would be descending by the time he reached our house. Then, as he came in to take a rest and heat himself by the fire, my father would ask if he had any post for the neighbours in Slanelough or Parkmore. He would check in the post bag and if there was post he took it out and examined it.

If the letters were only official letters like bills from the ESB or a letter from a government department, he gave them to my father, who placed them up on top of the mantelpiece and the next morning we children would drop them into the neighbours on our way to school in Moneystown. This would save the postman from having to push on for another half hour in the rain and darkness. But if the letters were handwritten, there was no question, but Jim would put them back in the bag and cycle on to deliver them. He knew they might contain very important family news that one of our neighbours might be anxiously waiting to hear. Also, if the official letter was thought to be the milk cheque from the creamery or co-op, it was deemed to be as important as the personal letter and would not be left on our mantelpiece overnight.

As the time approached for Jim McCabe to retire, people began to wonder who would replace him. When the news arrived that he was to be replaced by a man with a van, who would drive out from Wicklow town, there was consternation. Sure, he would be a stranger - a man from the Town - who would have no interest in the local farming people and would carry no news from around the locality. It was speculated that he would talk to nobody and would barely stop to throw the post in the door.

But when the man in the van arrived, it turned out all these fears were unfounded. The new postman was John Mitchell from Wicklow town and people soon found out that he was a very friendly, gentle and most kind man, who befriended everyone. At that time, many of the local people did not have cars, but walked or cycled everywhere. If they needed to post a letter or a parcel they had to make their way to Moneystown Post Office or Ashford Post Office. There was, and still is, a post box built into the wall in Ballycullen, but if someone had no stamps or needed to post a parcel it was not much benefit to them. Very soon after John Mitchell started as the local postman, he told everyone if they needed anything posted to give it to him, along with the money for the stamps and he would post it for them in Wicklow town. It wasn't long before John was also offering to bring out a pound of staples for the farmer who had run short while fencing, or stopping by the vets to pick up some medicine for a sick calf, or dropping a pair of shoes that needed mending into the cobbler in Wicklow town. The man with the van was proving to be very useful indeed and as well as delivering the post and the news; he was also now acting as a courier service. Everyone became extremely fond of John Mitchell and he continued on this route for quite a few years. He became very much part of the local community and when he retired, everyone was extremely sad to see him go and wished him well in his retirement.

By this time, life in the district had changed considerably. Almost every house had a telephone and their own transport and in many of the houses people were commuting every day to work. So there was no longer a strict need for the local postman to act as a courier service or to bring the local news from house to house. But still the role of the local postman as a friendly face calling to each house and keeping an eye out for anything amiss in rural homes, especially where someone is living alone, remains. The perpetually happy and cheerful man that replaced John Mitchell has continued to fulfil this role.

Lulu - the pet lamb who loved cornflakes
Each spring on the farm, my sisters and I would wait with great anticipation during the lambing season, to see if we would end up with a pet lamb. This great event came about when a new born lamb's mother died, or if for some reason, she was unable to feed the lamb or the lamb was very weak. Then it was given to us to bottle feed and look after. Some years we were lucky enough to end up with several pet lambs. We got much enjoyment out of looking after the little lambs and watching them grow up. Then, as they no longer needed bottle feeding they would become independent and go off grazing with the rest of the sheep and in time become integrated into the flock. But one of our pet lambs did not quite follow this annual and natural progression.

In the spring of 1969, around the time of the Eurovision song contest, we acquired a pet lamb which we decided to call Lulu after the Eurovision winner. Initially Lulu behaved like previous pet lambs, taking her bottle feeds and playing with us around the farmyard and grazing in the field beside the house. But as time progressed, she showed a reluctance to join the other sheep, preferring to hang around the farmyard with us.

It was around this time that we discovered she was particularly fond of cornflakes, which we used to pour into a bowl for her at the kitchen door. As that summer progressed, my father said she would have to go join the rest of the flock and with great effort she partially got used to being in the field with the rest of the sheep. But any opportunity she got, she would find a way in through the field gate into the farmyard and arrive at the kitchen door looking for a bowl of cornflakes. When we were sent up the fields to check the sheep, Lulu would always come running up to us, even when she had grown into an adult ewe.

1969: Ann and Mary Connolly with Lulu the pet lamb

Also, there were several times when she would hear us on our way to school and would manage to get out of the field and follow us. On these occasions, we would have to leave her with our neighbour Martha Lawler and collect her on the way home. So, I did truly get to live out the famous nursery rhyme in having a little lamb that *followed her to school one day* - actually, many days!

The story of Lulu continues in the next chapter "Chapter 14: The End of an Era", see section "Lulu Goes out to Pasture".

Strict Religious Rulings and Unhappy Friends and Neighbours

It is difficult to believe nowadays but in the early 1970s, the Catholic Church still retained a ruling that its members were forbidden to attend any non-Catholic religious services. In 1972, this ruling caused great distress to some of the Aghowle residents.

When William (Bill) Smith of Ballycullen took ill suddenly and died in February 1972, it brought shock and sadness throughout the locality. Bill was a very well-liked and respected man and was a central part of the local farming communities of both Ballycullen and Aghowle. He had been born in Ballycullen and farmed all his lifetime there and his father had been born and reared in nearby Aghowle Upper (in house no 5). Perhaps because of this, Bill had a very strong connection with the three farmers of Aghowle Upper – namely, Miley O' Brien, who lived and farmed where Bill Smith's father was reared, Bill Farrell and Patsy Connolly. All four men were born within a few years of each other, so they would have grown up farming together since their boyhood.

But along with the shock and sadness of Bill's sudden departure, the three Upper Aghowle men were also faced with a major dilemma, as they were Catholics and Bill was a member of the Church of Ireland. Under the Catholic ruling of the time, the men were not allowed to enter a Church of Ireland church to attend a service.

Although I was only 12 years old at that time, I still recall Miley O Brien, Bill Farrell and my father sitting in our kitchen, sadly brewing over the prospect that they could not go into Nun's Cross Church to attend Bill Smith's funeral. They even contemplated going against their religion and attending the funeral anyway. But these were men who had been born into the era of strict Catholic observance and indoctrinated with the fear that going against the church's teachings would banish them to hell and eternal damnation. So, in the end this upbringing won out and the three men stood with their caps in hand, along with other Catholic neighbours, on the roadside outside Nun's Cross Church while their friend Bill's funeral proceeded inside.

Miley O'Brien had been a particularly close friend of Bill Smith's, so it was with a very heavy heart he returned home that day and said to his wife Bridget *"there is something wrong in the world and with our religion, when a man cannot go inside a different church to see his old friend off"*.

Nun's Cross Church, Ashford

A very short time afterwards, the Catholic church changed its ruling on attending services in other churches and the three men were very disillusioned and they reflected *"Well weren't we the right fools to have listened to them and their rules and not followed our own hearts and just done what we knew was the right thing to do"*.

The Ecumenical Overcoat

While, as outlined above, the Catholic Church forbade its members attending Church of Ireland services up until the early 1970s, one of the local Catholic farmers was willing to chance wearing an overcoat that had attended a different church.

Billy Smith of Ballycullen told me the following story, which took place around the 1960s and relates to his father and his neighbour Dan Short of Aghowle Lane. In those days, most of the rural farming community could just about afford to have one good set of clothes, which were kept as their Sunday best to attend church or chapel and for other important events. Dan Short of Aghowle Lane came one Saturday evening to call on his good friend and neighbour, Bill Smith Senior of Ballycullen, the man whose funeral is referred to in the above section. Dan was in a predicament, as for some reason, he did not have an overcoat to wear to mass in Moneystown the following morning and he was wondering if he might be able to borrow Bill's overcoat.

Bill replied of course he could, but as he handed over the coat, he said to Dan *"But be sure now and hurry back with it after mass, as I will need it myself to go to service in Nun's Cross"* (the local Church of Ireland church). So, on the following morning, Dan Short wore Bill Smith's overcoat to 10 o'clock mass in Moneystown and had it back in time for Bill Smith to wear it to his church service at 11.30 am in Nun's Cross Church.

Hollywood comes to the Local Hillside

In 1964, a little piece of Hollywood appeared in the local district. At that time, Niall MacGinnis, who had appeared in such movies as *Captain Boycott* and *Martin Luther* had come with his family to live and farm at Ballycullen. Niall and his wife Eleanor were friends with Richard Burton and had appeared with him in *Alexander the Great* and it came to pass that in 1964 Richard Burton and Elizabeth Taylor appeared in the local area.

This is the story as told to me by Billy Smith of Ballycullen in March 2017:

"Back in the 1960s, Mahoney's old house and farm up on Ballycullen

Hill was up for sale and Richard Burton and Elizabeth Taylor were interested in taking a look at it. They arrived in their chauffeur-driven car to the MacGinnis's house here in Ballycullen to get Niall to show them the place. Niall called here at the gate to ask my father to go along with them, as he would know the area and the land very well. So off he went in the car with them and showed them the house and around the farm. Then Niall MacGinnis and Richard Burton decided they would walk, by a short cut back across the fields to MacGinnis's house and left the chauffeur to drive my father and Liz Taylor back to our farm. Afterwards the locals had a good laugh, saying that Bill Smith of Ballycullen had been seen out driving around the roads with Liz Taylor"

The house that Richard Burton and Elizabeth Taylor bought in Ballycullen

Richard Burton did end up buying the place in Ballycullen. It was said locally that it was to be a gift for Liz Taylor. While the couple did come to visit the place, they never came to live there. But for many years, until it was eventually sold, it was always referred to as "*Liz Taylor's place above in Ballycullen*" In the 1970s, if any strangers or any unusual cars were spotted around the Aghowle or Ballycullen area, it would be rumoured that the Hollywood couple were visiting.

A few years ago, I met a woman from Dublin who told me her mother used to love to say she had once been mistaken for Elizabeth Taylor. Back in the 1970s, her mother had driven down from Dublin to visit someone in the Moneystown area and on the way up from Ashford she stopped to ask a man who was driving cattle on the road for directions. Her car would have been rather flash for the local area at that time and so would her appearance, as she was wearing sunglasses, lipstick and a head scarf. The man directed her towards Moneystown and then rather sheepishly enquired: "*Excuse me Ma'am for asking, but would you be Elizabeth Taylor?*" The woman just smiled at him, rolled up the car window and drove on, leaving him none the wiser.

Chapter 13

10 Farmhouses
tell their story

When the Irish census was taken on the night of 31st March 1901, there were 10 occupied houses in the townland of Aghowle. While these census records give us an illuminating glimpse inside these 10 farmhouses and their households at that time, each of the 10 dwellings have a wider story to tell.

Using the census records as a starting point, I have tried to trace the history of each of these 10 houses back into the early 19th century and forward through the 20th century up to the point where each house ceased to be part of the local farming community. As we shall see, many of the people born beneath these roofs farmed here all their lives and saw out their final days in the same little farmhouses where they had first entered into the world.

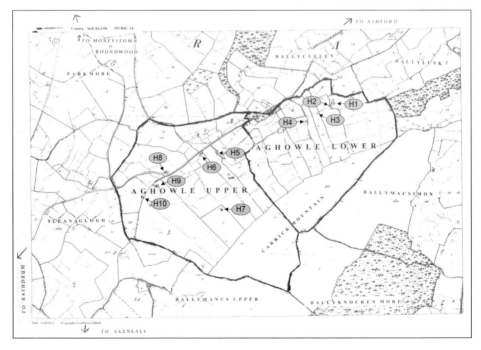

The 10 Houses of Aghowle

Being a rural community, there were of course no street numbers for the houses of Aghowle. Any mail would simply have been sent to such as "*The Shannon Family, Aghowle, Ashford, Co. Wicklow*" and the postman would safely deliver every time. However, for the sake of clarity and identification in this section, I have assigned numbers to the houses starting with No.1 at the bottom end of Aghowle Lower and working up to No.10 at the top end of Aghowle Upper. On the map, these are denoted as H1 to H10.

In this section, I follow the fortunes of all 10 houses up to the year 1960, by which time there were still seven houses remaining as occupied farmhouses. The section for each house starts with a summary of what was known about the house according to certain historical records, as follows:

Historical Record	Record Reference
1832 Land Records,	[NLI/MSS/11996-11997]
1839 OSI map	[OSI/1839]
1850 Glanmore Estate' Records	[FMP/LECR]
1854 Griffith's Land Valuation Records	[AAI/GVR]
1901 Census	[C/NAI]
1911 Census	[C/NAI]

In the penultimate section of this book, "Chapter 14: The End of an Era", I pick up their stories again as each of the seven farmhousess remaining by that time, one by one comes to the end of its days as part of a working farm.

House No. 1

Wedding Day outside Shorts farmhouse, 11th June, 1930
Seated: Bride and groom: Mary Byrne and Dan Short
Standing: Mary's sisters, Sadie and Lizzie and Bill Farrell, Aghowle

House No. 1 (McDaniel, McDaniel-Shorts, Shorts)

House No. 1 is located at the lowest end of the townland. At Aghowle Lower, there is a laneway in off the main Aghowle road on the Carrick Mountain side of the valley - this lane was always known locally as Aghowle Lane. House No. 1 is situated approximately half a mile up this lane, on the left-hand side.

Historical Summary	
Families:	McDaniel, McDaniel-Shorts, Shorts
1832 Land Records	Garrett McDaniel leasing 41 acres
1839 OSI map	A dwelling house and farm buildings marked here
1850 Glanmore Estate Records	Representatives of Garrett McDaniel leasing 61 acres
1854 Griffith's Land Valuation	Patrick Short leasing 61 acres of land
1901 Census	Garrett and Catherine Short and family, living in a two-roomed thatched farmhouse
1911 Census	Garrett and Catherine Short and family
Last family to farm here:	Daniel and Mary Short, until 1969

Family History

In the land records of 1832, Garrett McDaniel is recorded farming here. This McDaniel family (sometimes written as McDonald) are recorded in the local church records [NLI/PR/W] from at least the early years of the 19th century. While no actual address is recorded in those records, there are indicators that the family was living in the Aghowle Lower or Ballycullen area from that time.

In January 1842, Patrick Short married Garrett McDaniel's daughter Margaret and Patrick then moved in to live with the McDaniel family. Between 1844 and 1851, Patrick and Margaret Short had six children – Eugene (also known as Owen), Sarah, Mary, Garrett, Bridget and Margaret.

By 1854, Patrick Short is the named lease holder of the farmhouse and 61 acre farm here. On Patrick's death, the lease passed briefly to the oldest son, Eugene and two years later in 1883, it passed to the second son Garrett. As mentioned elsewhere in this book, Garrett had gone to work in the chemical industry in Widnes in Lancashire where he married Catherine Cassidy from Co. Offaly. The couple returned to the family farm in 1883 with four young children - Margaret, Mary, Bridget and Patrick.

In the following years between 1885 and 1896, Catherine Short gave birth to at least six more children here in the Short's two roomed farmhouse. Baptism records from Ashford parish record that Elizabeth,

Garrett, William, Catherine, Daniel and Sarah were all baptised in the local church at Ashford. In the 1911 census, Catherine Short records that she gave birth to 11 children in total, 8 of who were still alive in 1911.

The children of Garret and Catherine attended the nearby Ballylusk School. It appears Garrett took an active role in the local community, as his name appears on a list of persons present at the Board of Guardians meeting for the Rathdrum Workhouse, held on 6th May 1899 [WH&S/p.558].

In the 1901 census, details of the Short's dwelling house are recorded as a two-roomed thatched cottage with two windows to the front. It is the only dwelling at Aghowle Lower to be classified as a third-class dwelling. Details of the farm buildings show that there were four out-buildings: a stable, a cow house, a piggery and a fowl house. The only addition by the time of the 1911 census was one extra shed.

As the children grew to adulthood, they moved away from the family home to find work and to marry. Catherine Short died in August 1915 from a heart condition. The youngest son, Daniel, stayed living at home to assist his elderly father with the running of the farm. When Garrett passed away in December 1926, aged 78, Dan took over the running of the family farm.

A few years later in 1930, Dan married Mary Byrne of Knockrath (see photo at start of this section). Knockrath was quite a distance from Dan Short's home at Aghowle but the couple probably knew each other from childhood, as Mary Byrne was a niece of Ellen O'Reilly who lived very close to the Shorts home in Aghowle Lane and probably would have visited there regularly.

Dan and Mary were not blessed with children of their own, so they decided to foster a young boy named Joey Reilly, who came to live with them in 1947, when he was about 5 years old. Joey went to school in Moneystown and remained living with Dan and Mary until adulthood.

Dan and Mary ran the farm together and Dan also worked with his horse for the state forest. Dan was said to be a very strong man when he was in his prime and people recall he was one of the best men to pitch sheaves at threshing time. He is also remembered as one of the local men who used to play handball up at the Handball Rock on Carrick. He had a great love of hunting and as several of the photos here depict, he was rarely seen without his gun in his hand - it even appears in the photo (see colour section) taken in their kitchen!

Local people recall Mary Short cycling all around the neighbourhood on her bicycle as she visited neighbours and did her shopping and people remembered how well she kept their little cottage, always neat and gleaming inside with a beautiful flower garden around the house.

Dan and Mary Short pictured at their fireside, with Elizabeth Tighe centre.
Photograph taken from "Ashford, a Journey Through Time"
By kind permission of Sheila Clarke

Mary Short's brother, Jack Byrne, was a very regular visitor to the farmhouse. On Saturday afternoons, Jack would cycle from his home in Ballylug to Aghowle (a distance of about 10 miles) to visit Dan and Mary. When Jack's son, Tommy, was old enough to be carried on his father's bike, he would also make the journey each Saturday afternoon to visit his Aunt Mary and Uncle Dan.

Reflections: Tommy Byrne on Childhood Visits to Dan and Mary Short

Tommy Byrne now lives in England, but shared with me the following fond memories of those visits to the Shorts farmhouse in the late 1940s.

> *When I was a lad, from about six years old, my Dad would take me on the crossbar of the bike from Ballylug to Aghowle on a Saturday. Aunt Mary would make a big fuss and be all over me and Uncle Dan would say to me if he had known I was coming he would have baked me a cake.*
>
> *I remember the Gramophone with a big horn in the kitchen - His Master's Voice, I don't know what happened to it in the end. I can*

remember that each September we would get the horse ready and go to the field on the right-hand side of the lane, by the wood, to take out the potatoes. Joey would be there with us and sometimes Tess James that lived in Shannons' next door to Shorts. Then in the evening time when we were finished Aunt Mary would have a great dinner ready for us and apple tart afterwards.

Often on a Sunday Uncle Dan would go shooting rabbits, I went with him a few times. Dan and Mary used to keep a pig and every so often they would kill one and cure the bacon. Dan did other jobs as well, some forestry work, but in my memory not that much.

Back Row L-R: Dan Short's brother; Jack Byrne (Mary Short's brother);
Josie McGrath – a relative of Mary Short; Mary and Dan Short
Front: Tommy Byrne - Mary's nephew, who used to visit on Saturday afternoons in the
1940s
C.1946
Photograph courtesy of Tommy Byrne

Towards the end of the 1950s, some of the Aghowle farmers moved from farming with horses onto tractors and some even bought motor cars. But Dan remained farming by horsepower and both he and Mary continued to cycle to shop and to attend Mass. When Joey finished school, he worked locally for a while and then went to work in Dublin, returning home on his time off to visit Dan and Mary.

The story of House No.1 continues in the concluding chapter, "Chapter 14: The End of an Era", see section "House No.1: Short's".

House No. 2 (Shannon)

House No. 2 is located as a close neighbour to House No. 1, also on the left-hand side of Aghowle Lane.

Rear view of Shannons' farmhouse after it was sold and before it was renovated. Photograph courtesy of Ed. Ryan, the current owner

Historical Summary	
Families:	Shannon
1832 Land Records	Thomas Shannon leasing 18 acres here
1839 OSI map	A dwelling house and farm buildings marked here
1850 Glanmore Estate Records	Thomas Shannon leasing 23 acres
1854 Griffith's Land Valuation	Esther Shannon leasing 22 acres of land
1901 Census	Thomas Shannon and family, living in a three-roomed thatched farmhouse
1911 Census	Thomas Shannon and family
Last family to farm here:	Charlie Shannon and his niece Tess James 1962-64

Shannon Family History

This house was the home of the Shannon family for at least 130 years. The Glanmore Estate records show that Thomas Shannon was leasing 18 acres of land here at the start of 1832. Local parish records show that Thomas married Esther Devlin on 10th February 1834 and the couple had at least three children: Anne 1834, Bridget 1837 and Thomas 1839 [NLI/PR/W].

In the Glanmore Estate records of 1850, Thomas is recorded as the lease holder of 23 acres at Aghowle Lower but in the Griffith Valuation Records 4 years later, the lease has passed to his wife Esther, indicating that Thomas Senior has died in the meantime. Esther remained the leaseholder until her death in 1875, when her son Thomas took over the lease. Thomas was by this time married and the father of a young family.

In October 1870, Thomas married Catherine Toole, who lived in the neighbouring townland of Ballycullen. The couple had 8 children, 7 of whom survived to adulthood - Charles, Esther, Christina, Thomas, John, Kate and Bridget.

While Thomas was busy rearing his young family and farming, he was also one of the first people in the locality to join the National Land League and was also involved in the Fenian movement. We know from his obituary (reprinted below) that Thomas was an active member of the Land League and he came to the assistance of his neighbours, the Carey family, when they were evicted in 1887 and continued to assist them during their final years living in Aghowle.

In 1896, when Thomas and Catherine Shannon's oldest daughter, Christina was 23 years old, she died from a lumbar abscess

In the 1901 Census, details of the Shannon household are given as follows: Catherine and Thomas and their 6 remaining children are living in the family home, the youngest child Bridget is still at school, but all the rest of the family are involved in running the family farm. The farmhouse is described as a three-roomed thatched dwelling, with 4 windows to the front. There are 5 outbuildings, a stable, cow house, piggery, a fowl shed and a barn.

By the time of the 1911 Census, three of the Shannon children had left home. In 1909, Kate had married Thomas James from Wicklow Town; John was now living and working in Dublin and Esther had migrated to England. Bridget, Charles and Thomas were still living at home and helping to run the farm. The number of outbuildings had increased by three, to include a calf shed, a dairy and an extra general purpose shed.

Sometime around 1905 Esther Shannon migrated to England and went to work in London. Here she met her future husband, George Edward Lawrence and the couple married in December 1908 in London. The couple had their first child in England but within a few years George's work took him to India and so the family moved to live there for several years. For a woman who had spent most of her life on the small family farm in Aghowle, Esther must have found her new life in India very strange,

Esther Shannon born in Aghowle in 1878 and her husband Edward George Lawrence,
in their home in Hampshire, England
Photograph courtesy of Gerald Lawrence, Dorset

but her grandson Gerald Lawrence told me that during her years there she really embraced the Eastern lifestyle.

Despite the exotic location, she never forgot her Irish family roots. When her son was born, she chose her brother Charlie and sister Bridget (both still living at home in Aghowle) as his godparents. Perhaps to emphasise her strong Irish connections, she recorded her brother as Charles *Stewart Parnell* Shannon on the baptism record.

Esther and her family returned to live in England and her grandson remembered her fondly as a very interesting woman, who at one stage had slept with a loaded revolver under her pillow! She also kept in her home, in pride of place within a silver photo frame, a cutting from the Wicklow People newspaper claiming that her father had been 115 years old when he died – see obituary below.

Sometime between 1911 and November 1915, Thomas and Catherine Shannon's son John, who had been living in Dublin for a number of years, enlisted in the army and joined the 9th Battalion Dublin Fusiliers. John would have been in his late 30s when he enlisted, which would appear to be quite a mature age to join. It is not known if he took this decision for economic reasons, as many others did at the time, or whether he joined for patriotic reasons. We know his father was a very nationalistic-minded man, so perhaps if his son was of the same mind he may have been inspired by John Redmond's speech in Woodenbridge, Co. Wicklow, on 20th September 1914 which was to influence thousands of Irish men to join the British Army in the following months.

From records we know that John was in Blackdown camp in Aldershot Hampshire in November 1915, preparing to go to the front. While in the camp he wrote the following letter home to his parents in Aghowle:

Letter written from John Shannon to his parents on November 04th 1915.
Reproduced here by kind permission of The Director of The National Archives of Ireland
Ref: NAI, 2002/119 E267670, Soldier's Will, John Shannon.

Dear Father and Mother
Just a few lines hoping there is nothing wrong with you's as I am
rather annoyed as I have written two letters to you and I have got no
answer to either of them and if yous don't write soon I may not get one

from you at all as we expect to be going out in a few days
We made our will this week and we are quite ready to go out so you
may depend we won't be many more days here.
Whatever I should leave I left it to you mother so don't forget to keep
the regimental number and the letters I have written to you as they
might come in handy to prove your claim in case anything might
happen please god there wont.
But its best to be sure.
Tell all that I was asking for them
Don't forget and write as soon as you can
I have no more to say at present
Hoping that you's are well and I will hear from you soon

I remain Dear Father and Mother
Your affectionate son
J. Shannon

One hopes that John did receive his much-awaited letter from home before he went off to do his part in the Great War. Sadly, like so many other men he was never to return to see his family or to walk in Aghowle Lane to the little house where he had been born in 1876. John Shannon died in action at Mons in September 1916. His mother Catherine unfortunately did need a copy of John's letter transcribed above, in lieu of a missing will, to claim his belongings.

The following September the Shannon family lost another son, Thomas Shannon, who was single and still living at home in Aghowle, died from a lung condition.

Thomas Senior continued farming at Aghowle until his death in 1925. By this time, Thomas who

The fireplace in Shannons' farmhouse, a few years after the farmhouse was sold Photograph courtesy of current owner, Ed. Ryan

had been a nationalist and an active member of the Land League had lived long enough to see in his lifetime both his country gain independence and also to claim the proper ownership of the land his family had farmed for generations.

The Oldest Man Ever in Ireland?

But a strange conundrum exists regarding exactly how long Thomas Shannon's lifetime actually was.

Thomas passed away on 24th April 1925, and the death notice below appeared the following week in the Wicklow People newspaper:

> SHANNON – 24th April 1925, at his residence, Aghowle, Ashford, Thomas Shannon: aged 100 years: deeply regretted. Interred at Glenealy. R.I.P.

But when his wife Catherine registered his death in Rathdrum shortly after his passing, she recorded his age as 115 years and a short time later the following obituary appeared in the Wicklow People newspaper:

> DIED AT 115
>
> The death occurred recently of Mr Thomas Shannon Aghowle, Ashford, who was born in December 1809 and had attained the remarkable age of 115 years. He retained his full senses and exceptional virility to his final illness, which lasted only a few days.
>
> Throughout his long life, he resided in Aghowle and having seen the house he was born in live out its usefulness, he himself erected the stone dwelling that he died in, so that he practically never left the one spot in 115 years.
>
> He was a member of the Fenian organisation in his heyday: and all through the Land League agitation was a prominent and useful member; in fact, he was the first man in the locality to join its ranks and subscribe to its funds; and was among those who volunteered and carried out farming work on the Parnell estate when the chief was in prison.
>
> With ardent sympathy for the evicted tenants, he assisted them and fought for them in many ways, particularly about the Carey family when their turn came to be cast out on the roadside.
>
> He was also a member of the Co. Wicklowmen's '98 Association and carried his banner proudly in Wicklow town on the occasion of the laying of the foundation stone and the unveiling of the Billy Byrne

monument. His wife is a distant kinswoman of the famous Billy Byrne of Ballymanus.

His son, John Shannon, was killed at Mons in the Great War.

The funeral took place to Glenealy, where Rev. Father Costello C.C. Ashford, officiated. To his wife, children and grandchildren, sincere sympathy is extended in their bereavement.

So astonishing was the claim that Thomas Shannon of Aghowle had reached the great age of 115, that it also appeared in some of the international newspapers, such as the Lima News Ohio, the Fitchburg Sentinel (Massachusetts) and the Lancashire Evening Post.

Now all this seems confusing, as Thomas's age appears to be a bit of a movable feast. The only other records we have relating to his age are the 1901 and 1911 Census returns. In 1901 Thomas gave his age as 56 years and in the 1911 census he was 71 years – somehow managing to age 15 years in just a single decade!

It is a well-known fact that the ages people recorded in the 1901 and 1911 Census were often a bit inaccurate. This is said to be due to a number of reasons, one of which is that up until that time most people had little need to know their exact age during their lifetime, as it was not required or recorded for anything. Most people left school at 14 and other than showing they were full age at time of marriage, for the rest of their lifetime exact age was not relevant. Then as they got older they usually became quite vague about what their exact age was.

The introduction of the State Old Age Pension in 1909 brought about the need for people to try and prove what age they really were, if they were applying for the pension. As state registration of births only began in 1864, this caused problems all round. Some people could obtain a church baptism record to prove their age, but in many cases for those that were born in the first half of the 19th century, these records had not survived. The introduction of the pension in 1909 led to great discrepancies in ages recorded in the 1901 and 1911 census.

For some people, they had proved their correct age in 1909, so the 1911 record shows their actual age, but for others where no record existed, they often took advantage of the fact and declared an older age in order to claim the pension, or at least put an inflated age on record to which they could refer back to when they would be applying for the pension. But still the ages Thomas Shannon recorded in the census records are greatly at odds with his recorded age at death.

If we believe his recorded age at death, then he was born in December in 1809. This would mean he was around 60 at the time of his marriage and that he fathered 8 children after that. His youngest surviving child Bridget was born in 1885. This would suggest that he would have been 76 when she was born, which would have been unusual but not unheard of. It is said Michael Collins was born when his father was 75 years old. If Thomas was born in 1809, then in April 1901 he would have been 91 but only recorded his age as 57. And in 1911 when he should have been 101, he declared his age as just 71.

On his marriage record, Thomas's parents are recorded as Thomas and Esther Shannon [NLI/PR/A], so I was initially looking for a baptism record in the local parish for a Thomas born to a Thomas and Esther Shannon around 1809, but found none. However, in the local parish records I did find a baptism record for a Thomas Shannon born to Thomas and Esther Shannon who was baptised on 30 December 1839. Now this to me would seem a likely option for a record of Thomas Shannon's birth. If so, he would have been around 30 when he married, around 61 in 1901, 71 in 1911 (as per census) and 85 when he died.

If my theory is correct, then why was he said to be 115 when he died? I can think of a possible explanation for this, which relates to the fact that people did not know their exact age and many older people when they reached advanced years liked to add on a few years for effect. Although Thomas may have verified his age for his pension, as the years went on he may have then added some years to his age and it is possible that Thomas and his family thought he was around 100 when he died (as reported initially in the local paper just after his death).

Then perhaps, when they were going to register the death they located the copy of his baptismal record which he may have obtained when he was applying for his pension in 1909 As the handwritten baptismal record would have been 17 years old by then and perhaps difficult to decipher, the date December 1839 might have appeared to them as December 1809?

Of course, the other explanation is that perhaps Thomas really was 115 when he died and the record I found for Thomas Shannon born to Thomas and Esther Shannon in 1839 in the local parish records related to some other Thomas Shannon?

In any event, Thomas lived a long and active life and when he passed away in 1925, his wife Catherine became the owner of the farm. Catherine survived her husband by six years and after her death their youngest son Charlie took over the farm at Aghowle Lower.

Charlie Shannon remained a single man, but his sister Kate James and some of her children used often return and stay with him at the farm in Aghowle. As the years passed and Charlie became more advanced in years, Kate's daughter Tess, remained living with him in the farmhouse. It is said that Tess was much admired by the local young men but that Charlie was very protective of her and kept a sharp eye on the gentlemen callers. People also recall Tess, like most of the other local women, tending to the livestock and making butter and bringing it to the shops in Ashford to sell.

This photograph of the Ashford ICA group includes Tess James seated third from left in front row.
Photograph reproduced from "A Pictorial History of Ashford, Co. Wicklow, 1860s-1960s"
By kind permission of Sheila Clarke

As well as looking after her uncle in his advanced years, Tess helped to run the farm as Charlie got older. People recall that while Tess was living there the farmhouse was well kept with roses growing outside. In the early 1950s, Tommy Byrne of Ballylug used to visit his aunt and uncle, Dan and Mary Short, in the house next door to Shannons and he still recalls the Shannons farmhouse which had a magnificent large kitchen dresser stocked with an impressive array of fine delph. It would have looked something like the photograph below.

Tess also ran a little business from the farmhouse. She was an accomplished dressmaker and was much in demand with the locals for her skills. Her sewing machine was set up in the kitchen and during the 1950s and early 1960s, womenfolk who could afford to buy new material came to her to have outfits made in the current fashions. Those of lesser means, who may have got clothes handed on from relatives or sent in parcels from family working abroad, came to Tess to have them altered to fit themselves or their children.

The double dresser depicted here is reproduced from Wicklow's Traditional Farmhouses by kind permission of Christiaan Corlett.
All of the Aghowle farmhouses would have had a kitchen dresser, similar in style, but about half the width of the dresser depicted here.

At that time, the Garda Síochána were supplied with material and required to get their own uniforms made up. Sheila Clarke (nee Duignan) from Ashford recalls from her childhood that her father, who was Sergeant in Ashford Garda Station, used to go to Tess James to have his uniforms made. On one occasion, there was some material left over and Tess made for Sheila a small tunic coat, complete with brass buttons, similar to her father's uniform.

As Charlie advanced in years, his farming activities reduced, and several locals recall him as an elderly man walking about the house and farmyard with the aid of two sticks.

The story of House No.2 continues in the concluding chapter "Chapter 14: The End of an Era", see section "House No. 2: Shannon's".

House No. 3 (Reilly's / O'Reilly's)

House No. 3 was also located in Aghowle Lane. It was situated on the right-hand side of the lane, a little closer to the entrance of the lane than Houses 1 and 2.

Ellen O'Reilly outside the O'Reilly farmhouse, late 1940s.
Photograph courtesy of Terry Timmons.

Historical Summary	
Families:	Families: O'Reillys
1832 Land Records	Terence O'Reilly leasing 9 acres
	James O'Reilly leasing 8 acres
1839 OSI map	Shows a dwelling house and farm buildings at this location
1850 Glanmore Estate Records	Representatives of Terence Reilly leasing 15 acres
1854 Griffith's Land Valuation	Catherine Reilly leasing 14.3 acres
1901 Census	Bernard and Catherine O'Reilly and family, living in a three-roomed thatched farmhouse
1911 Census	Terence and Ellen O'Reilly and family
Last family to farm here:	Kate O'Reilly and her sons: Terry and Tommy, until mid-1960s

Reilly/O'Reilly Family History

NOTE: the name of this family in the 20th century is O'Reilly, but records from the 19th and some early 20th century records such as the 1901 and 1911 Censuses record the family name as Reilly. Within the local community this family is still often referred to as Reilly rather than O'Reilly.

The Glanmore Estate Land Records of early 1832 record two members of the Reilly family leasing land here - James and Terence. The local Catholic parish records show that Terence Reilly and Catherine Murphy had 4 children baptised in the parish between 1817 and 1832. No address is given for this family but when one looks at the named sponsors for these children, they match families that would have lived very close to the Reilly house at Aghowle Lower at that time. This would indicate to me that the Reilly family were living here from at least 1817. By 1850, the land records indicate that the two Reilly holdings have been joined together as one 15-acre holding and Terence Reilly is by this time deceased. In the land records of 1854 the lease is held by Terence's widow, Catherine Reilly.

In 1864, Terence and Catherine's son, Bernard (sometimes recorded in records as Bryan) married Catherine McCall of Carrigower, Roundwood. After their marriage, Bernard and Catherine lived in this farmhouse and had 5 children between 1869 and 1880, Catherine, Terence, John, Patrick and Mary Jane. These Reilly children, along with the children from the two neighbouring houses, the Shorts and the Shannons, would all have attended the small national school at Ballylusk. The pathway along Aghowle Lane to Ballylusk School must have been well trodden around this time, as records show that between 1869 and 1896, there were 21 children born between the 3 households of Shorts, Shannons and Reillys on Aghowle Lane.

Bernard Reilly took over the lease on their farm in 1877, after his mother's passing. In the 1901 Census Returns, the Reilly household is recorded as follows: Catherine and Bernard and four of their now adult children are living in the three-roomed thatched farmhouse, which has three windows to the front. All the members of the family are recorded as employed in running the farm and there are three outbuildings: a stable, a cow house and a shed.

By the time of the next Census in 1911, the composition of the household had changed dramatically. In March 1904, the mother Catherine Reilly died of bronchitis and in January 1905, her husband Bernard also died of bronchitis. After the passing of Bernard, the lease for the farm and house passed to the eldest son Terence.

Later that year Terence got married to Ellen Connolly, whose brother Patrick also lived in Aghowle in House No.10. Ellen Connolly had gone to Dublin to work in domestic service, but on her trips back home to visit Patrick, she and Terence must have formed an attachment. The couple married in Rathmines, near where Ellen worked, but then they came back to live in the Reilly farmhouse at Aghowle Lower. It is not known where Terence's brothers and sister were living, but by 1911 they are not living in the Reilly home.

By the time the census was taken in April 1911, the next generation of Reilly's/O'Reillys were well established. Ellen and Terence had four children: Kitty, Molly, Ben and Jinny. The description of the farmhouse is similar to 1901 but the number of farmyard buildings has expanded to six - the additions being a calf shed, a piggery and a fowl shed.

In 1914, the O'Reillys had another daughter named Liz and a few years later a son named Paddy. The six O'Reilly children, like their father before them, attended Ballylusk School and since the school closed in the late 1920s, they were among the last children to attend it. A number of the O'Reilly children are pictured in a school photograph in the section entitled "Schooling around Aghowle in the 1920s".

After the older girls finished their schooling, they headed to Dublin to seek employment and in time some of them moved on to work in England. The oldest son, Ben, worked locally for a while and then moved to the Rathdrum area where he worked in Avondale forestry. He also got married, but cycled back regularly to the family home to visit and help with the farm. Initially the two youngest children, Liz and Paddy, remained living at home. Paddy ran the farm and also did some work on the forestry and in time he got a job as a gardener in Barton's of Annamoe. When Kitty moved from her position in Dublin to work in England, Liz moved to Dublin to take up Kitty's job. But Liz always remained very connected to the local area and in time she married Lar Timmons, from the nearby townland of Parkmore and returned home to live there.

Ter O'Reilly - 1871 -1941
Photograph courtesy of
Terry Timmons

Ter O'Reilly and William Smith of Ballycullen used to walk over Carrick and down to Kilmacurragh to cut timber for the day and walk back again in the evening time. Ter is also remembered for carrying a sack of flour from Glenealy to his home in Aghowle, as he walked over Carrick.

Terence O'Reilly died in 1941 aged 70 years and his wife Ellen died 9 years later in 1950.

Ellen O'Reilly with granddaughter Jane Timmons c.1948
Photograph courtesy of Terry Timmons

Ellen is remembered in section "Reflections: Julia Byrne Reflects on Aghowle and Ballycullen 1920s-1940s") for her hospitality, especially at Halloween when she had a big pot of hot colcannon ready for those calling on the Vizards.[3]

4th and 5th from left- Paddy O'Reilly and his wife Kate
Photograph courtesy of Terry Timmons

---

3   "The Visards" was the name used locally for the practice of dressing up in disguise on Halloween night and calling to the neighbouring houses.

Meantime, Paddy O'Reilly, the youngest member of the family, married Kate Murtagh in 1947. But in January 1951, Paddy (aged just 35) died of heart failure. Billy Smith of Ballycullen, who was only a young lad at the time, clearly recalls his father and Dan Short of Aghowle helping to lay out Paddy O'Reilly's corpse in O'Reillys' farmhouse.

After Paddy's death, his young widow Kate was left to care for their two young sons, Tommy and Terry. During the 1950 and early 1960s, Kate ran their little farm and reared the boys, who went to school in Moneystown.

First Holy Communion Moneystown C.1955
Back Row 4th and 5th from left: cousins Terence (Terry) Timmons, Parkmore
and Terence (Terry) O'Reilly, Aghowle

Communion Day Moneystown 1958
Boy on right: Tommy O'Reilly Aghowle
Girls: Mary Molloy and Elizabeth McGovern
(who grew up in Aghowle
in the home of Bill and Mag Lee)

Reflections: Terry Timmons on childhood visits to O'Reillys and Aghowle
As mentioned, Liz O'Reilly had married and moved to live in Parkmore, but she regularly walked or cycled over and back from Parkmore to the family home in Aghowle, often bringing her two young children, Jan e and Terry with her. In April 2016, her son Terry, who still lives at Parkmore, shared with me some of his memories from childhood of his mother's family, the O'Reillys and the people of the Aghowle area.

All the children of Terence and Ellen O'Reilly went to school in Ballylusk. The school was very close to the quarry over there. My mother told me that the children used to be taken out of school and walked in a line up the road in the opposite direction when blasting was going on at the quarry. On one occasion, a window in the school was blown out when they were blasting the stone. A lot of the local men worked in the quarry, my uncle Ben O'Reilly worked there when he was a young man. They did all the drilling by hand in those days and it took three men to drill the holes, two men with sledges and one man turning the drill bit.

From when I was a young lad my mother used to bring myself and my sister Jane back down to visit her family home in Aghowle. I remember the house had a corrugated tin roof on the outside, it had been put on over the thatch and inside the house you could see the underneath of the original thatch. There were poles going across for holding up the roof and sods of big heather scraws that they had probably brought down off Carrick Mountain when the house was originally thatched.

They used to get the water for the house from the stream over where their neighbours, the Bradshaw family lived, but if there was very heavy rain then a little stream came down nearer to the Reilly's own house. There was a cow shed and a calf shed and a haggard at the back of the house with little ricks of hay in it and I remember there were apple trees as well.

The little farm was small enough and some of the land at that time was poor. The bottom field near the house used to be quite boggy back then, but has been drained now. The top of the field under Carrick was in ferns and only suitable for grazing. In my childhood, they kept a cow and some dry stock and didn't have any horses. I remember they put in a small corner of oats, about an acre and their neighbour Dick

Bradshaw would thresh it for them along with his own oats. They used to have a little meadow for hay and a patch for growing potatoes and vegetable for the house.

My uncle Paddy's wife, Aunt Kate, had a small little churn with a handle on the front for making butter and she was great for baking on the open fire. I can remember when I was a young lad down visiting there one year coming up to Christmas, seeing a row of round Christmas puddings all tied up in cloth, hanging over the fireplace.

Liz Timmons (nee O'Reilly) holding her son Terry
Her daughter Jane is girl in front beside bicycle.
Man with bicycle is Tom Shane
Photograph courtesy of Terry Timmons

When I was down there as a child with my mother, she would take me up on Carrick and tell me that when she was younger they would all gather up there on Sunday afternoons and meet up with the people from Glenealy that came up from the other side. She showed me the rock face where the men used to play handball. She also told me about the top road that ran under Carrick, I think she said it ran to Rathdrum, but I am not sure now. There were still old bits of walls and stones there when my mother was young, but even at that time it was nearly all disintegrated back into the ground and now you would never know it had been there at all.

My grandmother Ellen, like most of the women of her time, was a very religious woman and put great store in the holy water. My uncle Ben told me a story about one time when himself and some of the others was going to Ashford chapel, their mother asked them to bring her back a few bottles of holy water. But they forgot, so they filled up the bottles as they were passing in by the river in Aghowle Lane. Then when the mother would be taking out the holy water and shaking it and sprinkling it all around and praying, they would be having a great laugh to themselves.

My uncle Ben told me that he remembered when he was very young, that the British army were doing manoeuvres up on Carrick. They came in the lane from the Ballylusk side and went up near Reilly's house and out onto the mountain. Another lot came in from the Glenealy side. But Ben was only a little boy at the time[4] and was very frightened by the sight of all the uniformed men on horseback and the noise of all the horse's hooves coming in the lane, so he jumped into the ditch and hid in the briars until they had passed.

There used to be house dances in Reilly's house when my mother was a young woman. Of course, there was no television or radio in those days, so they would ramble around visiting houses and gathering at certain places. Uncle Ben used to talk about himself and the local men of the area gathering at the green triangle of grass outside the chapel in Parkmore.

When I was a young lad growing up I used to sometimes do bits of work in the summer holidays with the local farmers. I remember when I used to be working with Bill Farrell in Aghowle, he was living on his own by that time, so he would send me on ahead to go into the little farmhouse and get the fire going and boil the kettle for the tea.

I also remember when I was doing some work with Larry Timmons that he used to call the field on his farm that was there at Slanelough crossroads, the School House Field. Years later the local priest here, Father Nevin, who was interested in local history, was asking about it as he thought there might have been a school there once. But by that time Larry Timmons had passed away and no one could say why he

---

4   Ben was born in 1907, so this probably was around 1911-1913

knew it as the School House Field.[5] Miley O'Brien of Aghowle was a great machine man and if anyone wanted a bit of good ploughing done, he was the man. He had the first tractor around here, a Fordson I think, but it travelled very, very, slow, I don't think it even did walking pace. Once a week Miley would take out the tractor to come to Timmons shop here in Park to get tobacco. I remember I would hear the tractor for a good half hour before it got to the shop. As soon as it reached Slanelough crossroads, you would hear it tut tutting along, but you would have half an hour's work done before it arrived here at the shop.

The story of House No.3 continues in the concluding chapter, "Chapter 14: The End of an Era", see section "House No. 3: O'Reilly's".

House No. 4 (Hatton, McDermott, Kinsella, Symnes, Bradshaw)

House No. 4 is also located on Aghowle Lane, on the right-hand side of the laneway, and is the first house in from the main Aghowle road.

C.1890 The Hatton family outside their farmhouse in Aghowle
Photograph courtesy of Elizabeth Barratt, Carmel Historical Society, California

5   In December 2016 I recorded the following from Brendan Byrne of Garryduff: "*There used to be a field called the School House Field, up at Slanelough crossroads, where Larry Timmons of Park had the land. Larry's brother Bren used to say there had been a school there once. I am not sure if it was the field at the crossroads, on the Slanelough road, or if it might have been in the next field down this way towards Garryduff.*"

Historical Summary	
Families:	Hatton, McDermott, Kinsella, Symnes, Bradshaw
1832 Land Records	Holding was not identifiable
1839 OSI map	A dwelling house is located here at that time
1850 Glanmore Estate Records	Edward Hatton is leasing 26 acres of land
1854 Griffith's Land Valuation	Edward Hatton leasing 38 acres of land
1901 Census	George Hatton, living in a five-roomed slate roofed, two storey house.
1911 Census	McDermott family living here
Last family to farm here:	Bradshaw family until c.1964

Family History

Although a dwelling house is marked here on the first OSI map 1839, I was unable to identify from the land records of 1832 who was then occupying the house. The Glanmore Estate records of 1850 shows that Edward Hatton was living here at that time and leasing 26 acres of land. In the Griffith's Valuation records of 1854, his holding has increased to 38 acres.

Church records show that Edward Hatton and his wife, Ann, had been living in the Church of Ireland parish of Newcastle, Co. Wicklow in 1841 when their son James was baptised. Edward and Ann Hatton had 8 children in total, but I could only locate baptism records for four of their children. The Hatton children were James b.1841, Edward, William b.1849, George, Robert b.1854, John b.1855, Ann b.1858 and John b.1862. It is not known exactly when the Hatton family moved from the Newcastle area to live here at Aghowle Lower but the Glanmore Estate records show they had arrived by 1850.

The Hatton children would have attended the local Church of Ireland School at Kilfea. As recorded in the section "William Hatton: From Aghowle to a Californian Cattle Ranch" of this book, William Hatton (b.1849) left home at the young age of 13 and spent seven years at sea before settling in Carmel Valley in California, where he became a very successful cattle rancher and is still remembered for his dairy industries in the Valley.

William's great success in America seems to have influenced his siblings to follow a similar route. His brother Edward emigrated in the 1870s and settled in California, his sister Annie married Richard Dolan of Brocagh in 1890 and in 1892, Annie, along with her husband Richard and young daughter Ann went to join Edward in California. They departed from Moville, Co. Donegal aboard the Ethiopian. A year later the youngest member of the Hatton family, John, emigrated to join his sister and brother.

The year Ann married, her father Edward Hatton died aged 80 and was buried in Derrylossary cemetery. While his sons William and Edward were at this stage far away in America, they did not forget their father and had the following headstone erected over his grave.

Edward Hatton's grave, Derrylossary graveyard, Co. Wicklow

**ERECTED BY EDWARD AND WILLIAM HATTON OF CALIFORNIA
IN MEMORY OF THEIR DEARLY BELOVED FATHER
EDWARD HATTON OF AGHOULE
DIED SEPTEMBER 28TH, 1890 AGED 80**

Five years later, their mother Annie died, leaving George as the only living member of the Hatton family on this side of the Atlantic. In the 1901 Census, the Hatton household is recorded as follows: there are 3 occupants in the house, George Hatton who is single and his cousin John Hatton also a single man and Ephraim Faulkner.

Ephraim, who is described as a visitor, is a farmer and unmarried. It is unclear whether he was a temporary visitor or long-term lodger in the Hatton household. Ephraim was the leaseholder of a farm at Aghowle Upper, but the census records show his dwelling there was classified as uninhabited. Shortly after this census was recorded, Ephraim sold up the interest in his farm at Aghowle Upper.

From the 1901 Census description we know that the Hatton house is a five-roomed dwelling with a slate roof and has five windows to the front. There are seven out-buildings: a stable, a coach house, a cowhouse, a calf house, a piggery and a barn.

In 1903, George Hatton sold up the interest in his farm here to William McDermott from the Newcastle area of Wicklow, see sales notices below.

Hattons' farm was sold at auction and just over a month later there was a clearance sale of the contents of the farmhouse and farm.

It is not known what George Hatton did for the next 6 years, but in 1908 he migrated to America to join his brothers, Edward and John and his sister Annie. Alas, he did not live long to enjoy America, as he died in April 1911 and is buried in Salinas California. He shares a grave with his brother John who died the following year (aged 50) and his brother Edward who lived until 1924.

Their sister Annie and her husband are also buried in the same cemetery. Although Annie's married name was Dolan, her gravestone also records that she was Ann Hatton. In 2016, descendants of Annie Hatton and

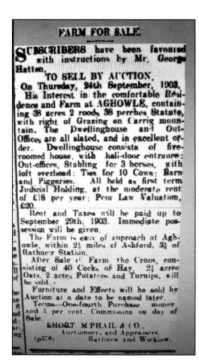

FARM FOR SALE

Subscribers have been favoured with instruction by Mr. George Hatton

TO SELL BY AUCTION

On Thursday, 24th September, 1903, His Interest in the comfortable Residence and Farm at AGHOWLE containing 38 acres 2 roods 38 perches Statute, with right of grazing on Carrig mountain. The Dwelling House and Out-Offices are all slated and in excellent order. Dwellinghouse consists of five-roomed house with Hall-door entrance: Out-offices with stabling for 3 horses, with loft overhead: Ties for 10 cows: Barn and Piggeries. All held as first term Judicial Holding, at the moderate rent of £18 per year: Poor Law Valuation £20

Rent and Taxes will be paid up to September 29th 1903. Immediate possession will be given.

The farm is easy of approach at Aghowle, within 2 ½ Miles of Ashford, 3 ½ of Rathnew Station.

After Sale of Farm, The Crops consisting of 40 Cocks of Hay, 2 ½ acres of Oats, 2 acres of Potatoes and Turnips, will be sold.

Furniture and Effects will be sold by Auction at a date to be named later.

MONDAY 29TH OCTOBER 1903

The Stock, Crops, Farm Implements and Household Furniture

STOCK

1 useful black cob, 14-hands, quiet in all work: 5-year-old donkey, 2-year-old do.,

1 cow, to calve in November; 3 backward springers 3 weanling calves, 1 sow on second litter, half gone in young; 14 hens, 10 Indian Runner Ducks.

CROPS

25 STACKS BLACK OATS, SOME HAY, ACRE POTATOES, ½ ACRE TURNIPS, LOT OF CABBAGE.

IMPLEMENTS

Dray, tumbling cart, van, croyden and sets harness, saddle and brindle, stone roller, 8 cwt., on frame; 2 ploughs, harrow, grubber, 2 moving machines, winnowing and threshing do., 4 dray and 2 trap axles, with metals; lot of very useful irons, 4 earthenware feeding throughs, wheel-barrow, 2 ladders, 2 sets cart harness, backbands, traces and single trees, 12 cow ties, lot of carpenter's tools, beam, scales and weights, turnip slicer.

USEFUL HOUSEHOLD FURNITURE

Including grandfather's clock, brass dial, over a century old, in oak case, in perfect order; piano, old oak presses and many other useful lots.

Sale to commence at twelve o'clock.

TERMS – Cash and 5 per cent commission.

SHORT McPHAIL &CO

Richard Dolan visited Aghowle and Brocagh to see where their ancestors came from. They told me that on their sitting room wall in America there hangs a framed photograph of Annie Hatton and Richard Dolan who left here in 1892, bound for California.

The story of the Hatton family is like the story of many Irish families of that time who were born on small tenant farms in this country and ended their days in America. Over the course of forty years, five members of this family left their farmhouse in Aghowle and settled in America. Their parents are buried in Derrylossary graveyard beneath a headstone erected by their two sons, who were living in California.

In 1903, William Mc Dermott bought the interest in George Hatton's farm and moved into his new farm at Aghowle as a single man. Within a very short time, he was joined by his new wife. He married Julia Sherlock in Ashford Church on 14th January 1904, and on the 30th October of that year the couple had a son, named Thomas.

In the 1911 Census, the farmhouse is now occupied by the McDermott family - husband William, wife Julia, their 6-year son Thomas and their niece Jane Dowling. In 1911, the house and buildings have remained the same except for the addition of a dairy. Shortly after 1911, the McDermott family move out of this farm and in the next few years they were followed by a Kinsella family and a Symes family, neither o f whom remained long living there.

By 1918, the Bradshaw family had arrived here from the Brittas Bay area of County Wicklow, the family consisting of parents William and Elizabeth and their young family. The Bradshaw family were to remain here for nearly half a century and they became a significant part of the local farming community. In Julia Byrne's reflections "Reflections: Julia Byrne Reflects on Aghowle and Ballycullen 1920s-1940s", she remembered that as a child she used to call to the farm for milk and was enchanted by the beautiful roses growing in the garden, while in Billy Smith's reflections, "Billy Smith Reflects on Local Families" he remembers his uncle

Aghowle c. late 1920s
Dick Bradshaw and Molly O'Reilly
Photograph courtesy of Terry Timmons

Dick and Florrie Bradshaw
Photograph from
"A Pictorial History of Ashford,
Co. Wicklow, 1860s-1960s"
By kind permission of Sheila Clarke

used to attend house dances here and he greatly admired the Bradshaw daughters.

In 1943, William Bradshaw's wife, Elizabeth, died at the age of 71. In the same year, William's son Richard (known locally as Dick) married Florence Sheane from nearby Ballycullen. As his father got older, Dick took over running the farm and William died in 1953 (aged 85).

During the 1950s, farming methods began to change with the introduction of tractors and more labour-saving machinery. Dick moved with the times and invested in a tractor and some farm machinery and with this machinery he set up a business and went out for hire to work for farmers in the local district.

Dick and Florrie had by this time 6 children: Eric, Laura, Evelyn, Sylvia, Victor and Greta. The Bradshaw children attended Nun's Cross School.

As we will later see the Bradshaw family moved from this farm in the early 1960s. Most of the Bradshaw children were still quite young at that time, but they shared with me a few of the childhood memories they have from their time living in Aghowle.

Nun's Cross School, 1959
Pictured: Laura, Evelyn and Silvia Bradshaw Aghowle
Also pictured: Mary and Margaret Mahon of Ballycullen.
Photograph from "The History of Nun's Cross School 1877-1997",
by kind permission of Margaret Bloomer

We recall our mother separating the milk and making butter. Cooking was done on the open fire and the bread was baked with the hot coals sitting on top of the lid of the bread pan. We also remember the Christmas puddings boiling for hours and then hung up in their cloths to drain. Threshing day was a very busy day in the kitchen as we tried to cook for all the men who came to help at the harvest.

    Larry Timmons of Park and Mick Harvey (Graham) of Moneystown used to keep sheep up in our top fields under Carrick and when they would go up to check them, they would always come in to the farmhouse for tea on their way back.

The story of House No.4 continues in the concluding chapter, "Chapter 14: The End of an Era", see section "House No. 4: Bradshaw's".

House No. 5 (Toole, Moran, Smith, Smith-Edge, O'Brien)

House No. 5 is located at Aghowle Upper on the Carrick side of the valley. It is approached by a short lane in from the Aghowle road.

Early 1960s The O'Brien family in front of the farmhouse

Historical Summary	
Families:	Toole, Moran, Smith, Smith-Edge, O'Brien
1832 Land Records	It was not possible to identify who was leasing this holding
1839 OSI map	A dwelling house and farm buildings located here
1850 Glanmore Estate Records	Patrick Moran leasing 27 acres, but unclear if he is living in the house
1854 Griffith's Land Valuation	Laurence Toole -size of holding unclear, recorded as 7 acres, but appears to be larger on the map.
1901 Census	Smith-Edge family, living in a four roomed, two storey slate roofed farmhouse
1911 Census	Smith-Edge family
Last family to farm here:	O'Briens, until 1980s.

Family History

It was not possible to identify who was leasing this property in the 1832 Glanmore Estate records. There is a dwelling marked here on the 1839 OSI map – this would have been a smaller residence than the two-storey house that survived into the twentieth century.

In 1850, Patrick Moran is leasing the house and land here, along with another holding in Aghowle Upper. By 1854, Laurence Toole is the householder. The records from the land valuation office [VOI/CB/AU] indicate that in 1862 the holding may have been split, with Laurence Toole holding seven acres and a small house, while George Smith holds 20 acres and a larger house. This house of George Smith's is the house that survived through to the twentieth century. It is possible that this house may have been constructed around 1862, but there is insufficient information to verify this.

In 1858, George Smith married Jane Storey in the Church of Ireland church at Nun's Cross. George had an address at Kilfea and was a school teacher, while Jane was the daughter of the local shoe maker, John Storey of Ballycullen. Church records show that between 1859 and 1862, George and Jane had two daughters christened in the Church of Ireland church at Enniskerry, Eliza in 1859, and Alicia in 1861, indicating that they may have started their married life in the Enniskerry area.

By 1862, the family had moved to Aghowle, as George is the recorded leaseholder of this house and twenty acres of land at Aghowle. It is not known if George was at that time working as a school teacher or a farmer, or both. What is known is that sometime before 1869 George died, as his widow Jane Smith is the named leaseholder in 1869. Jane remarried in 1871 to Edward Smith. Edward was the son of William Smith of Ballycullen and was a saddler by trade.

After his marriage, Edward moved into the house at Aghowle Upper and became the leaseholder. As well as farming here, he carried out his saddlery business. In the days when the horse was king on the farm, there must have been much business traffic coming and going to the house. Between 1871 and 1880, Edward and Jane had four children: William John Henry (1871), Frank Storey (1874), Martha Jane (1877) and Samuel Edward (1880). Eight years after Samuel was born, Edward's wife Jane died. In 1877, the new school at Nun's Cross opened and the Smith children would have attended school there.

Left: William Smith born 1871 in Aghowle,
pictured with a friend on Carrick rocks. C 1900
Photograph courtesy of Billy Smith

The period towards the end of the 1890s saw much change in this household. In 1898, Edward Smith's oldest son, William, married Ellen Hearn, who was widowed with two young children. William and Ellen lived for a short while at Tiglin before moving back to the Smiths' ancestral house at Ballycullen where their descendants still live and farm today.

Also around this time, the Smith's second son, Frank Storey Smith, decided to travel abroad to seek his fortune. Initially, he and his younger brother Samuel thought of seeking employment with their mother's brother, John Storey, who was by then a very successful sea captain in Australia. They also considered going off to join the Boer War but in the end, Frank went to New Zealand where he got work in the flax industry and a few years later Samuel followed him to New Zealand.

Also around the same time there were two marriages in the Smith household. In March 1900, Edward remarried. His new wife was Rachel Edge from Moneystown, a widow with two adult sons. A few months later, Edward's only daughter Martha, married Rachel Edge's son Thomas.

The 1901 Census reflected all these recent changes in the Smith household. On the night of the census, the occupants of the house were Edward Smith and his son Samuel, his daughter Martha Edge and son in law Thomas. On the same night, Edward's wife Rachel is counted in her former Moneystown home, presumably visiting her other son who was still living there.

The Smith farmhouse is described as a four roomed, slate roofed house, with four windows to the front. There are five farm buildings, a stable, cow house, calf shed, fowl shed and a barn.

When the census was taken ten years later, there are a number of changes recorded. Edward is widowed again, his wife Rachel having died the previous August. Samuel has migrated to New Zealand to join his brother Frank and Thomas and Martha now have 3 children, Elias (Pat) aged 9, Violet), aged 5 and Rachel) aged 2.

The farm house has one additional room, but the farm buildings are reduced to just three, a stable, cow house and fowl shed.

Martha Jane Edge nee Smith born 1877, Aghowle
Married Thomas Edge in Nun's Cross in 1900 Martha and her family left Aghowle in 1914 - she died in 1965 in New Zealand
Photograph courtesy of the Smith family, New Zealand

Rachel and Pat (Elias) Edge
in 1986

Violet Edge
on her 90th Birthday

Alice Edge

Adela Edge

In 1913, Thomas and Martha Edge had a fourth child, Alice. Around this time, they also began to assess their future. Making a living from a small farm in Wicklow was very difficult at the time and Martha's brothers Frank and Samuel were doing very well in New Zealand, so the couple decided that migrating to New Zealand might hold the best prospects for the future of their family.

Martha's brother Frank offered to travel back to Ireland and assist them in their journey to New Zealand. In April 1914, Frank Smith set sail from New Zealand for Ireland. He decided to keep a journal of his voyage back to Ireland and his return voyage from Ireland to New Zealand. Frank's handwritten journal still exists today as Frank passed it on to his son, Frank Henry. In 2015 Frank's family very kindly offered to transcribe for me the entries from this journal and gave me permission to include them in this publication. The Storey and Smith families also kindly supplied me with information and photographs relating to the Smith and Edge families who migrated to New Zealand from House No. 5.

Sadly, Frank Henry Smith passed away in early 2017, just before his 90th birthday.

The diary of his father's voyage back to Ireland and return to New Zealand contains daily entries and makes very interesting reading. Unfortunately, due to constraints of space, I can only include here a few of the entries from both of his voyages.

Extracts from:

Diary of Frank Storey Smith – Wellington to London 2nd May– 21st June 1914

2nd May

Departed Wellington SS "Moreki". 5pm blowing a gale, had tea, played cards until 10.00pm

Wednesday 7th May

Went to look at SS "Orieto". Found some of the New Zealand passengers aboard, so decided to sleep there until she sailed. Went out to Rosebury races, nothing but noise and confusion.

Saturday 10th May – Melbourne

Spent a lovely day seeing Botanical Gardens and Zoo in company with Mr. and Mrs. A., a very nice couple returning to England after a trip around the colonies. Spent another pleasant day seeing Public Art Gallery.

Sunday 17th May

Weather rough and passengers nearly all sick – distance travelled for 24 hours – 365 knots. No land in sight.

Monday 25th May

Not much excitement, only a fight between two lady passengers. Distance run –371 knots.

Thursday 28th May

Arrive Colombo. The weather is anything but good, rain accompanied with heavy thunder and lightning.

We go ashore as the weather seems clearing. We just get to the hotel before the rain comes down in torrents. Have a five-course breakfast for 2/-, we then take two rickshaws for a trip around the town. The weather is now gloriously fine. Town is simply beautiful. I mean of course the European parts of it, the native on the other hand is squalid enough for anything. Amongst places visited was the Museum and Buddhist Temple. We had to remove our boots before entering the latter place. I consider that the despised Buddhist religion better than any religion taught by the white races.

We were asked for alms on every hand. Little children running alongside your rickshaw throwing flowers in the chance of receiving a penny. Others crawling along on hands and one stump of a leg. A most pitiable sight. Others again having no arms and all asking "good masters help". Others again with all sorts and conditions of things for sale. For example, one had a fountain pen for sale. He wanted 10/- for it and eventually sold it for 1/-, however we had a real good time just the same.

I might here state for the benefit of those who do not already know. A rickshaw is a two-wheeled conveyance drawn by the natives, having numbers the same as our cabs. We sailed at midnight from Colombo.

Monday 1st June
Another quiet day, distance run – 368 miles. Just another passenger robbed of gold watch and chain.

Thursday 4th June
In Gulf of Aden and enter Red Sea, the heat is much greater.

Friday 5th June
Still in Red Sea and weather very hot, a good few people fainting and man operated on for appendicitis- everything quiet on board consequently.

Friday 12th June
Arrive Naples, the place is very beautiful from a distance but on closer inspection its very dirty, with the streets narrow and badly paved. A general strike is in progress here. The soldiers are busy keeping streets and shots can be heard in the distance, four rioters were shot tonight. However, we had a good spin around town just the same.

Just as we are leaving a fresh disturbance breaks out, windows broke and shots exchanged and altogether things are lively. We just manage to catch the boat which had left her moorings, but seeing a big crowd of passengers coming she waited for us.

Saturday 13th June
A passenger committed suicide by jumping overboard in the night.

Monday 15th June
Arrive at Gibraltar, the great key to the Mediterranean Sea. We were not allowed to go ashore here, however I managed to get some fair cigars for 4/- per hundred.

Arrive at Plymouth. We get our first glimpse of Old England here and very pretty it's the nicest place and coast sighted the whole way.

After disembarking some of our passengers, we proceed on our way to London.

Saturday 20th June
I will never forget the rush of getting through the Customs Officers. I had to carry my own luggage through the crowd. A portmanteau and trunk. And then get the same amount through for a lady friend. The hardest hour's work in a long time and then just in time to catch a train for Euston.

Frank stayed at home in Aghowle for three and a half months. While he was at home, two major events took place. On the 12th August, Frank married May Hearn in Nun's Cross Church - May was the step daughter of Frank's oldest brother, William Henry.

At the start of September, England joined the Second World War. As mentioned earlier in this book, May Hearn's brother Harry was in the army (see section "Harry Hearn") and just three weeks after England joined the War, Harry was killed in action in France on the 19th September. It is not known if word had reached his family of his death before May and Frank set sail for New Zealand on 7th October, but it would seem not, as Frank does not make any reference to it in his diary entries.

On the 7th October, Frank and his new wife May, together with his sister Martha Edge, her husband Thomas and their four children (ranging in age from twelve to under two years) all set off for New Zealand. The following are some extracts from Frank's diary of the trip:

Diary of Frank Storey Smith – Dublin to Wellington October-November 1914
After a delightful stay at home and having the pleasure of getting married we book passage in the good ship "Orontes" sailing from London on 9th October.

7th October

Leave Dublin North Wall. Had a very pleasant trip. We had on board a thousand troops bound for the front.

Friday 9th October –London

Arrived at Tilbury docks. Here we had to pass the doctor and as we were only third class of course we had to wait until first and second class were aboard before the pompous officials could look at us. On board these liners it is the custom when there is a crowd of passengers to have two sittings at meals. If you are fortunate enough to get into the first sitting for the first meal you remain in the same sitting and seats throughout the voyage. Being an old hand, my wife and I got seats for the first sitting.

9th October

Sailed at 1.00pm arriving in Plymouth after 11.00am the next day. Here we took on board the mails and received one letter and two postcards from friends in Ireland.

15th October.

Lovely weather, smooth sea, all quiet. My wife who has been suffering from sea-sickness since coming on board has now recovered and is getting quite the sailor. Sight Sardinia at 2.pm.

The sea which was delightful an hour ago is now swelling waves and causing our ship to roll and pitch in a most uncomfortable manner.

6.pm nearly all the passengers are sea-sick, my wife and friends are very bad.

Friday 16th October

9.00am sight Naples. Go ashore in the company of my wife, who has somewhat recovered and Mr. E. (Thomas Edge- Frank's brother- in -law.)

Frank gives a detailed account of their day sightseeing in Naples and their unsuccessful attempts to buy some decent tea to take on board.

Tuesday 20th October

Arrive Port Said about 7.am. After breakfast wife and I go ashore. After a pleasant visit which Mrs. S and I appreciated very much we get onboard again where everything is coal dust, noise and confusion preparatory for sailing.

24th October

4.00pm rough sea, passed Purim Island, a fort near the south Coast of Asia. 5p.m. met a fleet of 35 troop-ships escorted by three men-of-war. Troops coming from Australia end-route to the war. A lovely sunset with all the ships in the distance. The artist who could paint it would make a fortune.

Monday 26th October

7.30 slight altercation amongst lady passengers owing to the presence of a German cruiser in these waters. The Company don't take any risks and onsequently order all lights out after sundown.

Monday 9th November

Expect to reach Freemantle tomorrow, the first Australian port of call. The monotony of long stages will now be broken and we will reach a port every three or four days.

Tuesday 10th November.

Arrive Freemantle. A lovely day, the town is a nice clean little place. The people are nice and civil, quite a treat after Naples, Port Said and Colombo.

"Stop Press" Just before leaving Freemantle we heard that the German cruiser "Emden" was sunk by HMS Sydney near Cocos Island.

Wednesday 18th November

A lovely day with bright warm sunshine. Duly arrived in Sydney on the 19th, had a good dinner at Sergeants, Circular Quay, also tea and returned on board at 10pm. Sailed per Huddard Parker liner "Ulimaroa" for Wellington. After an uneventful trip lasting 4 days we duly arrived in Wellington on 24th November and so my scribble ends and lived happy ever after.

Signed Frank S. Smith.

The Smith family settled in New Zealand and were very happy there. Frank worked in the flax industry. He lived a long and active life and served in the Home Guard in the Second World War. While they never managed to visit Ireland again, Frank and May always retained a very strong connection and association with Ireland and their Irish family roots, which they passed on to their children and grandchildren - who have made the journey back to the ancestral home in Aghowle. Their oral family history recalls that each year when New Zealand celebrated St. Patrick's Day by playing Irish music and song on the radio, May Smith would sit for the day in her kitchen and cry with the memories of her family and friends back in the valley under Carrick. Thomas and Martha Edge and family also settled and prospered in New Zealand, and nine years after their arrival they had another daughter, Adela.

L-R: Frank Storey Smith, born in Aghowle 1874,
His wife May Smith nee Hearn, whom he married in Nun's Cross Church in August 1914,
son Frank Henry Smith b. 1927 and daughter Eileen b. 1915.

The O'Briens

A short while after the Edge family left for New Zealand in 1914, another family came to live in House No. 5. They were Michael and Ellen O'Brien and their two young children.

To continue the story of this house, I am fortunate enough to be able to get the history of the O'Briens' time in Aghowle first hand from the last member of the family to live in the house. She is Catherine O'Brien[6] who was born in 1959 and in March 2016, Catherine shared with me her recollections of the O'Brien family's time here.

The first section, which is in Catherine's own words, recounts how her family came to live in this house and a little further into the story she also recounts the work her father and grandfather did to reclaim part of their farm. The rest of the family story I have written up from information Catherine has shared with me. Later on, in "House 5: O'Brien's" in "Chapter

---

6   Catherine and I are friends since early childhood and grew up together in Aghowle. We were the last two children to grow up in the Aghowle farming community. I would have spent much of my childhood in the O'Brien's farmhouse.

14: The End of an Era", Catherine picks up the story again with a personal account of her family's final years living and farming here.
Narrated by Catherine:

My grandfather, Michael O'Brien, was from Monageer in Co. Wexford. He was from a very good farm but was the youngest of twelve children, so by the time he left school he had to go out to work as a farm labourer. He was working as a ploughman and around that time a new type of plough was coming into Ireland. He got a job on a farm in Co. Galway working with this new plough. He was over in Galway for about a year, but before he had left his home in Wexford, he had been courting a girl by the name of Ellen Dempsey from nearby Bellcarrick and so he was anxious to get a position back nearer home.

In 1911, he applied for an advertised position in Knockrobin in Ashford Co. Wicklow. When he came up for the interview he realized the position was for a married man, so he lied and said that he was married. He was offered the job and then hot footed it down to Bellcarrick and proposed to Ellen. Within a month he and his new wife were back to take up the position in Knockrobin, with granddad working outside on the farm and granny working in the house.

Michael and Ellen O'Brien
Photograph reproduced from "A Pictorial History of Ashford, Co. Wicklow, 1860s-1960s"
By kind permission of Sheila Clarke

That was September 1911 and my father Miley O'Brien was born the following August. Just over two years later in October 1914, their second child Peg was born at Knockrobin. Shortly after this they bought the farm in Aghowle.

Granny's mother in Wexford bought them a cow so they would at least have a supply of milk for the children on the new farm. They set out from Ashford for Aghowle on the pony and trap, which contained their few belongings, along with a little two-year-old boy and a small baby and the cow tied to the back of the trap. Granny used to say it was with a very heavy heart that she arrived into the farm in Aghowle. The place had been unoccupied for a while and it was a dreary cold winter's day and as they came down the lane it probably seemed very lonely and isolated. She recalled there was just an old clay floor in the kitchen. Shortly after, when they were replacing this floor they dug out lots of bits and pieces of leather, so this must have been where Edward Smith had sat for his lifetime doing his saddlery by the light of the kitchen window.

As the O'Brien family settled into their new home, there were increases in the family. On Easter Monday, 24th April 1916 (the day of the Rising) their third child, Nell, was born. Nell's mother used to say she was a very unsettled child due to the time of her arrival. Nell was joined in the following years by Sheila, Mary, Lar (Larry), Kevin and Nance (Nancy).

As well as the O'Briens' eight children who survived into adulthood, Ellen O'Brien also gave birth to two daughters who died either at birth or soon afterwards. At that time, such children were not afforded a normal funeral or burial in a graveyard and were often buried in secret. On the deaths of both O'Brien children, their father Michael made a small wooden box and laid his dead infant in it. Then under the cover of darkness he carried the little box several miles to the old graveyard in Kilfea. Here in the dark of night he buried his baby by himself and then walked back home again.

By the mid-1920s, the family had increased to 8 children and Michael and Ellen were working hard to build up the farm and improve the quality of the land. The farm was divided into two parts: one section consisted of the land on the Carrick side of the valley that surrounded the farmhouse and stretched up to the foot of the mountain; the other portion of the farm lay on the upper side of the Aghowle Road and stretched up towards the boundary with Slanelough. This portion above the road was known as the Raheen, due to the rath or fort that stood near the top of the farm.

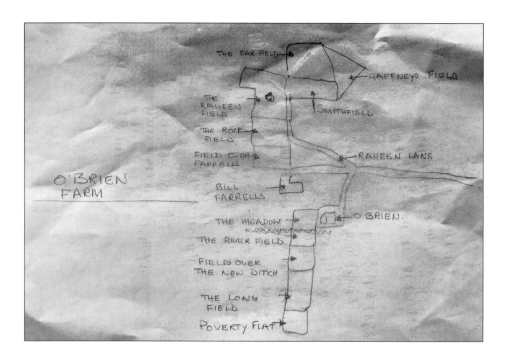

The field names on O'Briens' farm as recorded by Catherine O'Brien, 2017

When the O'Briens had bought the farm the Raheen section of the land was not arable due to the preponderance of stones and rocks and an overgrowth of furze bushes. Here Catherine recounts how the family reclaimed this land:

> *When my father, who was the eldest, was about 13 years old he was taken out of school, as he was needed to help his father with the work of reclaiming the Raheen. They started at the bottom of the land and had to work their way up painstakingly field by field. All the work of clearing was done by hand using mattocks and slash hooks. They also had some kind of long implement with a head on it, for getting down to the roots of the furze bushes and pulling them up out of the earth. So, each small section was done by a process of cut and burn and cut and burn.*
>
> *The laneway up to the Raheen was steep and rocky and it could be slippery in some places where water flowed across it. One day when they were going up this lane to work they had the two horses with them and the horses were pulling a heavy load behind them. The weight pulled the horses backwards and one of them, Jack, slipped and fell*

back awkwardly and injured himself so badly he had to be put down.
This was a huge loss for my grandfather and for the farm at that time,
it remained very vivid in my father's memory for many years after.

But in time they did manage to reclaim the land up there and in my
childhood it was very good land and we grew barley, potatoes, hay and
turnips and there was good grazing pasture for sheep up there too. The
work of reclaiming the land continued on into the 1960s, I remember
a lot of work being carried out on the top field under Carrick, which
my father used to call Poverty Flats. That field had a lot of furze bushes
that had to be removed. Then some crops were planted in it for a couple
of years to bring back the heart into the soil. But after that it was used
for grazing, as it was so near Carrick, the deer kept coming down to
eat the crops.

All the O'Brien children went to school in Moneystown. As well as doing
well academically they were also very musical - it was said they inherited
this talent from both their mother and father's side of the family.

Pictured below are three members of the O'Brien family at the Wicklow
Féis in 1933.

Feis 1933, Wicklow
Back Row: Sheila O'Brien, Maureen Doyle, Maura O'Brien, Jim Lawlor.
Front Row: Nellie Byrne, Rosie Timmons, Kevin O'Brien
Photograph from "A Pictorial History of Roundwood, County Wicklow, 1870-1970"
By kind permission of Joseph McNally

Some of the older people of the locality with whom I spoke recalled seeing Ellen and Michael O'Brien going down to shop in Ashford in their pony and trap and people remembered them as a lovely couple. Ellen O'Brien was known as a kind and generous woman and one of her many acts of kindness was to care for and assist the traveling women at their time of confinement. As the word spread of her help to the expectant mothers it became commonplace for the traveling families that passed near the townland to plan their route so that they would be arriving in Aghowle around the time a baby was due. They would usually set up camp near the top of O'Brien's lane and Ellen would give them food and even blankets if needed and was there on hand to help the mother during her delivery, if necessary.

As the young O'Brien family grew up and finished their schooling it was clear that the farm could not support them all, so each in turn found their own path in the world.

Miley, who was the oldest son, stayed farming with his father on the family farm, but he also got some work with the State Forest when it was planting the lands it had purchased at Aghowle around 1930. This provided very welcome regular money coming into a household that was providing for 8 children. Miley was very enterprising and as a young man of 26, he set himself up with a tractor and threshing mill and in the autumn time went out for hire. Miley and his threshing mill is covered in more detail in the section "Threshing Time in Aghowle".

Peg O'Brien and Paddy Barry on their wedding day
Photograph courtesy of the O'Brien family

Peg O'Brien went to work in England and there she met and married a Cork man named Paddy Barry. After a while the couple moved back to farm in Mitchelstown and had a family of 9 children.

Sheila O'Brien went to Dublin and became a nurse, a profession she followed for a number of years, including nursing in America for a year. When she was working in Dublin, she would visit her sister Peg in Cork regularly and while visiting there she met her future husband, Ned Touchstone who was a cousin of Peg's husband. So, both sisters ended up living near each other in Co. Cork.

Sheila O'Brien and her husband Ned Touchstone
Photograph courtesy of the O'Brien family

When Mary was finished school, she went down to stay with her mother's relatives in Bellcarrig Co. Wexford to look after her uncle and keep house for him. While living here, she met Alec Hobbs and they married and settled in Co. Wexford - the couple had three children. The Hobbs family were very frequent visitors back to the family farm in Aghowle. In 1998, Mary Hobbs died on the 5th May, and her husband Alec died 9 days later, on the 14th May.

Kevin worked with a company installing telegraph lines and this work took him away to many foreign locations, including the Middle East. But while he

Mary O'Brien and her husband Alec Hobbs
Photograph courtesy of the O'Brien family

traveled to far away locations, Kevin returned back home very regularly, often timing his visits to coincide with helping Miley at hay making or harvest time or when there was potato picking on the farm.

As a young child, I remember that when Kevin O'Brien returned to Aghowle from his foreign travels he would always come to visit our family. Long before the big cheerful red headed man would arrive at the kitchen door, we could hear him. His loud singing voice would be belting out a ballad, perhaps Whiskey in The Jar or Among the Wicklow Hills, as he came sauntering up the road towards our farmhouse.

Kevin O'Brien and his mother Ellen in O'Briens' farmyard 1940s
Photograph courtesy of the O'Brien family

Unfortunately, in the mid-1960s, Kevin was diagnosed with lung cancer and died in the prime of his life in 1967. He spent his last months back in Wicklow being cared for by his sister, Nancy and her family in Ashford. Kevin's niece, Ellen Hobbs Kenny supplied me with the following:

> *A little story my mother, Mary O'Brien, told me:*
> *"Mylie, Kevin and Lar O'Brien went to Rathdrum one Saturday evening and Granny told them to bring her home a can of paint. Sunday morning after mass when they were getting their breakfast Granny asked about her paint and all three had forgotten about it. Granny was cross and asked them "What do ye be thinkin' about when ye are out?" to which Kevin replied "Women".*

Nell O'Brien married Pat Clarke from Clonmannon in Ashford and for the earlier part of their married life they lived in Ireland. Then in 1963, the entire family emigrated to Goulburn, New South Wales, Australia, where the family settled and prospered. Nell was always remembered as a very resourceful girl, and her friends and neighbours who had attended

Moneystown School with her always liked to recount the following story: After Nell moved to Australia she applied for a job. The application form required her to fill out her college/university education. Nell proudly filled in she had graduated with honours from Moneystown College in Ireland. When she got the position her common sense and her Moneystown education saw her well able for her new position.

Nell Clarke (nee O'Brien) with her Husband Pat Clarke and their family
Photograph courtesy of the O'Brien family

Lar O'Brien remained around Aghowle for a while after finishing school and during this time he played in a local band with Des Fitzgerald of Moneystown. But in time, he went to work in England and got a position in the RAF. Here he met his wife Ivy, who was a WREN at that time. The couple married in 1947, their wedding photograph appears in the Big Snow of 1947 section "The Big Snow in Aghowle" of this book. The couple settled in Stoke, where Lar worked in the potteries. He also played music in the local pubs and folk clubs. He was a founding member of the Potteries Folk Festival and its logo featured a picture of Lar sitting on a three-legged stool playing music.

Shortly after Lar got married, his father Michael O'Brien died in 1948. He was aged 79 and his wife Ellen died four years later, aged 83. By this time the only members of the family remaining at home in Aghowle were Nancy and Miley.

The following year, 1953, Nancy married Sonny Manning and the couple went to live nearby in Cronroe. Nancy and Sonny had 6 children and Sonny would later go on to be Head Gardener in Mount Usher gardens in Ashford. Johnny Keneally had a small but significant (and profitable!) role to play in their courting – see section "Reflections: Johnny Kenneally On Childhood Visits to Farrell's in the 1940s/50s".

After Nancy's marriage, Miley remained a bachelor for just a few years. His sister Sheila was at this time still nursing in Dublin and on one of her trips back home to Aghowle she brought a nursing friend with her.

Nancy O'Brien and Sonny Manning
on their wedding day in Bel-air Hotel Ashford

Her friend was Bridget Glynn from Co. Galway and romance blossomed between Miley and Bridget. In 1957, many of the O'Brien family traveled to attend the wedding of Miley and Bridget in Tuam, Co. Galway. After their honeymoon, the couple returned to start their married life together in the farmhouse in Aghowle.

The following year, tragedy was to visit Miley and Bridget as their first-born child, Michael, died at birth and he was laid to rest with his grandparents Ellen and Michael in Rathnew graveyard. Much nervous anticipation surrounded the arrival of their second child the following year. But this time all was well, and their daughter Catherine was born safely in September 1959.

The Farrell family lived on the next farm to the O'Briens (House No.6) and by this time Sarah Farrell was a woman in her late eighties. She was very relieved and delighted that the new baby in the O'Brien farmhouse had arrived safely. As a gift to celebrate the baby's arrival, Sarah dug up some of her daffodil bulbs and brought them over to the new parents, who planted the bulbs along the laneway approaching the farmhouse. In the following spring, Sarah's gift produced cheerful golden blooms.

Within a few months, Sarah Farrell passed away in her 87th year. But in springtime each year when the daffodils came into bloom along the laneway, the O'Briens fondly remembered their neighbour Sarah and her gift to celebrate the safe arrival of their daughter.

By the early 1950s, all the O'Briens except Miley had moved off the farm, some settling nearby, while others were further afield. But the desire to come back to their childhood home remained very strong and they all returned to visit as often as they could. Sometimes they would all try to gather in the farmhouse at the same time and then the house would once again fill with music, singing and card playing very late into the night.

As the years progressed, the O'Brien families who had settled in different locations produced children of their own and they too became part of the regular visitors to the farmhouse in Aghowle.

Miley O'Brien and Bridget Glynn on their Wedding Day, 1957
Photograph courtesy of the O'Brien family

The story of House No. 5 continues in the concluding chapter, "Chapter 14: The End of an Era", see section "House 5: O'Brien's".

Sheila, Mary, Nell and Peg O'Brien 1961

House No. 6 (Moran, Cunniam, Farrell)

House No. 6 is located at Aghowle Upper, on the Carrick side of the valley. It is approached by a very short laneway in from the Aghowle road.

There is just a small field separating House No. 5 and House No. 6.

Farrells farmhouse early 1970s, unoccupied after Bill Farrell sold it.
Photograph courtesy of Seamus Corcoran – current owner.

Historical Summary	
Families:	Morans, Cunniams, Farrells
1832 Land Records	Simon Moran leasing 61 acres
1839 OSI map	A dwelling house and farm buildings located here
1850 Glanmore Estate Records	Sarah Moran leasing 71 acres
1854 Griffith's Land Valuation	Sarah Moran leasing 70 acres of land
1901 Census	William Moran and extended family, living in a three-roomed thatched roof farmhouse
1911 Census	Jeremiah and Sarah Farrell and family
Last family to farm here:	Bill Farrell, until 1967

Family History

This house and farm has a long association with the Moran family and its history can be traced back further than any of the dwellings in the townland. The earliest surviving local Catholic Church records date back to 1747 and the records from this period show the Moran family was well established in the townlands of Aghowle and Ballycullen at that time. From the local Catholic parish register [NLI/PR/W], we know that in 1812 Simon Moran married Sarah Smith. No address was recorded on this record, but a year later when the Moran's first child, Winifred, was baptised, their address was recorded as Ahoule/Aghowle. As surviving church records are incomplete, we do not know how many children the couple had, but Winifred had at least three other siblings: Edward William and Mary.

In the Tithe Applotment land records of 1832 [NAI/TAB], Simon Moran held three holdings totalling 61 acres at Aghowle. The land records of 1832 show that, as well as Simon Moran's three holdings in Aghowle, four other members of the Moran family held land here. In total at that time, there were eleven land leases in Aghowle held between five of the Moran family. There were also Morans leasing lands at Ballycullen. I believe all these Morans were part of the one original family and several members held leases in both townlands.

From the Glanmore Estate records of 1850, we can see that the house and surrounding 71 acres of land was leased by Sarah Moran. While there were 5 members of the family leasing 11 holdings in the townland in 1832, by 1854 there were only three members of this family remaining and they held leases for four properties.

It would appear therefore that between 1832 and 1854, some of their previous smaller holdings had been consolidated into larger ones. In 1854, Sarah Moran's farm of 71 acres is the largest farm and Sarah continued as the named leaseholder until 1882, when the lease passed to her son William. Sarah died in 1887 and her death record states she was 103 and died of old age. As already mentioned, people were quite vague about their actual ages at that time, so Sarah Moran was probably not exactly 103, but she may well have been approximately 100 years of age at the time of her death. We know she married in 1812, seventy-five years before her death and it is quite possible she may have been aged twenty or more when she married.

Sarah's son William married Anne Shannon in 1872. Ann was a member of the Shannon family living at Aghowle Lower, in House No. 2. The following year the couple had their only child, Sarah. A few weeks short of her eighteenth birthday in November 1891, Sarah married Andrew Cunniam in the Catholic Church at Ashford. Andrew was from Ballycullen and his family had lived in the local area for well over two centuries, so both Sarah's and Andrew's families had a long history of farming in the valley and I imagine their marriage would have been approved of as a good match for both of their families.

The couple had two children, Greg born 1894 and Nan born 1896, but just two years later in 1898, Sarah aged 25 was left widowed with two small children. Andrew Cunniam died of an abscess of the throat, a condition that would be easily treated nowadays with antibiotics.

In the 1901 Census, the Moran household consists of William, his wife Anne, their widowed daughter Sarah Cunniam and Sarah's two children Greg and Nan. The farmhouse is a three-roomed thatched house with three windows to the front. There are eight farm buildings: a stable, a cow house, a calf house, a piggery, a fowl shed, a barn, a turf shed and a general shed.

The census was recorded on 1st April 1901. Just three weeks later on the 21st, William Moran died, aged 81 years.

Two years later, Sarah remarried. Her husband was Jeremiah Farrell of Ballycullen. The couple had two children: Bride born in 1904 and Bill born in 1907. In the meantime, Sarah's mother Anne died in 1906. In the 1911 Census, the household now consists of Sarah and Jeremiah Farrell, Sarah's two children from her first marriage and the two children from her second marriage. The composition of the farm

Jeremiah Farrell and Jimmy Connolly, in Farrells farmyard, C.1930

buildings has changed to a stable, a coach house, a cow house, a piggery, a fowl shed and a barn.

The Cunniam children went to school in Ballylusk, using a pathway that went across the fields from their farmhouse to Aghowle Lane. Bride Farrell also started school in Ballylusk, but she and her brother Bill completed their schooling in Moneystown School, perhaps because by that time their neighbours the O'Brien children and the Connolly children were attending Moneystown school.

When Greg Cunniam completed his schooling, he went to work in Dublin and here his step nephew Johnny Kenneally remembers him:

> *Greg left Aghowle at 15 and went to work for the Tram Company in Dublin. His first job was looking after the horses as a stable boy for the horse drawn trams in Dublin, then he graduated to driving the horses and later on he drove the electric trams and then the petrol trams and he ended up driving the diesel buses.*
>
> *He stayed there till he was 65 and when he retired he got a great write up in the papers and a long-service silver medal, which he left to me. I remember visiting him in Dublin after he retired and even then, he sat on his chair and his head would move from side to side as if he was still driving and looking out for traffic. He was a lovely old man.*

His sister Nan remained living at home and alongside her mother, she took a very active role in running the house and farm. She is remembered for her weekly trips to Wicklow town to sell butter and eggs and also rearing turkeys for the Christmas market. After finishing school, Bill remained at home to assist in running the family farm. In time, as his father became advanced in years, Bill took over the main running of this farm.

When Bride Farrell finished school and became a young woman, she moved to Dublin and got a position as a children's nurse. Here she met her future husband, John Kenneally from Co. Cork, who was at that time in the army and had been a bodyguard for Éamon De Valera. When they decided to get married, John came down to Aghowle to ask Bride's parents for permission to marry. He arrived dressed in his full army uniform and the entire neighbourhood was very impressed with Bride's future husband. When they married in 1934, John left the army and the couple opened a little shop in Cork selling tobacco and sweets. But it was difficult to make a living from it, so after the birth of their first son Vincent, the couple moved to England to stay with John's sister who had secured a position for him over there.

There in 1938 they had their second son, Johnny. Although Bride had settled in England, she always kept a very close connection with her family home in Aghowle. Even when the boys were very young, she brought them over to stay each summer and she continued to return back home each year until finally in her older years, ill health prevented her from travelling.

On these childhood holidays to the Farrells' farm, Bride's youngest son Johnny developed a deep love for the local area and he too continued to make the trip back from England regularly, even after he grew up and married.

When Johnny's Uncle Bill was retiring and selling the farm, he retained one field which he left to Johnny. Then in later years, Johnny and his wife Jeanette built a home on this site. Now they currently divide their time between their English home and their Aghowle home.

Johnny Kenneally at Lady's Well, Ballymanus, 2016

Reflections: Johnny Kenneally On Childhood Visits to Farrell's in the 1940s/50s

In April 2016, I visited Johnny in his Aghowle home which he has nostalgically named "The Farrells" and which looks across on the fields stretching up to Carrick where his mother spent her childhood years. Johnny re-lived for me some of his fond memories of his summers on Farrells' farm in the late 1940s and the 1950s.

> *I came over to the farm in Aghowle from the time I was a young boy, but I think there was a gap of a few years around the wartime that we couldn't come over. The first time I clearly remember was when I was about 10 or 11 years of age. The whole family came that summer and*

as there would not be enough space for all of us in the little farmhouse, we brought a big ex-army bell tent for our family to sleep in.

I remember the excitement of the journey as we came across on the ferry boat and then caught a steam train down from Dublin to Rathdrum. Our uncle Bill was there to meet us with a hired taxi. It was a big American car. I think it came from a garage just on the way into Rathdrum.

When we got to the farm, my grandmother would be standing out on the roadside waiting for us. She would be all dressed up in her Sunday best clothes. What surprised me as a child was that while it was clear that she was really delighted to see us, there was no hugs and kisses, I was used to my aunties and uncles in England giving us a cuddle and a big hug. But my granny in Aghowle was not that sort of person, even though we knew she was very excited about us coming to stay.

When we arrived, she would fuss about us and bring us in to the kitchen and we would all sit down to a big tea. Then after the tea, she would go and change back into her everyday working clothes.

Living on the farm at that time was my granny and my granddad and my Uncle Bill and Auntie Nan. My grandfather seemed very old to me back then and he walked with a limp and had a walking stick. I think he broke his leg at some stage. It seemed to me that there were several people around Aghowle who had broken their leg and I think they were not much for going to see the doctors back then. As my grandfather could not walk very far, he kept a single telescopic eye glass that he used for counting his sheep in the fields up under Carrick. We used to be fascinated with this eye glass and when grandfather died it was passed on to my older brother.

My auntie Nan had broken her leg at one stage as well, but she would never go to visit a doctor as they were all men, she used to wear long skirts down to her ankles and would never let a man anywhere near her. She ended up with a bad limp and walked with a stick, then she put on a lot of weight and that made things worse for her. Uncle Bill, who was a quiet sort of man, ran the farm, I enjoyed going around with him on the farm and when I grew up we always kept in contact and I remained very fond of him.

The year we came over with the bell tent we put it up in a field beside the farmhouse, but it was missing a central pole to support it, because the pole was too heavy to carry with us on the journey over.

My uncle Bill helped cut down a branch of a tree and we used that instead. But then one night during a bad thunder and lightning storm the tent blew down. Miley O'Brien who was the next door neighbour came to the rescue and took me down to their house and put me in to his sister Nancy's bed. She was a young woman at the time and was not well pleased with my arrival. But years later we used to have a good laugh about it when I would tell her she was the first woman I ever slept with.

Then for the rest of our stay we had to all sleep in the farmhouse. I was in the upper room, squashed in with my grandfather and Uncle Bill. My grandfather used to smoke a pipe all the time and I remember that he would get ready for bed and then sit on the side of the bed smoking away for a while before he lay down to go to sleep.

In those days, there was of course no bathroom in the house. So, we used to be taken down to the river to the place where they used to wash and dip the sheep. We were able to stand up in the water there and wash ourselves. One year I had a brace for my teeth and I took it out to wash it and it floated away down the river. My father was very cross because he thought I had thrown it in the river on purpose. We searched all down the way but could not find it.

The water for use in the house came down in a little stream close by the farmhouse; I remember it was beautiful clear water. Sometimes in summer the stream dried up and we used to have to go to O'Brien's well for the drinking water.

My brother Vincent, who was about 13 at the time, decided that we should have a toilet near the house. So he cut branches and constructed quite a good framework in at the back of the house, my grandmother was not very impressed with the idea so she stood watching him with her arms folded. When he had it completed he set it up with a bucket inside, but it never got used, as my grandfather came and grabbed the bucket away as he needed it for milking the cows.

The back of the farmhouse used to be thatched at that time, while the front had corrugated iron over the thatch. I remember one summer we went with the pony and cart to visit a family called Timmons that lived in the Bog in Ballycullen. The purpose of our trip was to get some rushes to re-thatch the back of the house. We got to their house by going in a pathway that was down past O'Brien's Raheen and we went up over the hill to Ballycullen. When we got there, I remember Sarah Timmons made a great fuss of myself and my brother, but she warned us on no account to go near their well as it was the deepest and most dangerous one in all of Co. Wicklow. So of course, the first thing we did was to sneak out and go find the well.

A big event during our stay used to be the hay making. When they had the hay saved they piled it up into big cocks and tied a rope around it and then they used the horse to drag, or slig it, down into the barn. I used to be allowed to sit on top of the hay cock when they were bringing it down from the meadow to the barn.

When any big job was undertaken on the farm, Bill's two neighbours Miley O'Brien and Patsy Connolly would come to help out. One time during our stay, Uncle Bill had decided to rebuild and upgrade his milking parlour. They made wooden casings and then they made up fresh cement and poured it into the casings and left it for several days to dry out. When it was dry they removed the wood. I recall there was some dispute about the best way to build it. Miley was mechanical minded and was the ideas man, but I recall on this particular occasion my uncle Bill declared it was going to be his milking parlour and they were going to build it his way.

At that time on the farm they had two horses, Jess and Lil. Jess was the mother and Lil the daughter. As Jess was the quietest one I was allowed to ride on her. They also had a pony and trap and over the summer I was shown how to handle it. Once a week Auntie Nan took the pony and trap to Wicklow town to sell her eggs and butter and buy the groceries.

One day when she was taking us with her to Wicklow we had got as far as Rathnew village when suddenly there was a big thunder and lightning storm. The pony got frightened and took off at high speed and threw a shoe. Eventually Nan got her under control, but then we had to turn up a lane near Rathnew to go find a blacksmith. In the end we never got to Wicklow town because the money for the groceries was spent on re-shoeing the pony.

Each Sunday we would go to mass in Moneystown. Granny and Nan would go in the pony and trap and the rest of us would walk. We preferred to walk anyway as it was a great social event as we joined with everyone else along the way to the church. There was a little shop across from the chapel where we used to buy sweets. One Sunday when no one was watching, my brother bought some cigarettes and later we hid out in the field and tried smoking them. I didn't like them at all and could not see what the attraction was.

One particular Sunday when we were walking back from mass as we got nearer to Farrell's farmhouse we could see smoke rising up into the air. Then suddenly Miley O'Brien realised his house was on fire. There were flames billowing up out of the chimney. We all ran down to the house and Miley grabbed the ladder that was up against the hay rick and put it up to the chimney. He had a water hose rigged up in the milking shed and he was able to get the water down the chimney and quench the flames. Of course there were no carpets or anything to get ruined by water in those days. His quick thinking saved the farmhouse.

I remember sometimes at night uncle Bill and Jimmy Connolly used to go out hunting rabbits. Jimmy Connolly was a great shot and I remember one night they brought me with them up through Farrell's fields and I was amazed how Jimmy was able to hit a rabbit from such a distance in the darkness.

My grandmother and Auntie Nan reared turkeys to sell at Christmas time. Each Christmas they would post us over a turkey to England. One year during the war time the turkey arrived late on Christmas Eve, but luckily it was all plucked and ready for the oven. So next morning my mother put a bit of sausage meat stuffing in it and cooked it. But when we sat down to dinner and she went to carve it and remove the stuffing, she found that Auntie Nan had already partially stuffed the turkey with some sweets for us children and a few packs of Woodbine cigarettes for my parents, as they were hard to get during wartime. But by then the gifts were all cooked into a horrible brown mess.

One year when I was over staying on the farm I had an unexpected source of income. A young man called Sonny (Miley) Manning was coming to court Nancy O'Brien who lived next door and they used to go walking up the Raheen lane. Nancy's brother Miley used to give me a shilling and tell me to follow them up the Raheen and keep a good eye on them and report back to him. But then Sonny Manning used to spot me and also give me a shilling to go away and not tell Miley anything. So, I did very well from the deal and in the end so did Sonny and Nancy, as they later got married.

One summer my brother and myself and our grandfather went to the bog to bring home the turf. My grandfather was a very elderly man at that time, but he hitched up the pony and cart and we set out for the bog. We stopped by our turf bank and was getting ready to start loading the turf, but the next thing we knew was that the pony and cart was sinking quickly down into the bog.

My brother acted very quickly and unyoked the pony from the cart and we managed to pull the pony up out of the bog on to solid ground and got her free. Then with much effort and time, we managed to get the wheels of the cart back up out of the bog as well. My grandfather was very impressed with my brother's quick thinking and was grateful they were not at the loss of the pony and cart. But after all the commotion there wasn't much turf saved that day.

My brother and I used to go over to O'Brien's next door to see Miley's threshing engine. It used to fascinate us. He also had the first tractor in the area and one time he turned it over going up the Raheen lane and it was so heavy he had to get all the local men out to help him get it upright again.

Uncle Bill told me that during the War of Independence, the local IRA men were hiding out up on Carrick Mountain and that his father used to carry bread up to them.

Bill Farrell and his nephews Vincent and Johnny Kenneally
Farrells' farmyard Aghowle c. 1939

My grandmother told me this story which happened one day sometime after her first husband had died and there was no man living in the farmhouse. A tramp came to the farmhouse and knocked at the half door asking her if she could spare a slice of bread and a drop of tea. She cut him a slice off the fresh bread she had just made; he then asked if there was anywhere he could put his head down for the night, so she told him he could sleep in the barn.

Unfortunately, at that time there were some bottles of stout stored in the barn, as it was a cool place to keep them. The tramp found them and drank them all and became quite drunk.

Later that night when she had gone to bed, the tramp entered the farmhouse and tried to get passionate with her. She managed to get the broom and poked him in the stomach with it. While he was recovering, she got the fire poker and hit him in the groin with it. He then ran out of the house and up the road. He went up the back road past where the Rocher Doyle lived and somewhere around there he tried to enter another house. No one is sure what exactly happened at that house, but he set fire to it and the elderly woman inside died.[7]

Farming at Aghowle, 1960s.
L-R: Joe Beale, Bob Smith, Georgiana Crofton, Dan Short and Bill Farrell.
Photograph from "A Pictorial History of Ashford, Co. Wicklow, 1860s-1960s"
By kind permission of Sheila Clarke

---

7 Author's note – So far, I have not been able to establish which house the tramp is said to have entered and set on fire, nor who was the woman who is said to have died inside. I have not come across any newspaper reports from that period describing such an incident.

> *The locals were alerted and chased the tramp but he escaped up towards Carrick and was never caught. Later they found evidence of where he had been hiding in the cave up in the rocks.*
>
> *We used to love coming to stay on the farm for our holidays and hated going back home at the end of the summer. The first summer we came my brother and I were really disappointed when we were told it was time to go back home, we had thought we were going to stay forever on the farm. So, we decided to run away and hide. This plan did not go down very well with the adults, as the hired taxi was standing waiting to take us to the train in Rathdrum.*

In 1955, the Farrell household lost two of its family members. In March, Nan Cunniam died aged 58 and in November, her step father Jer Farrell also died, aged 83.

The story of House No. 6 continues in the concluding chapter, "Chapter 14: The End of an Era", see section "House No. 6: Farrell's".

House No. 7 (Rutledge (Relish), Doyle)

House No. 7 was located about four fields above House No. 6, on the hillside beneath Carrick Mountain. Its ruins are currently surrounded by the Forestry.

Artist's impression of House No. 7 from the 1901 census records and remaining ruins
Illustration by Róisín Beirne

Historical Summary	
Families:	Rutledge (Relish), Doyle
1832 Land Records	John Rutledge/Relish leasing 14 acres
1839 OSI map	A dwelling house and farm buildings marked here
1850 Glanmore Estate Records	Laurence Rutledge leasing 20 acres of land
1854 Griffith's Land Valuation	Laurence Rutledge leasing 21 acres of land
1901 Census	John Doyle and family, living in a two- roomed thatched roofed house
1911 Census	House no longer exists
Last family to farm here:	Last farming family to live here: Rutledge c.1890
Last family to live here:	John and Mary Doyle and family 1905

Family History

The first family that could be identified living here is the Rutledge family – but there is some confusion about this family's surname. After researching the available records, combined with local oral history, I believe the name Rutledge was originally pronounced locally as Relish.

In the tenant records of Glanmore Estate from 1832, there are two conflicting entries for the list of tenants at Aghowle. In one, the 14-acre holding is leased by Laurence Rutledge, while another list for the same year gives the leaseholder as Laurence Relish. I found similar conflicting entries in church records and petty court records and have concluded Relish was the local way of pronouncing the name Rutledge. Even in my childhood, long after the Rutledge family had left here, the local people referred to where the Rutledge family lived as "Relish's old place".

From Catholic Church records, I believe the Rutledge family came from the townland of Ballinakill about 3 miles from Aghowle and are first recorded in the Aghowle townland in the land records of 1832. In the following year, Richard Rutledge married Winifred Moran, who was the eldest daughter of Simon and Sarah Moran (House No. 6) - the Moran's farm bordered the Rutledge's farm.

Richard and Winifred lived in House No.7 and had at least 7 children: Richard, Winifred, Simon, Eliza, Margaret, Bridget and Sarah. The leaseholder's name is still recorded as Laurence Rutledge/Relish in the 1854 Griffith's valuation records, but following records show that it had transferred to Richard Rutledge (senior) and then on to Winifred by the early 1860s, indicating Winifred was widowed by this time.

In January 1872, Winifred's son Simon married a local girl named Eliza Mullens from Ballycullen and the following year, their first child Richard was born in Aghowle. Soon after that, Simon and his family moved to

Wicklow Town where they set up and ran a successful dairy business. Descendants of Simon and Eliza Rutledge still live in Wicklow Town today.

Records show that Winifred and Richard's other son, Richard, married Eliza Crawford early in 1880. They were living in the family home at Aghowle when their daughter Winifred was born on Christmas Day later that year. Around this time, Richard also became the named leaseholder. Church records show that Richard and Eliza were still living here in 1886 when their son Richard was born. This Richard also appears in the section of this book "Richard John Joseph Rutledge" relating to local casualties in the First World War.

Sometime during the following years, the family moved to the Ashford area and records show that when Winifred Rutledge Senior died in 1893, she was living with her married daughter Bridget in Ballinalea. The lease for this holding was transferred back to Simon Rutledge who was now living in Wicklow town where he carried out his dairy business and he sub-let the house here. In early 1899, when John Doyle from Aghowle Upper (House No. 9) married Mary Mansfield of Saggart, Co. Dublin, the couple rented this cottage from Simon Rutledge. Later that year their first child, Mary, was born here.

In the 1901 Census, John and Mary Doyle and their daughter Mary, are recorded living here. The house is described as a two-roomed, thatched cottage, with two windows to the front and with one outbuilding, a fowl shed.

Between the time of the census in April 1901 and September 1904, Mary and John Doyle had three more children: Henry in May 1901, John in June 1903 and Patrick in September 1904.

Their second son, John, was born on 23rd June 1903, but just 4 days previously their oldest son Henry, aged 2 years, died from tuberculosis (TB) or consumption as it was commonly called at that time. Unfortunately, this disease visited many Irish households. Within a few months of Henry's death, another neighbour Kate Connolly (aged 33) in Aghowle Upper (House No. 8) also died from TB.

A Fire Tragedy
Sadly for Mary and John Doyle, the loss of their son Henry was not the only loss they were to experience. On the 28th September 1905, a terrible tragedy was to befall their family.

At that time, a bread car from Wicklow town used to pass through the townland once a week, bringing fresh bread to the local families. Each week, Mary Doyle along with the other neighbours in the area would go down to the main Aghowle road to buy their bread from the passing bread car. On this particular Thursday, a disaster was to happen while Mary Doyle made her journey down across the 3 or 4 fields from their house to the main road. Before leaving her cottage, she secured her two oldest children in the bedroom and carried her baby Patrick in her arms. There was no fire lighting in the kitchen and Mary believed the two children secured in the bedroom were safe. But while she was away, the house somehow caught fire and the children perished.

The following are the details of the event as recorded in the local Wicklow Newsletter newspaper dated 30th September. It would appear that sensational tabloid headlines were in use even in those days. The report goes into very graphic detail of the tragedy and makes gruesome reading, but it does provide us with a detailed historical record of the fire and the inquest on the following day.

TRAGIC DEATH of TWO CHILDREN
ON CARRIG MOUNTAINSIDE
LOCKED IN AND ROASTED ALIVE IN A COTTAGE
A PATHETIC INCIDENT

On Thursday evening, a shocking tragedy took place by Carrig mountainside, some four miles from Ashford and about a quarter of a mile from Ballycullen main road up a hill. A labourer named John Doyle, aged about 40 years, resided with his young wife and three children in a thatched cottage on the land of Mr. S Rutledge, Wicklow. Doyle worked for the small farmers around him, while his wife earned a few pence rearing fowl, besides minding the children and house. As usual, the father left home in the early morning for his work and returned about five in the evening to find two of his children burned beyond recognition, the house and all its contents entirely consumed, along with some £8 in cash, which had been hidden away in a delph jug. A heartrending and pathetic scene was then witnessed. In one corner of the room lay two small black figures, the charred remains of Doyle's two children – Mary, aged 6 and John, aged 2. The body of the child, Mary, was lying against that of her little brother, as if she would protect him from the cruel flames and her arms- or what remained of them- were raised as if embracing him. She had evidently thrust him under the iron bed in the corner, in hope of rescue before the burning roof would fall in on them. It appears that Mrs. Doyle went down to the main road to meet the bread van, taking her baby with her and leaving the other children shut up in the room. There was no fire on the hearth and there appeared not the least danger. During her absence, the house caught fire from some cause or other and before anything could be done to rescue the children, the roof fell in and the whole cottage was a mass of burning flame.

Yesterday, an inquest was held on the bodies by Mr. James Murray, J P, Coroner for East Wicklow, in the farmhouse of Mr. Jeremiah Farrell, which is situate by the roadside, at Aghowle Upper. The bodies of the children had been conveyed upon a door down to Mr. Farrell's barn and were there viewed by the jury. Head Constable White, of Wicklow, Sergeant Wills, Constables Brennan and Madden, of Ashford, were in attendance. The following were sworn on the jury- Messrs. George Byrne, RDC foreman: James Turner, John Turner, Denis Turner, Thomas Shannon, Thomas Shannon jun; Andrew Byrne, James Toole, John Colquhoun, William Byrne, Michl. Doyle and Thomas Edge.

The first witness was Mary Doyle, a woman of about 30 years of age, mother of the deceased children. She stated that shortly after 4 o'clock, she left the cottage to meet the bread cart on the main road. Before leaving, she placed the two children in the bedroom, latching the door upon them. She then took the baby in her arms and went for the bread. She was about three-quarters of an hour away. When she was returning she saw fire bursting from the kitchen chimney at the back of the house and knowing that there was no fire upon the hearth when she left, she became alarmed and hastened to the cottage. There she found the house was in flames. She saw two of her neighbours – Mr. Farrell and Mr. Edge – trying to force the door in. She told them about the children inside and they burst in the door, but could go no further. Once a week, the bread cart passed and she was in the habit of leaving the children in the cottage while she went for the bread.

Mr. Farrell, examined, stated that, observing flames from the cottage roof, he and Mr. Edge ran to the spot. They burst in the door but could see nothing but fire. The roof then fell in. Sergeant Wills, examined, said the occurrence having been reported to him, he, accompanied by Constable Terrett and Brennan, hastened to the scene. They found the whole cottage burnt to the ground and that the roof and portion of the walls had fallen in. They commenced to look for the bodies of the children and after some time succeeded in finding them under a bedstead in the corner of the room. The bodies were very much burnt: in fact everything in the room had been consumed.

Dr. J H. Halpin, medical officer of Wicklow, deposed that he made a superficial examination of the bodies. They were greatly burned and death was due to shock from the extensive burns received.

The Coroner said it appeared to him to have been an accident, pure and simple. Whether the mother had acted wisely by shutting the children up by themselves in the room, was a matter of opinion, but she appears to have done the same thing many times before. She stated that there was no fire upon the hearth, but it was likely that the children may have found matches and there was no telling what children, when left alone, will do. Were the jury of the opinion that the fire was accidental?

Foreman– Yes and that we leave no blame to anyone.

A verdict was then returned in accordance with the medical evidence. At the close, Mr. George Byrne made an appeal to the jury and those present for some small subscription to assist the unfortunate parents, who had lost everything they had in the world. They were without clothes, food, money or a home and this was one of the hardest cases he had ever met and he hoped a generous public would help in the effort to provide Doyle and his poor wife with a fresh start in life. The appeal was responded to by everyone present.

Extracts of this harrowing *Wicklow Newsletter* report were published by some of the British newspapers in the days following the event, including the Whitby Gazette, Manchester Courier and the Shetland Times. The twelve men that were sworn on the jury can all be identified as neighbours of the Doyle family from the townlands of Aghowle and Ballycullen. This indicates that many of the local men had gathered on the day at Farrell's small farmhouse for the inquest. It is also likely that many of the local women folk would have been there too, to support and comfort Mary Doyle. Mary was a young woman of twenty-four years of age at the time and three of her close neighbours were, like herself, mothers of young children. All three had given birth within the last year. Sarah Farrell had three children, Martha Edge two and Annie Connolly (my grandmother) had just given birth to her first child a few months earlier.

One cannot imagine how the devastated parents, Mary and John Doyle, were able to endure the proceedings of the inquest on the day following the deaths of their two children and the loss of their home and all their possessions in the fire. Mary Doyle's own family were living many miles away in Saggart, Co. Dublin. She no doubt did have the support of her husband John's family who were living close by (in House No. 9) and the support of all her neighbours.

With the help of their neighbours and friends, the Doyle family were re-housed a few miles away in Ballycullen. The newspaper report of the inquest noted an appeal was made for assistance to the family and acknowledgement notices that appeared in the Wicklow People newspaper over the following weeks showed that many people from the local area, as well as throughout the county, had made donations to help the Doyle family.

The following is a letter of thanks from John Doyle that was printed in the Wicklow Newsletter on November 18th, 1905.

In 2016, when a group of people gathered in remembrance at the site of the Doyles' cottage, the remains of a glass sugar bowl (illustrated right) was found inside the ruined walls, where it had most likely lain since the day of the fire. A descendant of Mary and John Doyle took the piece to place it on the Doyle family grave.

The 1911 Census records tell us that Mary and John Doyle and their surviving

---

THE AGHOWLE FIRE

TO THE EDITOR

Sir, - Would you kindly allow me space, through your columns, to return my most sincere heartfelt thanks to the many sympathising contributors who so generously subscribed to the fund raised on my behalf, on the occasion of the recent fire at Aghowle, whereby my two children lost their lives and my little homestead was burnt to the ground. I wish to return special thanks to Messrs. George Byrne, RDC Ballycullen: John Britton Glenealy: John Byrne Barnbawn; and Jeremiah Farrell Aghowle, who, at great personal inconvenience acted as collectors for the fund.- Yours gratefully,

John Doyle
16th November, 1905

Remains of Doyle sugar bowl
Illustration by Róisin Beirne

---

child Patrick are now living in the neighbouring townland of Ballycullen, in a four-roomed slate roofed house with out-buildings of a fowl shed and a piggery. John Doyle is the named leaseholder. Their son Patrick is now attending school and the couple also now have two daughters, Kate born 1907 and Molly born 1909. In the year after this Census was taken, the couple had a third daughter Rose (b. 1912).

Their son and three daughters went to Ballylusk School and Rose Doyle is pictured in a school photograph in section "Schooling around Aghowle in the 1920s".

Mary and John Doyle's three daughters born in Ballycullen in the years after the fire grew into adulthood, married and had families of their own. After the tragedy Mary and John had known, this must have brought them great consolation.

But life was also to bring Mary and John Doyle yet more sadness. When their son Patrick, whom Mary carried with her in her arms on the day of the fire, had reached 15 years of age in 1919, he too died from TB. So, the four children that the couple had brought into the world in their cottage in Aghowle were now all deceased.

Left: Mary Doyle; Seated: her daughter Kate, born 17 months after the fire; Standing: Kate's daughter Ellen. Photograph courtesy of Mary Doyle's granddaughter Ellen O'Leary

After the fire, only some ruined walls remained of the burnt-out house and a few decades later the land around the ruins was purchased by the State Forest and planted with trees. As these trees grew up, no physical reminder of the tragedy was visible. But the memory of the two little children who lost their lives there was not forgotten and lived on in the folk memory of the townland. Sixty years later, in my childhood, the local people still remembered them and spoke of their deaths with great sadness.

In April 2016, a small group of people gathered to remember the two children, Mary Doyle and her little brother John, who lost their lives in their cottage in 1905. A ceremony of remembrance was held at the site of the ruins of their house and also at the nearby Holy Well. Those that gathered there included: descendants of the children's sister Kate Doyle

*2017 -The ruined remains of the wall of the house
where the Doyle children lost their lives in 1905*

(b.1907); descendants of some of the people who were living in Aghowle at the time of the fire; and some people who had a very close connection to the children's mother, Mary Doyle, in her later life. Also, one of the people there was a grandson of Jeremiah Farrell, one of the men who had run to the scene of the fire and tried to rescue the children.

I have written a poem in remembrance of this tragedy and the children that lost their lives – see "Echoes in Sunlight" in the Poetry Appendix.

Since House No. 7 was destroyed in 1905 and never lived in again, this concludes its history.

*2016 Remembrance ceremony
for the Doyle children.
Front centre: Ellen O'Leary who is a niece of the
children;
Left: Ellen's daughter Catherine,
Right: Ellen's granddaughter Shannon.*

House No. 8 (Power, Edge, Doyle, Connolly)

House No. 8 is located at Aghowle Upper and of the 10 houses featured, it was the only one situated on the side of the valley opposite Carrick. It is situated beside the Aghowle Road, and across the road from the farmhouse is a laneway that comes out at the Slanelough road beside the Wart Stone. This laneway was known as The Back Road, and predated the current road that comes out at Slanelough crossroads.

This was the house that I grew up in.

Connollys' farmhouse, c. 1935
Man holding horse: Patsy Connolly;
Man on horse: Joe Murray, Patsy's brother in law; Child: Joe's son Paddy

Historical Summary	
Families:	Power, Edge, Doyle, Connolly
1832 Land Records	Not possible to identify the occupant at that time
1839 OSI map	A dwelling house and farm buildings located here
1850 Glanmore Estate Records	James Power leasing 48 acres of land
1854 Griffith's Land Valuation	Charles William Edge leasing 54 acres of land
1901 Census	Patrick Connolly and siblings, living in a three-roomed thatched roofed farmhouse
1911 Census	Patrick and Annie Connolly and family
Last family to farm here:	Patsy and May Connolly and family (including myself), 1971

Family History

As there were quite a lot of changes in the farm holdings in Aghowle between 1832 and 1850 and there are no records relating to these changes, I was unable to identify who was the leaseholder of this house and surrounding land in 1832. The dwelling house and out-buildings are marked on the 1839 OSI map and in 1850 James Power is the recorded leaseholder.

The Powers did not stay very long as James has left by 1854, when Charles William Edge is leasing the house and 54 acres of land here. In October 1847, Charles William Edge had married Jane Faulkner in the local Church of Ireland church at Nun's Cross. Charles was from the townland of Knockrath (about 6 miles away) and Jane was from Aghowle Upper. Her family lived in a house close to House No. 5. Aghowle Upper. (The Faulkner's house is recorded as uninhabited by the 1901 Census, but a member of the family is recorded as lodging in House No. 4, Aghowle Lower).

Jane and Charles William Edge also did not stay long here in this house - records from 1858 show that James Doyle was by then the lease holder. In April 1859, Charles and Jane Edge make an appearance again, this time in the other side of the country when their names appear in the church records for the Church of Ireland parish of Athenry, County Galway. Here on the 16th April 1859, the couple have 4 of their children christened on the same day: Mary aged 8, Archibald aged 6, Elizabeth aged 4 and Jane aged 18 months. Looking at the ages of these children, it seems likely that some of them may well have been born in the house in Aghowle when Charles and Jane were living here.

The next occupants of this farmhouse were James and Anne Doyle and their family, records showing that the Doyle family lived here from 1858 to 1896.

James Doyle married Ann McGuirke of Raheen, near Roundwood, in the Roman Catholic parish of Glendalough in January 1853 and the couple was still living at Raheen when their daughter Ann was baptized the following year. Sometime before August 1858, the family had moved to this house at Aghowle Upper, as their daughter Eliza was born here that year. Their neighbours, Bridget and James Byrne (House No.10) were sponsors for baby Eliza.

The couple had at least five more children while living here: Laurence, James, William, Patrick and Bridget. James Doyle remained the leaseholder for this house and 54-acre farm until 1896/7. Not much else is known about this family. As the name Doyle was (and is) very common in Wicklow, it was difficult to definitively identify members of this family in available records. Also, it is not known where James and Ann moved to in 1896, so they and their children could not be identified in the 1901 census records.

It would appear that at least some of their children may have migrated to America, as this notice printed in the Boston Globe in February 1902 would indicate:

> *MISS A. DOYLE, who left Aughoule, Ashford, Co. Wicklow, Ire, Spring 1892. for Boston, please address her brother Boston Daily Globe – Boston, Massachusetts, United States of America.*

In 1892, there were two Doyle families living in Aghowle - House No. 8 and House No. 9. There was no child with initial "A" in House No. 9, while James and Ann Doyle in House No. 8 had a daughter Ann born in 1854 - so one assumes this notice must relate to tha t Ann Doyle.

The Doyle family sold up the interest in their farm at the end of 1896. The following is the sale notice for the house and farm, as it appeared in the Wicklow People newspaper in November 1896.

AGHOWLE ASHFORD

Sale of small farm, stock, crops, etc.
Subscriber is favoured with instruction from Mr. JJ Doyle,
who is changing his residence,

TO SELL BY PUBLIC AUCTION

His interest in and to his farm at Aghowle, containing about 33 acres, 2 roods, 1 perch, situate about 3 miles from Ashford, as held by him from E. Synge E.s.q. under judicial agreement, at the rent of £16 per year: valuation, £19 5s, The farm has a southern aspect and there is a comfortable thatched dwelling house, cowhouse, barn, stable, piggery and shed, beside the county road: also 22 brood ewes, 20 lambs, 1 ram, 1 cob mare, 4 years old, by The Ranger, trained to all work, gentle and fast in harness,:2 cows, 1 a springer: 1 calf, 2 store pigs, fowl, 2 stacks of black and white oats, rick of first crop hay, plough and harrow, new dray and harness and the usual furniture of a Farmers house.
Sale on Monday 23rd day of November
At 11 o'clock

The tenant rental records show that sometime between the end of 1896 and 1898, the lease of this house and farm changed from James Doyle to Patrick Connolly - my grandfather. Patrick and his family had been living and farming at Knockraheen near Roundwood, about 9 miles away. At that time, Dublin Corporation was preparing to undertake the second phase of the Vartry reservoir and as part of this work they acquired the land the Connolly family was leasing in Knockraheen.[8] The family members who relocated to Aghowle were Patrick and his sisters Kate and Jane. Patrick's sister, Ellen, who was still single at that time, was working in Dublin and would return from time to time to the new family home at Aghowle.

In the 1901 Census, Patrick Connolly is recorded as the head of the household and living with him are his sisters Kate and Jane and a farm servant, George Manley. Although it was not uncommon at that time for people to be a little inaccurate in knowing and recording their exact age, the three Connolly siblings have greatly underestimated their ages on the Census returns. Patrick recorded he was 29, although he was about 40 at that time. Jane recorded her age as 23 while she was in fact 32 and Kate gave her age as 21 while she was really 30. One wonders if this underestimation might have been connected to the fact that all three were not yet married and had recently moved to a new area where they were not well known. Perhaps they felt their marriage prospects might be increased by reducing their ages by about a decade?

The dwelling house is described as a three-roomed thatched house with two windows to the front. There are 7 out-buildings: a stable, a cow house, a piggery, a dairy, a fowl shed, a turf shed and a general-purpose shed.

In the autumn of 1903, the household underwent major changes. In September, Kate passed away, having been ill for several years with TB. This was just a month before her brother Patrick was to marry Annie Dempsey in Ashford church. Annie, as we will see shortly, was living close by in farmhouse No. 10, housekeeping for her elderly uncles. A month after Patrick married, his sister Jane married Thomas Byrne of Knockrath and moved from Aghowle to live in Knockrath, about 6 miles away.

In the 1911 Census, the household consists of Patrick and Annie Connolly and their three children: Molly (b.1905), Paddy (b.1907, known to family and close friends as Patsy and who would become my father) and Jimmy (b.1910). The dwelling house now has three windows to the front and the thatched roof has now been changed to a corrugated iron roof. The farm buildings remain the same.

In the following years, the Connolly children along with the Farrell and O'Brien children attended Moneystown School – see group photograph in "School Days 1919".

8   Most of my grandfather's original land at Knockraheen is now under water, but a small patch of dry land still exists north of the R765 road, right beside an old hand pump on the road and running down to the shore where there is a large overflow drain to the Lower Lake, close to the dam on the Upper Lake.

When Patsy left school, he began farming with his father on the family farm. By this time, the family was no longer just there as tenants but were owners of the farm. Patsy and his father set about building up their farm and making it more profitable and improving the land by clearing areas of rock and furze bushes. A map of the fields of Connolly's farm is illustrated below.

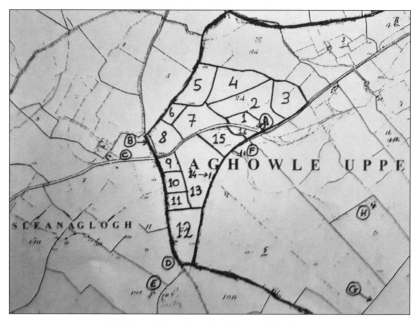

Fields and Landmarks of Connolly's Farm

Field No.	Field Name
1	The Calf Field
2	The Bank Field
3	The Rock
4	The Three-Cornered Field
5	The Top Field
6	The Clover Field
7	The Brow
8	The Field Over the Crossroads
9	The Field Under the Crossroads
10	The Split Stone Field? (or possibly The Field Across from the Split Stone)?
11	(Name lost in the mists of time)
12	The Bushy Field
13	The Bank Over Franks
14	Franks Place/Frank's Walls
15	The Bog
16	The Little Field

Landmarks

A   Connolly's Farmhouse
B   Giffney's Bank
C   The School House Field
D   Joe Ryan's Gate
E   Loughlin's Walls
F   The Rocher Doyle's Place
G   Mooney's Ditch
H   Relish's Place

His two neighbouring school friends, Bill Farrell and Miley O'Brien, also stayed at home to help their fathers run the family arms and as noted elsewhere in this book, these three families worked very much in cooperation with each other throughout the entire farming year.

Sometime after he left school, Jimmy Connolly went to work in Laragh House in Annamoe, where part of his job was to trap rabbits, which had become very plentiful in the countryside and were causing much damage to farm crops. It is said that Jimmy was very skilled at rabbit hunting and spent a lot of his time both day and night engaged in catching rabbits and selling them to the dealers who bought them for the Dublin market. The Late John Timmons, whose family ran the local shop at Parkmore had the following recollection of Jimmy during the 1940s:

> *I remember Jimmy Connolly, during the war he was alwayss out hunting rabbits, he had a load a dogs, one of them he called Hitler. When he would come back in the evening he would have all the dogs sitting outside the shop door, you would be afraid to go in by them. He would have a ferret in a sack on his back, with two little holes cut in the sack for the ferret to breathe out through. He was a great man to chew tobacco, he would chew, and chew, and eventually he would spit out a big thick black spit, and if you had chippings you could tar the road with it.*

He was also very athletic and won road races, as well as playing on the minor football team for Ashford in the early 1930s (winners of the 1931 Co. Wicklow Championship – see photo). Later, he played on a winning Moneystown senior football team in the late 1940s.

After Jimmy migrated to Australia in 1950, the memory of his athletic achievements became legendary and perhaps grew somewhat with the re-telling. I remember hearing during my childhood many stories of how he won road races. These stories recounted how he would be out all night

Ashford Minor Football Team 1931 – Winners Co. Wicklow Championship
Jimmy Connolly, first in kit from left in front row

hunting rabbits and get 1 or 2 hours sleep before decking out in his farm work boots and cycling an old bicycle to the starting point of the race in Roundwood. He would arrive just in time for the starting pistol and would reach the finish point in Bray well ahead of the other runners and have a pint of stout drank in the nearest pub before the second man arrived at the finish line. It was also recounted that Jimmy had an unusual way of checking his time when he was training for the road races. This was before stopwatches would have been common place and it appears Jimmy did not even have a pocket watch - instead he would take a large clock off the kitchen wall in the farmhouse, place it in the ditch at the side of the road and use that to measure his "lap times" as he ran the roads nearby.

After she finished school, Molly Connolly went to work in Dublin as a priest's housekeeper. In 1931 she married Joe Murray, who worked in St. Ita's Hospital, Portrane. Molly and Joe settled in Dublin and went on to have seven sons, but as we will see from the piece below by her son George, she always kept a very close connection to the family farm where she was born.

In 1937, Anne Connolly passed away, aged 68 years. For the next 10 years, the farmhouse was home to the widowed Patrick and his two bachelor sons Patsy and Jimmy, although Molly and members of her family make regular visits down from Dublin to the farmhouse.

In a strange twist of fate, Molly who settled in Dublin had a family of 7 sons, while her brother Patsy who remained running the family farm at Aghowle had a family of 3 daughters. Molly retained a lifelong connection back to her family farm and over the years Molly, Joe and their sons were regular visitors to Aghowle. As soon as Molly's older sons reached 9 or 10 years old. they came down to spend their summers on the farm.

In May 2016, I visited Molly and Joe's third son, George, at his home in Adare, Co. Limerick. George was born in 1936 and from the time he was aged around 10, he spent his summers on Connolly's farm. Now nearly 70 years later, he recalled for me some of his vivid and treasured memories of those summers.

Molly Connolly and Joe Murray on their wedding day in 1931

May 1939- sheep shearing on Connollys' farm Aghowle
Back L-R: Patsy Connolly, Molly Murray (nee Connolly) and Patrick Connolly
Front L-R, Molly's four sons: Joe, Paddy, Tom and George

Reflections: George Murray Recalls Summers on Connolly's Farm in the 1940s

We were brought down to the farm from the time we were very young children. The first trip where I was old enough to remember was with my mother. We got the bus from Aston Quay in Dublin down to Ashford. From there we walked up to the farm. I was probably about 8 or 9 years old at the time and to a small boy the 4-mile journey up all those hills seemed an interminably long trek. But the journey was made more pleasurable by my mother stopping here and there along the way to pick wild cherries for me, from the roadside trees. She of course knew where such treasures grew from her own childhood days. I recall there were some near the way up to the Devil's Glen and around Ballycullen near Baird's house.

On this trip, or perhaps another time when she and I stayed in Aghowle, we also walked from the farmhouse on paths through the woods out across Carrick and down to visit my mother's aunt Roseanna who lived in Glenealy village. We stayed the night in aunt Roseanna's little house and I slept in a tiny attic room.

In the summers after that trip with my mother, I used to go down either with one of my older brothers, Tom or Paddy, or sometimes by myself. My father was very good with his hands and he used to make up bicycles from the individual parts and sell them on. When we were old enough to go down to stay on the farm he made us a bike each, as then we would have some form of transport and could be useful for running messages for Uncle Patsy and Jimmy.

When we went in to Aston Quay to get the bus, these bikes were put on a cradle on the top of the bus with the luggage and taken off for us when we reached Ashford. So, then we would be able to cycle up to the farm. After that, when something was needed for the house or the farm, Tom and I would use them to cycle to Ashford or Wicklow Town. I remember we would race one another at high speed down all the hills from Aghowle to Synnotts' shop in Ashford and sometimes we would head on into Wicklow Town if we had to get something in Delahunts' general store. I remember one of the things we used have to go there to get was a new filament for the tilly lamp. On the way back, we would carry all the messages on the handlebars of the bikes and have to walk up some of the hills from Ashford.

Living in the farmhouse at that time were my grandfather and my

Uncle Patsy and Uncle Jimmy. I remember my grandfather as a kind and gentle old man, who was slightly balding and always wore a waistcoat. He used to smoke a white clay pipe which was quite fragile and could very easily get broken. My uncle Jimmy was very athletic and won road races and was on a Wicklow Football team. He worked in Laragh House in Annamoe as well as spending a lot of his time hunting rabbits. He was a bit of a lady's man and would head out every Saturday night with his thick curly hair dripping with Brilliantine. I remember one night he had no Brilliantine so he went down to the cart shed at the bottom of the yard and got some axle grease to put in his hair. I imagine the smell of it was not very attractive to the young ladies that night. My uncle Patsy ran the farm, he was a quieter man than Jimmy. I was very fond of him. He was one of the nicest men I ever knew.

When myself, or one of my brothers, were down staying on the farm for the summer, Uncle Patsy used to put us in charge of preparing the dinner in the middle of the day. This meant he could stay longer working in the fields and come in when the food was ready. This system usually worked very well, except when my older brother Paddy was staying there. Paddy was very fond of reading and always had a novel or two on the go. So, he would sit in the sunshine in the haggard and get engrossed in his book and forget about the time. Then only when he would hear the clip clop of Patsy and the horse coming in from the field, would he jump up and run to the water spout to wash the spuds.

The food on the farm was simple but fresh and tasted lovely. They had their own freshly dug potatoes and they kept a little garden with cabbage and other vegetables and they cured their own bacon. I always felt a bit sorry for the pig on the farm because I knew very soon he would be getting the knife and would become a side of bacon hanging up in the fireplace. When they killed the pig, they would keep the pig's bladder for us to use as a football. It was like a big balloon and you tied it at the neck and Tom and I would play football with it out in the fields until it would eventually burst on a furze bush.

As there were only men in the house at that time, they did not churn butter or bake bread. A van came around once or twice a week and brought fresh bread and they got butter from the O'Brien family that lived nearby. Nancy O'Brien made lovely butter. I can remember going in to the little dairy room they had on their farm on churning day and seeing Nancy there in a big white apron with all the slabs of butter she was after churning. The taste of that butter on fresh new potatoes was lovely.

I also remember sometimes when we were down in O'Briens we would go up to their Long Field which was a great place for picking mushrooms. We would bring some home and put a bit of butter and salt in them and cook them on the hearth of the fireplace. Other times we would go up onto Carrick and pick the ripe fraughans and they tasted wonderful. On the road up from the farmhouse going towards Slanelough crossroads we used to find little wild strawberries. They were small but very sweet and tasty.

I mostly remember Miley and Nancy in the O'Brien household, but at that time Sheila and Kevin would sometimes come back home too. Kevin was friendly with my older brothers, Tom and Paddy. I remember when Kevin became ill and died quite young that my brother Tom was very upset.

Everything was very free and easy on the farm during the week, but when Saturday evening came around I had to have a bath, so that I would be clean and respectable for mass on Sunday morning. There was of course no bathroom or running water in the farmhouse. The drinking water was got from a spring well in the bog going towards Slanelough crossroads, the water they used for general household washing came down from the bog and out at a water spout across the road from the farmhouse. They also collected rain water that came off the roof into a barrel at the front of the house. I realised on my first Saturday night down there that this barrel of water was my bath. Patsy told me to go strip off and get into the barrel and wash myself. Although not many people used to pass along the roadway by the house, still I was terrified someone might come past when I was having my bath in the barrel. One of the summers when I was a little older and had become a young teenager I was particularly worried that an attractive young girl that I had taken a fancy to in one of the neighbouring houses, might pass by during my bath time.

I also remember every Saturday evening my grandfather would call me out into the yard and then he would fish around in his waistcoat pocket and produce a shilling and give it to me to spend in the shop after mass the next morning.

We usually walked to mass through the fields, we went up the Bank Field behind the house and through a corn field into Coneran's farm and out onto the road near their house and then over to the church in

Park. If the grass was very wet, we would go the long way all round by the road. After mass, I would go and spend grandfather's shilling in Timmons shop.

On a Sunday evening Patsy used to go to Coneran's house in Slanelough to play cards. The people that gathered there were the neighbours from Slanelough and Parkmore. The card game they played was called dawn and they would play for small amounts of money. I was too young to play so I would sit and watch them, or sometimes the woman called Martha who lived there would take me with her to visit some neighbours. She usually took me along a pathway through the bog that led out onto the Parkmore road.

Martha Lawler nee Byrne, pictured polishing Mr. Coneran's shoes. George Murray remembers Martha taking him across through the bog to visit neighbours in Parkmore. Photograph courtesy of Bernadette Lawler

One summer's evening in particular I remember the woman we went to visit gave me a big thick slice of Christmas pudding. It was full of treacle and was very dark and sticky, but I decided I should eat it all to be polite, but then she went and cut me another big slice. When we were finished visiting we returned along the path through the bog. By this time, it was getting dark and you could hardly see the path at all. I was amazed how Martha could find the way back across, I was afraid we would end up in a big bog hole, but we never did.

The three local farmers, Miley O'Brien, Bill Farrell and Uncle Patsy, used to always work together to help one another on their farms. One of the major events on the farm during my stay used to be the hay making. The meadow was cut using a horse and a mowing bar. They would start at the outer edge of the field and cut in towards the centre. The rabbits that were hiding in the meadow and the corncrakes that were nesting there, would keep running in towards the centre. But when there was only a little bit of meadow left in the middle they would run out and scatter in all directions. The corncrakes were just beginning to decline in numbers then and the farmers didn't like that they had to disturb them nesting, but still they had to get their hay cut. In time, the corncrakes died out in Wicklow and most parts of the country as well.

When the cut grass dried out and turned into hay it was heaped up into big cocks around the field, then they would yoke up Billy the horse and attach a linked chain under the hay cock and tie a rope around the base of the cock. When they had it attached, they let me sit up on top of the cock of hay as Billy sligged it down from the Top field out onto the roadway and down into the haggard. By the end of the day, after sligging in all the hay cocks, the road would be littered with rolls and wisps of hay.

Uncle Patsy also taught me how to make hay ropes using a little implement called a twister. You attached a metal hook that was at one end of the twister into the hay and then as you twisted the handle the hay twisted into a rope and you kept feeding the hay along towards the hook until you had the length of rope you wanted. After the hay was heaped up into haycocks in the field these ropes were used to tie it down and secure it until it was drawn into the hayshed.

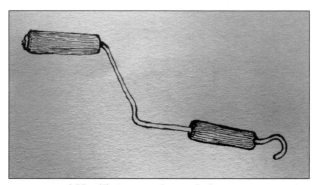

A Hay Twister used to make hay ropes
Illustration by Róisin Beirne

At that time on the farm they had up to six cows milking. I learned how to milk and during the summer I would milk the Kerry cow as she was the quietest. I remember at milking time the cats would be lined up and waiting for their share of the fresh milk which would be poured into a container for them at the cow house door. But some of them couldn't wait that long so they would come sit with their mouth open at a particular spot in the cowshed and we would squirt the milk directly from the cow into their mouths.

Uncle Jimmy was a great man for hunting rabbit. He would often come in with a dozen or more rabbits hung across the crossbar of the bike. I remember once he brought me along on one of the night time lamping expeditions. It was probably a dangerous thing to do but it was a great adventure for me.

Jimmy always kept several dogs for rabbit hunting, including the terrier called Skipper that came from our house in Dublin. He used to keep his three ferrets in a jute sack, tied at the neck. Before he would send a ferret into the burrow after the rabbits, he would put a long lead around its neck and attach a bell to it. Jimmy nearly always got his ferret back. Although sometimes he would have to follow the sound of the bell and dig him out of the burrow. When the rabbit bolted from the burrow, the dogs were ready and waiting. Jimmy kept special heavy-duty gloves for handling the ferrets.

There were a lot of rabbits in the countryside at that time and people made good money catching them and selling them to the dealers. Once a week the dealer's van used to call to the farmhouse to buy the rabbits, also some of these dealers used to sell bread and other household supplies. In the summers I was staying there I can remember two different vans calling, Staffords and Wholohans.

I had my own little source of income from the rabbits. Very soon after I started going down to stay on the farm Uncle Patsy showed me how to set a gin rabbit trap. Looking back now as an adult it seems very cruel to the poor rabbit but at the time the rabbits did a lot of damage to the crops on the farm and also they provided a much-needed source of income during the 1940s when people had very little money. So as a child I just accepted that trapping rabbits was another part of life on the farm. As well as learning how to trap rabbits to sell them, I also learned how to skin the rabbit after you killed it and how to gut and wash it and then cook it.

Sometimes instead of a rabbit, you would catch a stoat or a weasel in the trap. Then you would have to make sure they were dead before you took them out as they could attack you. Uncle Jimmy made a lot of money from hunting the rabbits and he used to add this money to his savings which he kept in a press that was built into the wall of the bedroom.

When I first started staying on the farm there were no ceilings in the rooms of the farmhouse, it was just the exposed timbers of the old angled roof. Then one summer when I came to stay they had put in low plywood ceilings in the rooms. One of the consequences of this improvement was that my bedtime now became very noisy and a bit frightening. The back of the house was built up against the earth bank of the old orchard. The soil came up quite near to the eaves of the house. After the plywood ceilings were put in mice and perhaps sometimes rats were able to come in from the orchard under the eaves and down on to the upper side of the new ceilings. Their scurrying on the plywood made a terrible racket and was quite frightening at night time.

The putting in of these new ceilings had a much more detrimental effect for uncle Jimmy. The rodents were now able to come in through the eaves onto the ceiling and from there they made their way down through the old walls into the press in the bedroom where Jimmy kept all his money rolled up in a big wad of notes. One day when he went to put some more of his rabbit earnings into the press he made the grim discovery that the mice had chewed through his life's savings. He was devastated at the loss, he brought the chewed remains of the notes into the bank in Wicklow where the manager tried to salvage anything he could from the shredded remains.

It was not too long after that, that Jimmy emigrated to Australia. By this time his father had passed away and Patsy was running the farm. Whether his decision to emigrate was as a result of losing his savings and Patsy taking over the running of the farm, or perhaps he had already planned to go to Australia anyway and his savings were to help him to get set up there when he arrived.

In the summer of 1947 I was 11 years of age and was staying down on the farm. One day I was standing in the porch at the front of the house looking out into the farmyard while Jimmy and Patsy were sitting in the kitchen. My grandfather was walking across the yard and suddenly I saw him fall down. I called to Patsy and Jimmy that granddad had fallen and they ran out to him. But when they got to him they realised he was after having a heart attack and was dead.

I was quickly removed inside and over the next couple of days I was shielded from all the preparations for the funeral. A few days after the funeral my mother took me with her back home to Dublin.

Sometimes in the evening time some of the neighbours might drop by. A regular visitor to the house was Mick the Rocher Doyle. Mick was an elderly man who lived on his own in a little house just inside the woods off the lane near Connollys' farm. He would come visit at least 2 or 3 evenings in the week and he would sit with Patsy and Jimmy by the fireside and they would smoke and talk for hours, Mick used to smoke a little clay pipe. Sometimes he would make himself very comfortable by stretching out on the settlebed beside the fire, with a pillow under his head.

The settlebed depicted in this photograph is very similar to the settlebed that the Rocher Doyle would have rested himself on in Connolly's farmhouse. This photograph is reproduced here by kind permission of Christiaan Corlett, who photographed the settlebed in a house in Killiskey, Co. Wicklow.

The neighbours in Aghowle always watched out for one another. Uncle Patsy would never let a morning pass without going out into the farmyard and looking over towards the trees around Mick the Rocher's house and checking for a little plume of smoke. Then he would know that Mick was up and about and all was well.

When I started going down to the farm for my summer holidays they had a big thundering horse called Billy. Then one of the summers when I went down Billy was gone. He had died during the wintertime and uncle Patsy told me he had buried him in a field on the farm beside the ruins of Kate Dempsey's house. Another summer I was there Patsy went to the fair in Ashford to buy a new horse. He bought the horse for £20 from a man who lived near Bray and the man assured him that the horse was very suitable for farm work. But when he got him home the horse was very flighty and could not be yoked.

Patsy could not afford to be at the loss of his money, so he had to take the horse all the way back to Bray. In the end the man agreed to take the horse back and gave Patsy back his money.

While all the farm work around the townland at that time was done by horse power, Miley O'Brien was ahead of his

time and had a tractor. To a young boy like me this was a big powerful machine. One day, Miley was going with the tractor over to collect his turf from the bog in Moneystown and he brought me along with him. As there was no traffic on the roads at that time he let me sit beside him and drive the tractor on the way over to the bog. I was delighted with myself until suddenly, out of nowhere, a motor car appeared around a corner. Miley, myself and the car driver all got a terrible fright and Miley quickly pushed me aside and got control of the tractor before we all ended up in the ditch.

The roads at that time were not tarred but were surfaced with small stones and gravel. A local man called Bill Lee, who lived in the little cottage below O'Brien's farm, was employed by the County Council to help upkeep the stretch of road from Ballycullen to Aghowle. He used to break the stones for the road and he always wore a big pair of goggles. He had to work no matter what the weather, so if it was raining he would be all dressed up in his oil skins. I often used to stop and chat to him on the roadside as he was working.

I also remember at that time tinkers used to call to the farmhouse and repair buckets and such things. In those days, they were very skilled tinsmiths and very valued by the farmers for their work around the farmyard.

There were always dogs on the farm for herding the sheep and cattle and Jimmy kept dogs too for hunting rabbits. One time when Patsy came to visit our house in Dublin he became very attached to a little terrier dog we had called Skipper. My father wanted to give Patsy the dog to bring back to the farm, but my younger brother Jim was very fond of the dog and was not happy at all when he heard the dog was going to Wicklow. So, my father got around this by telling Jim that the dog was not been given away at all, but he was just going down to stay for just a little while on the farm to learn how to catch rabbits. Jim seemed happy with this and proudly told everyone that Skipper was down in Wicklow getting trained by uncle Jimmy's dogs to kill rabbits

I was not usually down on the farm at harvest time, but I do recall that one time I was there for a meitheal.[9] My mother was there too and she and the other local women were working away in the kitchen preparing food for the men. The big threshing mill stood in the haggard and all the local men had turned up to help. There was a lot of noise and activity and people were trying to keep me away from all the dust and chaff that was flying about. Although I was just a young lad I remember marvelling at this system of everyone coming together to get the job done.

Each summer I looked forward to the school holidays as I knew I could then go down to the farm in Aghowle for the summer and at the end of each summer, I hated having to leave and come back to Dublin. But when I reached about the age of 14 or 15 my idyllic summers on the farm came to an end. By that time I was old enough to get employment for the summer picking fruit in Lamb Brothers, which later became Fruitfield, in Donabate. As I was the third oldest of seven boys any extra income coming into the household helped to provide for and educate, myself and my 6 brothers.

Although my long summer vacations on the farm had come to an end, my connection with Aghowle and the Connolly family has remained all through my lifetime. I made many visits back to the farm until it was sold in the 1970s and then I continued to visit Patsy and his family in the bungalow they built at Slanelough crossroads. Now nearly 70 years later, my memories of those childhood summers on the farm and the people of that close-knit farming community, are still very much alive in my mind.

During the 1940s, as his father entered old age, Patsy Connolly took over more of the responsibility and active running of the farm while Jimmy worked in Laragh House and engaged in his rabbit hunting business. Then in 1947, as Patrick was reaching his late 80s, he passed away.

The following few years saw significant changes on the farm. Just over

---

9   A meitheal (pronounced *meht*-hill) is an old tradition where people in rural communities gathered together on a neighbour's farm to help save the corn, hay or some other crop. The community would work each farm in turn.

three years after his father's death, in December 1950 Jimmy Connolly migrated to Australia along with another local man from Castlekevin, named Alf Belton. The two men left for their voyage in style, as May Curley of Castlekevin used to recall that she had washed and ironed their shirts for them the night before they left. The hot climate in Australia did not suit Jimmy and after some time he left and came back and settled in England, but did not make contact again with his family for nearly 30 years. Sadly, the whereabouts of Alf Belton remain unknown as he lost contact completely with his family.

Also around the same time, Patsy met and married a young woman from a few miles away. She was May Pierce, a farmer's daughter from Ballinastraw. The couple married on the first of August 1951. Patsy used to joke that the wedding date had been fixed to suit the activities on the farm – it was between the saving of the hay and the cutting of the corn.

Patsy Connolly and May Pierce (centre) on their wedding day outside Rathdrum Church.
Also in picture are Bill Farrell Aghowle, and May's sister Peggie

In the following years, the couple had three daughters, Ann born 1954, Mary 1955 and myself, Margaret, in 1959.

The story of this house continues in the concluding chapter, "Chapter 14: The End of an Era", see section "House 8: Connolly's".

House No. 9 (Mooney, Doyle)

House No. 9 was located a short distance off the left-hand side of the laneway known as the Back Road that ran from opposite House No. 8 through to the Slanelough-Barnbawn road, to a junction beside the Wart Stone.

Artist's impression of House No. 9 based on the 1901 and 1911 census records and the author's childhood memory of the house.
Illustration by Róisín Beirne

Historical Summary	
Families:	Mooney, Doyle
1832 Land Records	Lease holder could not be identified
1839 OSI map	2 Dwelling houses and farm buildings close by, but are most likely not the later farmhouse here.
1850 Glanmore Estate Records	Darby/Jeremiah Moran is leasing 51 acres of land
1854 Griffith's Land Valuation	Darby/Jeremiah Moran leasing 51 acres
1901 Census	Henry (Rocher) Doyle and family, living in a three roomed, slate roofed, house
1911 Census	Henry (Rocher) Doyle and family
Last family to farm here:	Most likely Peter Mooney, possibly through tenants
Last family to live here:	Mick (the Rocher) Doyle late 1950s

Family History

The early history of this house is unclear. The Ordnance Survey map of 1839 indicates two dwellings in the general vicinity of this house, but it appears that the house that was here in the later part of the 19th century and into the 20th century may have replaced one of these dwellings. As there were considerable undocumented changes in the land holdings at Aghowle Upper between the 1830s and the 1850s, it is not clear who may have leased the surrounding lands in the 1830s.

By 1854, Griffith's Valuation records show that Jeremiah (also known as Darby) Moran was leasing a house and 51 acres here. Records from the early 1860s show that Jeremiah Moran is no longer recorded in the townland, but his holding and some surrounding lands appear to now be leased by Peter Mooney *Big* who has a lease for 92 acres here. Peter Mooney *Big* was from the nearby townland of Tomriland, which was another part of the Glanmore Estate and he also held leases for land and several houses there. Another branch of his family recorded as Peter Mooney *Little* also held land in Tomriland.

It is not certain that Peter Mooney himself lived in this house, or whether he resided in Tomriland and managed this farm from there - he may have employed a herdsman to live here and manage his lands at Aghowle. There are indications that he may at one stage have rented out this house, which he was leasing from the Glanmore Estate. Petty Court records show that in 1884 he took a case against a Mr. Gormley who had failed to quit Peter Mooney's cottage at Aghowle.

Who occupied the dwelling between 1884 and the late 1880s is not known but sometime around 1890, a man named Henry Doyle, along with his family, began renting the house from Peter Mooney Big. This Doyle family was to continue living here for the next 70 years.

Henry Doyle had married Sarah Kane in the Roman Catholic parish of Wicklow in 1863. No address was given for the bride or groom, but baptism records identified for a number of their children show that the family was living at Newbawn near Rathdrum in the late 1860s and in the 1870s. In the 1911 Census, Sarah Doyle recorded that she had given birth to 9 children, 5 of which were still alive at that time. The Doyle's children were: Henry, Mary, John, Ellen, Mary, Michael, Julia, Patrick and Sarah.

When the Doyle family moved to live in Aghowle around 1890, they rented this house from Peter Mooney Big. It does not appear that they were leasing any land, other than perhaps a garden or small field around the house. It is however possible that Henry had come here as an employee of Peter Mooney, to work on Peter's farm at Aghowle.

The only record for Henry Doyle here in the townland during the 1890s, is his dog license record.

In the 1901 Census, the household consists of Henry, his wife Sarah and three of their adult children, Henry, Michael and Patrick. Their adult son John is married and living in House No. 7. The house here is described as a three-roomed slate roofed house, with three windows to the front. There are two farm buildings, a fowl shed and a cow shed, so perhaps the Doyle family did have the use of a small garden or field around the house on which to graze a cow.

By the time of the 1911 Census, there are only three of the Doyle family remaining in the family home, parents Henry and Sarah and son Michael. There are still two outbuildings but they are now described as a fowl shed and a general shed. I did not find a record for Henry Doyle's death, but his wife Sarah lived a long life and died here in 1928, aged 89 years.

When I was a child in the 1960s, I remember some of the older neighbours still recalled Sarah Doyle and told how she used to like sitting by the fireside smoking a little clay pipe. If a neighbour dropped in unannounced, as was often the custom at the time, she would quickly hide the pipe under her apron. But as she sat there in conversation with her visitor, the telltale smoke would begin to appear from under the apron. Like the surname Byrne, Doyle was also very common in Wicklow, so each family had a nickname. These Doyles were known as "The Rocher" Doyles, but I have not as yet been able to find out how they got this name.

After Sarah and Henry Doyle passed away, their son Mick the Rocher remained living here in the house and working as an agricultural labourer in the local area. He is remembered as a slightly eccentric man, who was well read and had extensive knowledge of the local turf banks and was an expert on everybody's turbary rights. The late John Timmons whose family ran the local shop in Parkmore recalled Mick coming into their shop in the 1940s:

> *Mick the Rocher Doyle, he was King of the Bog, for he knew everybody's turbary rights. He was retired by that time and he used to spend a lot of time in Joe Ryan's of Slanelough. Mick would come into the shop on a Saturday evening, there would be a lot of lads in the shop, he would stand in the corner and start giving out at the top of his voice about the government, the football, or maybe the bog boundaries. But sure, people would be doing their shopping and nobody would be paying any heed to him at all.*

Mick remained renting the house here and over time the ownership of the house passed from Peter Mooney Big to his sister Esther Mooney and in time Mooney's land and house was bought by the Tighe family of Rosanna.

The Tighe family continued to rent the house to Mick. Then around 1930, when Tighes sold the surrounding land to the Ministry of Lands for tree planting, an agreement was reached with Mick that he could remain renting the house for his lifetime. The only stipulation was that he had to vacate the house briefly each year in order that he did not establish squatting rights. My father told me that once a year an official from the forestry would arrive and put Mick outside his house and lock the door and when Mick had stayed out for the specified time, the official unlocked the door and Mick returned to his house for another year.

The land around his house was planted with forestry trees. In time as the plantation grew up, Mick's house became surrounded by the trees. People with whom I spoke, who recalled visiting the house remember it as a dark and strange place just a little way inside the forest. But Mick appears to have been happy here, where he had lived since he was a young boy. Like everyone else in the townland at that time, Mick had no electricity or water in the house. He used to go a short distance through the trees to the spring well in Farrell's bog to get a supply of fresh water.

The general picture that formed from people's recollections gave me an initial image of an eccentric elderly bachelor who lived in his house in the woods. But my mother's memory of him gave me a different view of the man. When my parents married in 1951 and my mother moved into the farmhouse, Mick the Rocher who lived nearby was a regular caller to our farmhouse.

When my oldest sister Ann was born in January 1954, she was the first child born in Aghowle Upper for about 30 years. Mick the Rocher was by that time a man in his 80s, who had never married and who had lived for many years on his own. My mother recalled how the summer following my sister's birth, Mick the Rocher would call regularly to the farmhouse to take the new baby out in her pram and he would wheel her up to Slanelough crossroads and back.

With the help of his neighbours, Mick remained living at home in his house in the woods well into his 80s - but as his health deteriorated in the latter half of the 1950s, he had to move into the care of the County Home in Rathdrum, where he saw out his final days. Mick passed away in the summer of 1960 and is buried in Glenealy cemetery.

The now unoccupied house reverted back to the Forestry and in the 1960s and 1970s it was used as a shelter for the forestry workers and also for the timber men who had begun to fell the now mature trees in this area of the forestry. With a ready supply of timber, they were able to light a good fire in the big open fireplace - on cold or wet days they would sit and warm themselves as they brewed up tea in their billy cans and sometimes played cards around the fireside. The upper room of the house was also used at times to stable a horse for the timber men.

With the passing of time the roof began to deteriorate, then in time the walls also began to fall and a large laurel hedge that had been planted at the back of the house began to grow around the ruins.

Recently while rooting around to discover how much of the ruins remained, I came across some relics of the time when the Doyle family had lived here. I found the remains of some fancy patterned delph, which may have dated back to Sarah Doyle's time living here, some of these pieces appear as if they may have been the good china taken out for special visitors.

Also among the ruins I found a brown bottle embossed with the words Halls Tonic Wine. This product appears to date back to the 1920s when its contents were said to fortify and strengthen the body. Sarah Doyle had given birth to 9 children and died at the age of 89 years in 1928, so perhaps this drink, as well as smoking her clay pipe may have contributed to her long life.

Hall's Tonic Wine bottle found at the ruins of the Rocher Doyle house, 2017 Photograph by Róisín Beirne

Remains of delph which were found at the ruins of the Rocher Doyle house in 2017 Photograph by Róisín Beirne

In my childhood during the 1960s, my sisters and I used to play in and around this house. At that time, it was unoccupied and only used by the forestry men and their horses. By then, the vegetation around the outside had begun to grow wild. While I knew a family named Doyle had lived here, I did not realize as a child that it had been the family home of the Rocher Doyles for over 70 years and was inhabited until shortly before my birth in the late 1950s.

I only ever knew it in a state of disrepair - hence I was very surprised to learn that at the start of the 20th century, this very cottage had won prizes for its upkeep and appearance. While researching through some old copies of the Wicklow Newsletter newspaper, I came across a copy of the Wicklow Newsletter and Arklow Reporter, dated Saturday October 1st, 1910. In it, there is a report of the allotted prizes by the County Wicklow Committee of Agriculture for the competition of cottages and plots, throughout the county.

The results show that the county was divided into different divisions and classes and that in the division covering Wicklow/Delgany/Powerscourt/Newcastle and Glendalough, Henry Doyle's cottage and plot at Aghowle was awarded fifth place in the Class 1 category. To get some idea of what the judges were looking for in this competition, here is an extract from the judge's report, printed with the list of prize winners:

The gardens in most places were clean and well cultivated with a good variety of vegetables, fruit and flowers; the general arrangement of the garden, walks and fences was fairly satisfactory. The cottages were well kept, clean and neat and everywhere the importance of light and fresh air seems to be much appreciated. Many competitors appear to imagine that a large number of little ornaments are necessary. While this is not so, it adds very much to the labour of keeping the place clean. Paint seems to be used to advantage on the gates and woodwork of the premises.

The quality of the poultry was generally good, but the houses in many cases were not satisfactory, not clean or whitewashed. The manure heaps in general were neat and well arranged and in a few cases tanks for the collection of the liquid was set down with much benefit, as could be seen by the fine collection of vegetables in those places.

From researching through the Wicklow newspapers dating from the first decade of the 20th century, I noted that Henry Doyle's cottage at Aghowle appeared a number of times among the list of prizewinners, although never actually gaining the coveted first prize. But finding it listed among these prizewinners helped me to realize that the abandoned stone cottage I played in as a child had once been an exceptionally well kept and cared-for family home.

Since House No. 9 has not been occupied since the end of the 1950s, this concludes its history.

House No. 10 (Byrne, Dempsey)

House No. 10 was located on the right-hand side of the laneway known as the Back Road in Aghowle Upper.

Artist's impression of House No. 10 based on the 1901 and 1911 census records and people's memories of the ruined walls.
Illustration by Róisín Beirne

Historical Summary	
Families:	Byrne, Dempsey
1832 Land Records	Francis Byrne leasing 11 acres land here
1839 OSI map	A dwelling house and farm buildings marked here
1850 Glanmore	Estate Records Francis Byrne leasing 23 acres of land
1854 Griffith's Land Valuation	Francis Byrne leasing 18 acres
1901 Census	4 Byrne brothers, living in a three-roomed thatched farmhouse.
1911 Census	2 Byrne brothers remaining.
Last family to farm here:	Andrew Byrne 1925 and his niece Kate Dempsey 1935

Family History

The history of this house and land can be definitively traced back to the land records of 1832, when it was occupied by the Byrne family. From the local church and other records, there is evidence of the same family living here earlier in the 19th century and possibly much earlier.

The local church records show that Francis Byrne married Mary Moran in 1821 and the couple had at least 6 children: Rose, Bridget, James, John, Francis and Andrew. It is likely that Francis Byrne's family had been living in this locality for some time, but it is difficult to establish for certain.

Byrne was an extremely common name in Wicklow, so it is difficult to distinguish individual families. In the Hearth Money Rolls of the mid-1600s, there were 3 Byrne families recorded in the townland. The church records from the mid-1700s also show quite a few entries for Aghowle marriages and baptisms with the Byrne surname. Given the timings, it is quite likely that Francis was a descendant of one of these families. Likewise, Francis's wife, Mary Moran, was a member of the well-established Morans of Aghowle and Ballycullen.

The Glanmore Estate list of tenants for 1832 records a Francis Byrne leasing 11 acres of land at Aghowle, while the Ordnance Survey map shows there was a dwelling house and farm buildings here in the late 1830s.

According to the Griffith's Valuation land records of 1854, Francis was leasing 18 acres of land and a dwelling house here. Five of Francis and Mary's six children did not marry and they remained living for their lifetime on the family farm. In August 1864, Bridget (who was my great grandmother) married a shoemaker named James Dempsey in Ashford church[10] and their marriage was registered in the Ashford registration district. Bridget's husband, James, was from Co. Wexford but was living in Rathnew at the time. The couple started their married life in nearby Parkmore and after a number of years they moved to Glenealy. Bridget and James had 7 children, of which only three daughters survived. Later, two of these daughters came here to House No. 10 to care for their aging uncles.

The lease for this house and farm transferred from Francis to his eldest son James in 1885, indicating that Francis died around this time and it is likely that his wife Mary was also deceased by this time. In 1898, Rose, who was single and living here with her brothers, died aged 70 years.

The five Byrne siblings seemed to have lived quiet hardworking lives here on their farm - apart from always paying their rent on time and renewing their dog licence, there are few records relating to the family. Francis, or

---

10 In August 1991, some 127 years later, I would myself get married in that same church - certain traditions and practices manage to survive through many generations!

Frank as he was often called, did appear to be either a very religious person or a very well-liked person - or perhaps both. As I was researching the families in and around the townland, I was struck by the number of times Frank's name appeared as a sponsor on baptismal records. Over about four decades, he was named as a baptismal sponsor for nearly every family in the surrounding neighbourhood.

Although perhaps he was not always very pious as in 1902, he did appear once in the Petty Court records, when he was charged six shillings for being found drunk on the public road in Wicklow Town while in charge of an ass and cart. At that time, his niece Annie Dempsey (my grandmother) was housekeeping for Frank and his brothers. This entry in the Petty Courts conjured up for me a vision of my grandmother sitting in the late evening in the Byrne's farmhouse with a dried up burnt dinner as Frank merrily weaved his way up Aghowle with his ass and cart!

In the 1901 Census records, the household consists of the four single Byrne brothers, James, John, Andrew and Francis (Frank). Also living in the house as a housekeeper is Annie Dempsey, the daughter of Bridget Byrne. The house is described as a three-roomed thatched dwelling, with three windows to the front. Although the Byrne farm is smaller than those of their neighbours and a good portion of the ground is boggy, the farm buildings reflect the long history of the family farming here. There are 8 farm buildings: 2 stables, a cow house, calf house, barn, piggery, dairy and a turf shed.

By 1911, two of the elderly brothers are deceased. In 1904, John died aged 71 and in 1910 James died aged 81. Remaining in the house are the brothers Francis and Andrew, both now in their 70s. The description of the house is still the same, but the farm buildings are reduced. There is only 1 stable now and the piggery is gone. In 1913, Francis, the third brother, died aged 72. Andrew, the remaining brother, lived on until 1925. By then, his other niece Kate Dempsey had come to care for him and help to run the farm (her sister Annie having left to marry my grandfather in 1903 and now living close by in House No. 8). Andrew was 87 when he died in 1925 and was the last member of the original Byrne families to live in the townland.

The 5 Byrne siblings, Rose, James, John, Frank and Andrew, all lived their entire lives in this house where they had all been born. On his passing, Andrew willed the house and farm to his niece Kate, who had come to care for him. Kate Dempsey also did not marry and she remained living here and farmed the land until her death in 1935. Julia Byrne of Ballycullen, in her reflections of the 1930s (see section "Reflections: Julia Byrne Reflects on Aghowle and Ballycullen 1920s-1940s"), recalled Kate as an elderly woman who used to dress in black and lived in the thatched farmhouse here. When Kate passed away, she was the last descendant of the Byrne family to live and farm here. We know her grandfather Francis Byrne was living here from at least 1821, but it is likely the family's association with the townland went back much further.

Kate Dempsey C.1890s (?)
This photograph, handed down through our family, is believed to be Kate Dempsey, or perhaps her sister Annie or Rosanna. It is believed from the style of dress that it dates from around the 1890s.

When Kate Dempsey died in 1935, she left this farm and house to her sister Annie Connolly (nee Dempsey) and her brother-in-law Patrick Connolly, who were living in House No. 8. The main part of Connolly's farm lay across the road from the Byrne-Dempsey farm and several separated fields of Connollys land actually lay at the top end of the Byrne's farm, bordering Slanelough. Byrne's farmhouse was not lived in again and in time became ruined.

My father told me the following story relating to this house. A number of years after the house became vacant, my father was returning alone one dark night from a card game in Slanelough. As he was passing down the roadway by the Byrne's abandoned house, he heard noise from within and a strange eerie sound. He became very frightened and hurried home convinced that some of the Byrne's ancestors were not at rest and perhaps their spirits had returned to the house. The next day before dusk descended, he decided he should try and put his fears at ease and go over to check the house. Upon entering the abandoned farmhouse, he discovered the disturbed spirits were actually a nest of owls in the old chimney. The strange sound he had heard on the previous night was the calling of the adult owls and the chirping of their chicks.

As the surname Byrne was so common in Wicklow, each family was given another name to distinguish them from one another. The Byrne family that had lived here were known as the *Frank* Byrnes, because of the name Francis, which was not that common in this locality. When the Connollys inherited the Byrne's farm, that new section of the farm was known as Frank's place. The field where the house had stood became known as Frank's Walls and the field above it was the "Bank over Franks".

The field around the ruined house and the bank above it was good grazing land and as children we were regularly sent off in the evening time with the sheep dog to go over to "Franks "to bring home the cows for milking. So, while the Byrne family had died out in the townland several decades before my sisters and I were born, their presence still remained throughout our childhood.

In time, the ruined walls of the old farmhouse disappeared back into the landscape. But in recent decades, a new family have made their home very close by the site of where Byrne's old farmhouse stood. The last of the Byrne children were born in the late 1830s, but after over 150 years, a new generation of Aghowle children were to grow up on this patch of land.

Since House No. 10 has been unoccupied since the mid-1930s, this concludes its history.

The following section gives the final story of how the seven remaining farms of Aghowle gradually ceased their farming activities during the 1960s

Chapter 14

The End of an Era

By the early 1960s, the final chapter in the story of Aghowle's traditional farms and its farming community was beginning to unfold. House No. 7 had burnt down in 1905 and Houses 10 and 9 had been unoccupied since the 1930s and 1950s respectively. So, at the start of the 1960s, there were seven farming families remaining in the townland.

House No. 2: Shannon's

In April 1962, Charlie Shannon died at House No. 2. Charlie, like his father before him, had lived into old age and Charlie died in the house where he had been born 87 years earlier. In his final years he was still pottering about the house and farmyard on his two walking sticks, but it was his niece Tess James, who was living in the farmhouse with him at that time, who was looking after the farm. As well as looking after Charlie and the little farm, she also ran her dress-making business from the house. For the last year or two of his life, Charlie spent most of his time on the settlebed by the kitchen fire, where he sat chatting to visitors during the daytime and slept by the heat of the fire at night.

On his passing, Charlie left the house and farm to Tess, who had remained there to care for him in his old age. After his passing, Tess stayed for a few years and continued to run her dressmaking business, but the location was very quiet and remote. She decided to sell up and move to Bray where the demand for dressmaking would be better. The following is the auctioneer's sale notice as it appeared in the Wicklow People newspaper, giving details of the auction on Wednesday 4th March 1964:

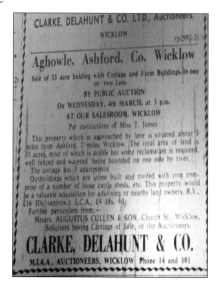

When Tess James closed the door on House No. 2, it ended the last chapter

---

Aghowle, Ashford, Co. Wicklow
Sale of 35 acre holding with Cottage and farm buildings, in one or two lots

By PUBLIC AUCTION
On WEDNESDAY, 4th MARCH, at 3p.m.
AT OUR SALEROOM WICKLOW
Per instruction of Miss T. James

This property which is approached by lane is situated about 3 miles from Ashford, 7 miles from Wicklow. The total area of land is 35 acres, most of which is arable but some reclamation is required, well fenced and watered being bounded on one side by river.
The cottage has 3 apartments.
Outbuildings which are stone built and roofed with iron comprise of a number of loose cattle sheds etc. This property would be a valuable acquisition for adjoining or nearby land owners.
R.V. £6 –10s, L.C A £4 18s 10d
Further details from –
Messrs. AGUSTUS CULLEN & SONS, Church Street Wicklow
Solicitors having Carriage of Sale, or the auctioneers

CLARKE, DELAHUNT & CO
M.I.A.A. AUCTIONEERS WICKLOW phone 14 and 101

---

in the life of this dwelling as a farmhouse. She was the last member of the Shannon family to live and farm here - it was the end of at least 130 years of continuous occupation by the Shannon family. Her mother Kathleen (or Kate as she was known) had been born here in April 1883 and her grandfather was also born here.[11] Her great grandparents Esther and Thomas are recorded farming here in the Glanmore Estate records in 1832.

Tess James died in September 1968 in Bray, Co Wicklow.

The land was bought by a farmer from one of the surrounding townlands but as he had no need for the dwelling house and farm buildings, they were separated from the land, and after a while they were sold on. The farmhouse remained vacant for several years.

During this time, the weeds grew up around the farmyard and garden and at times sheep from the surrounding land would make their way into the dwelling house. But after a few years, the house was bought by a family from Dublin and over time they lovingly restored and upgraded the house and made it habitable again, and the house is now currently occupied.

---

11 Whether that was in 1809 or 1839 is somewhat unclear - see the story of House No.2.

Shannon's unoccupied farmyard 1970s
Photograph courtesy of Ed. Ryan, the current owner.

House No. 4: Bradshaw's

Around the same time that Tess James sold the Shannons' farm and house, another local farmer was also on the move. The Bradshaw family had originally moved to Aghowle nearly 50 years earlier in 1918. In 1943, Dick Bradshaw and Florrie Sheane had married and by the early 1960s, the couple had 6 children. While continuing to farm the land at Aghowle Lower, Dick had also realised that farming was moving away from the use of horses to the use of tractors and more technical machinery. He had invested in a range of farm machinery and went out for hire to work for local farmers who had not the means or the interest in investing in machinery themselves. As time progressed, Dick realised that making a living from the hilly fields under Carrick was very difficult and that he would be better putting his efforts into just working for hire with his machinery. So the Bradshaws decided to sell their farm at Aghowle and move down to live at Nun's Cross.

It is not known when exactly the Bradshaw family sold their house and farm and I did not manage to locate the sale notice, but the land valuation records [VOI/CB/AL] show that both the house and the land changed hands a number of times from the mid-1960s into the early 1970s. I did locate the auction notice for when a Mr David Pearson Myles was re-selling the house and lands in May 1969 – see below.

To the best of my knowledge, the Bradshaw family were the last family to live in this house and farm here. In 1973, the now current owners bought the old farmhouse which was beginning to fall into disrepair and they restored and upgraded the house and the remaining farm buildings and it has been their family home ever since. While there have been some changes to the exterior, it is still quite similar in appearance to the house depicted in the photograph of the Hatton family living here c.1890 (see the story of House No. 4).

Aghowle, Ashford, Co. Wicklow

Sale of Compact Farm of 47 acres with Residence and Out -Buildings in poor repair.
BY PUBLIC AUCTION ON FRIDAY, 30th MAY
AT 3PM
AT THE GRAND HOTEL WICKLOW.
Per instruction of David Pearson -Miles Esq.

The property is situated about 3 miles from the weekly livestock market at Ashford, 7 miles Wicklow and 31 miles Dublin.

The two storey slated house, which is in very poor condition, is approached by a short lane and comprises the following accommodation: Sitting room, Kitchen, 3 Bedrooms and Dairy. The house occupies a pleasant position, has a small garden in front and could be made quite attractive. Main electricity and never failing water supply by gravitation. New 3 span Hay Shed with lean-to, other Out-Buildings in poor repair. The total area of land is 46 acres 3 roods and 10 perches, which is dry and of good sound quality, with the exception of about 3 acres of rough grazing. The lands which are all under grass, have been heavily limed and manured and are in wonderful heart, good fencing and an ample supply if water from stream.

The entire is held subject to Land Annuities amounting to £11 0s 10d. approximately R.V.£21 6s on land and £2 10s on buildings.

Further particulars from J.H. McCarroll & Co. Church Street, Wicklow, Solicitors having Carriage of Sale, or the Auctioneers.

House No. 3: O'Reilly's

In the mid-1960s, as the above two farms on Aghowle Lane were sold and their farmhouses left vacant for some time, a third dwelling also became unoccupied. In this case, the farm land was not sold off. In January 1952, when Paddy O'Reilly died at the young age of 35, his widow Kate was left with two very young sons to care for. Kate remained living at Aghowle and farming the O'Reilly land while rearing her sons, Tommy and Terry.

When the boys had finished their education, they went off to work and around the same time a relative of their mother's in Co Wexford became ill. Kate left the farmhouse here to go care for her relative, leaving the O'Reilly's farmhouse vacant. After a number of years, when Kate no longer needed to stay in Wexford, she moved back to live in the Rathdrum area of County Wicklow and in time the farmhouse here fell into ruin.

But the O'Reilly family always retained their land here and have the distinction of being the only Aghowle family from the 19th and 20th centuries to still hold their original farm. While most of the O'Reilly farmland is leased out, a descendant of Paddy and Kate O'Reilly has in recent years returned with their family to the O'Reillys' farm at Aghowle and have built a new family home here close by the site of the original farmhouse. They are now residing on the same land where their ancestors Terence and James O'Reilly were living and farming in 1832 and where other O'Reillys' may possibly have lived for many years before that date.

House No. 6: Farrell's

The next farmhouse and working farmyard that was to disappear from the townland was the Farrell-Moran farm at Aghowle Upper. In October 1960, Sarah Farrell, at a few weeks away from her 88th birthday, died in the farmhouse where she had been born and lived all her life. After Sarah's passing, her son Bill who had not married was left living alone in the farmhouse. By 1967, Bill was sixty years of age and he began to contemplate his future. At that time, farming methods were beginning to change. The era of the horse and small mixed farming was quickly disappearing. The future lay in mechanisation and larger more intensive methods of farming. Bill was a single man approaching old age and did

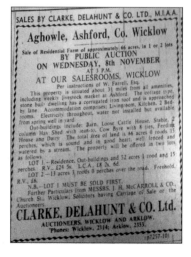

not see his future in this new way of farming. Bill's step-brother Greg Cunniam, who lived in Dublin, suggested that perhaps Bill should sell the farm and move to Dublin where he had family.

After much consideration, Bill did decide to sell up and go join his step-brother's family in the Rathgar area of Dublin. This must have been a very difficult decision for him, as he had lived and worked all his life on the farm. In November 1967, Bill sold his farm and house and headed for Dublin.

On the day Bill Farrell headed for Dublin, latching the farmhouse door for the last time and closing the farm gate behind him, he was leaving the place where his mother Sarah, his grandfather William and his great

---

Aghowle Ashford Co. Wicklow

Sale of Residential farm of approximately 66 acres in 1 or 2 lots
BY PUBLIC AUCTION
ON WEDNESDAY, 8TH NOVEMBER
AT 3 P.M.
AT OUR SALES ROOMS, WICKLOW
Per instruction of W. Farrell Esq.

The property is situated about 3 ½ miles from all amenities, including weekly livestock market at Ashford. The cottage type stone built dwelling has a corrugated iron roof and is approached by lane. Accommodation comprises: Living room Kitchen, two bedrooms. Electricity throughout, water not installed but available from spring well in yard.

Out-buildings include: Barn, Loose Cattle House, Stable, 2 column Hay Shed with lean-to, Cow Byre with 8 ties, Feeding house and Dairy. The total area of

land is 66 acres 0 rood and 15 perches, which is sound and in good heart, well fenced and watered by a stream. The property will be offered in two lots as follows,

LOT 1 – Residence, Out-buildings and 52 acres 1 rood and 15 perches. R.V., £24.5s. LCA., £8 2s 6d.

LOT 2 13 acres 3 roods 0 perches, over the road. Freehold. R.V., £6

N.B. LOT 1 MUST BE SOLD FIRST

Further particulars from MESSRS. J.H. Mc Carroll &co., Church St., Wicklow. Solicitors having carriage on sale or the Auctioneers.

CLARKE DELAHUNT & CO. Ltd.
AUCTIONEERS, WICKLOW AND ARKLOW.
Phones: Wicklow, 2314 Arklow, 2353

grandfather Simon, had all lived and farmed and the place where they had all drawn their last breath. He was the last descendant of the Moran family to farm here in Aghowle and we know from church records that the family were well established here by the mid-18th century. From available records, Bill's ancestors can be traced back to living on this farm from at least 1813, but it is likely they were farming this land before that date.

While Bill left the townland to move to Dublin, it was not a complete departure. He knew he could return whenever he wanted and stay in either Miley O'Brien's or Patsy Connolly's homes. His black Morris Minor remained a very frequent sight in the townland as Bill returned very frequently at weekends to stay in either O'Briens or Connollys. Then Bill, Miley and Patsy would once again head to Ashford or Rathdrum for a pint on the Saturday night. On the weekends he visited, Bill would also return to his old spot outside the chapel in Parkmore on Sunday mornings to catch up on all the local news.

Farrells' farm land was bought by a farmer from a neighbouring townland and the farmhouse was rented out for a short while, but then lay unoccupied for some years before it was sold on.

The Corcoran family and friends picnicking outside the old farmhouse c.mid 1970s
The Corcorcan family purchased Farrell's farmhouse in the early 1970s.

In the early 1970s, when it was beginning to fall into disrepair, it was bought by the now current owner. This family saw its potential and recognized its history and over time they put much labour and love into restoring the farmhouse, endeavouring to retain as much as possible of its original features and reinstated its thatched roof of old. The new owner also preserved any of the original farm buildings that were still intact, and they got a new lease of life as store rooms and studios.

This spy window, part of the old farmhouse, has been preserved
and retained as a feature by the current owner.
Most of the Aghowle farmhouses were "lobby entry",
i.e. as you entered from the front door into the kitchen there was a wall
screening the fireplace, and the spy window was set into this wall.

2017 - A Return Visit after 170 Years

In June 2017, John Moran of Ohio USA, accompanied by his wife Jan, fulfilled a lifelong wish and came to Ireland to visit the place where his great, great grandfather Thomas Moran left in 1847. As covered in the famine time emigration section of this book "The Moran Family Who Never Forgot Their Townland", Thomas and Ann Moran and their 7 children left Aghowle Upper around 1847 to go to Canada and after a short period moved down to settle in America. Thomas was a member of the Moran family who were well established in Aghowle from at least the mid-18th Century. It is not known if Thomas was born here in House No. 5, but other members of his family definitely were. In records from 1841, [NAI/VOB/AU] when Thomas would have been married with a family of his own, he is recorded living in a house close by this house at Aghowle Upper.

John Moran standing at the home where his Moran ancestors lived from at least 1813
(June 2017)

House No. 1: Short's

In just over a year after Bill Farrell locked up his farmhouse and sold his farm, another homestead of long standing in the townland also came to the end of its farming life. During the 1960s, Dan and Mary Short of House No.1 had continued to farm at Aghowle Lower. Joey Reilly, the boy that had grown up with the family, had completed his education and moved to work in Dublin.

By the 1960s, some of the local farmers had moved on from horse power to tractor power and swapped the bicycle for a car or small van, but Dan and Mary were happy to continue the lifestyle they had enjoyed all their lives. Both were familiar sights as they cycled their bicycles down to the village in Ashford, or over to Moneystown to shop and attend mass. In later years, if Dan needed some heavy work done around the farm one of the neighbours with a tractor would come in to help him and their neighbours were always on hand if either Dan or Mary needed a lift somewhere.

By 1969, Dan Short was seventy-four years of age, but with the help of Mary he was still doing a little bit of farming and was quite active. So, it was a great shock to the local community when he took ill at the end of January and died suddenly. The entire neighbourhood turned out to say farewell to a man who had been part of their local farming community all his life, as his father and his grandfather had been. After his death, Mary, who was sixty-four, found herself living alone in the little farmhouse after thirty-eight years of married life. In the weeks after Dan's sudden passing, her neighbours and relatives called frequently to the house to keep her company and check if she needed anything.

Dan and Mary Short outside their farmhouse in the late 1960s.
Photograph courtesy of Tommy Byrne

One of the regular callers was the local postman, John Mitchell. As John knew Mary was now on her own he would drop into the farmhouse as he was passing, whether he had post to deliver or not. One morning in April as he called to the house, he became concerned. In those days no doors were locked, and callers would come straight into the kitchen. This morning when John saw no sign of Mary about the place and no fire lighting he knew something was amiss. He discovered Mary in the bedroom where she had taken ill during the night. John called for an ambulance and Mary was taken to hospital, but passed away soon after.

So, it came to pass that just ten weeks after the community had turned out to bury Dan, they came out again to lay Mary beside him in Glenealy graveyard and their farmhouse lay closed up and vacant. In January 1969, when Dan Short passed away he had lived out his 74 years in the house where he was born. His father Garrett Short had also been born there in 1848 and Dan's grandfather Patrick Short had lived there from the time he had married Margaret McDaniel in the mid-1840s. Although no address was recorded, an entry in the local church register indicates that it is very likely that Dan's grandmother Margaret McDaniel was born in the same house on 24th October 1818. The family's association with this house and farm spanned a hundred and fifty years.

Joint memorial card for Dan and Mary Short, 1969
Courtesy of Tommy Byrne

Five months after Mary Short's death, the farm and farmhouse was put up for auction. Below is the auctioneer's notice that was printed in the Wicklow People Newspaper.

Again, the land was purchased by a farmer from a neighbouring townland and the farmhouse was separated from the farm and sold on again as a private dwelling. It appears to have changed through a couple of owners in the following years before the house became occupied again. This new family wished to make it their family home and retain many of the original farmhouse features. They also kept some horses, so the original farm buildings were once again in use as

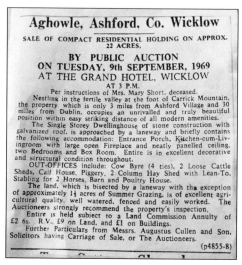

Aghowle, Ashford, Co. Wicklow

SALE OF COMPACT RESIDENTIAL HOLDING ON APPROX. 22 ACRES.

BY PUBLIC AUCTION
ON TUESDAY, 9th SEPTEMBER, 1969
AT THE GRAND HOTEL, WICKLOW
AT 3 P.M.

Per instructions of Mrs. Mary Short, deceased.

Nestling in the fertile valley at the foot of Carrick Mountain, the property which is only 3 miles from Ashford Village and 30 miles from Dublin, occupies an unrivalled and truly beautiful position within easy striking distance of all modern amenities.

The Single Storey Dwellinghouse of stone construction with galvanized roof, is approached by a laneway and briefly contains the following accommodation: Entrance Porch, Kitchen-cum-Livingroom with large open Fireplace and neatly panelled ceiling, two Bedrooms and Box Room. Entire is in excellent decorative and structural condition throughout.

OUT-OFFICES include: Cow Byre (4 ties), 2 Loose Cattle Sheds, Calf House, Piggery, 2 Column Hay Shed with Lean-To. Stabling for 2 Horses, Barn and Poultry House.

The land, which is bisected by a laneway with the exception of approximately 1¼ acres of Summer Grazing, is of excellent agricultural quality, well watered, fenced and easily worked. The Auctioneers strongly recommend the property's inspection.

Entire is held subject to a Land Commission Annuity of £2 6s. R.V., £9 on Land, and £1 on Buildings.

Further Particulars from Messrs. Augustus Cullen and Son, Solicitors having Carriage of Sale, or The Auctioneers.

(p4855-8)

Aghowle Ashford, Co. Wicklow
SALE OF COMPACT RESIDENTIAL HOLDING ON APPROX. 22 Acres
BY PUBLIC AUCTION
ON TUESDAY 9TH SEPTEMBER 1969
AT THE GRAND HOTEL, WICKLOW
AT 3 P.M.
Per instructions of Mrs. Mary Short deceased.

Nestling in the fertile valley at the foot of Carrick Mountain, the property which is only 3 miles from Ashford Village and 30 miles from Dublin, occupies an unrivalled and truly beautiful position within easy striking distance of all modern amenities.

The single Storey Dwellinghouse of stone construction with galvanized roof, is approached by a laneway and briefly contains the following accommodation: Entrance Porch, Kitchen-cum-Living Room with large open Fireplace and neatly paneled ceiling, two Bedrooms and Box Room. Entire is in excellent decorative order throughout.

OUT-OFFOCES include: Cow Byre (4 ties) 2 loose Cattle Sheds Calf House, Piggery, 2 Column Hayshed with Lean-To, Stabling for 2 Horses, Barn and Poultry House.

The land, which is bisected by a laneway with the exception of 1 ½ acres of Summer Grazing, is of excellent agricultural quality, well watered, fenced and easily worked. The Auctioneers strongly recommend the property's inspection.

Entire is held subject to a Land Commission Annuity of £2 6s R.V., £9 ON Land and £1 on Buildings.

Further Particulars from Messrs. Augustus Cullen and Son.
Solicitors having Carriage of Sale, or The Auctioneers.

---

stables. One imagines if Dan Short, a man who had farmed nearly all of his lifetime with horses, was looking down from above, he would have been very pleased to hear the clip clop of hooves about his old farmyard once more.

Six weeks after the initial auction, there was a clearance sale of the contents of the farmhouse and farmyard at Aghowle. Overleaf is the notice for the sale, as it was printed in the Wicklow People.

These items listed represent the lives of several generations of the Short family who lived and farmed here. Farmhouse items such as the painted dresser, iron beds, iron kettles and forms (wooden stools), were beginning to belong to a bygone era. In the farmyard, many of the farm implements listed related to the days of farming with horses, which by now was almost a thing of the past.

AGHOWLE, ASHFORD, CO. WICKLOW

CLEANANCE SALE of Furniture, Horse Implements, Hay, etc.

BY PUBLIC AUCTION

ON WEDNESDAY, 22ND OCTOBER

At 2 p.m.

Per instructions of Daniel Short, Deceased.

Lots briefly include: Mahogany Drop-leaf Table, Sideboard, Mahogany Dining Chair, Cane Table, Wooden Armchair, Pye Electric Radio, Bed Settee, 2 Double Iron Beds, Springs and Mattresses, 2 Wardrobes, Mahogany Dressing Mirror, Chest of Drawers, Pillows, 2Kitchen Chairs, Painted Dresser, Press, 2 Kitchen Tables, 2 Forms, Quantity of Delph, Glassware and Kitchen Utensils, Oil Lamp, Tilly Lamp, 4 Iron Kettles, 3 Iron Pots, Bread Bin, Shoe Last, Plastic Bucket and Basin, Lino, Pictures, Curtains, Etc.

Outside: D.M.B. Plough, Drill Harrow, 3-part Pin Harrow, Root Pulper, Wooden Ladder, Wooden Oats Bin, 3 dozen Sacks, Potato Basket, Tumbling Rake, Stone Roller, Old Mowing Machine and Dray. Hay Forks, Slash Hooks, etc. Sundry Tools, 2 hay Royes, Gent's Bicycle, Small Hand Churn, 2 Milk Buckets, 3 Milk Crocks, Quantity of Scrap Iron and Timber.

Approximately 2 Tons Loose Hay in Shed. Quantity of Farmyard Manure.

ON VIEW MORNING OF SALE

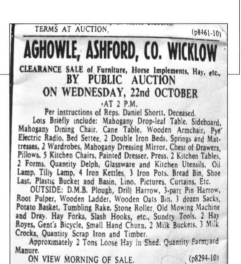

At the end of the clearance auction that day, as the house and farmyard contents were sold and drawn away, most of the evidence that the Short family had lived and farmed here for well over a hundred years, disappeared into the evening dusk.

House 8: Connolly's
During the 1960s, five of the traditional working farmhouses and farmyards in the townland had ceased farming. By the start of 1970, there were only two remaining working farms in the townland of Aghowle, belonging to the O'Brien family and to my own family, the Connollys. My father had married when he was 44 and

Connolly Family outside their
farmhouse, 1970

now as he was in his early sixties, he too was beginning to make decisions about his future in farming.

He had been blessed with three daughters and my two older sisters were by this time out working. Like his neighbour and lifelong friend Bill Farrell, he felt there were many new changes coming in to farming and at his age, he would be better to retire. He and my mother decided that they would sell the farm and farmhouse and keep a small area of land to build a new house on. As well as carrying out mixed farming all his lifetime, my father had also built up over the years a side business of selling cabbage and cabbage plants to half of County Wicklow. My parents decided if they kept a few acres of land they could continue doing this, as well as branching out into sowing a variety of vegetables to sell from the house. The Field Under The Crossroad at Slanelough was ideally suited as the location for the new bungalow and market garden business as it lay at the end of the farm and could be easily separated from the rest of the land. One of the last events to take place on our farm was the shearing of the sheep. On a sunny day in June of that year, my father organised with my school teacher, Arthur Hall, for me to take a half day absence from the national school in Moneystown, so I could go with him to Rathdrum to sell the last load of wool from our farm. After Vincent Pierce inspected the wool and paid my father, we then returned some of the money back to the Pierce family, by going into Pierce's public house where we sat on two tall stools at the bar and my father bought himself a glass of stout and a Club Orange and a bar of chocolate for me.

By the summer of 1971, the new house was completed, and the farm was put up for sale.

This is the auction notice from the Wicklow People newspaper:

AGHOWLE, ASHFORD, CO. WICKLOW
SALE OF A COMPACT FARM OF 70 ACRES
WITH COTTAGE RESIDENCE AND GOOD OUT- BUILDINGS,
BY PUBLIC AUCTION WEDNESDAY 2ND JUNE, AT 3PM
AT THE GRAND HOTEL, WICKLOW
Per instructions of Patrick Connolly Esq.

This good roadside holding is situated about 4 miles south west of Ashford village, 3 miles Glenealy and less than an hour's drive from Dublin. The stone built cottage residence could be made most attractive and briefly comprises: Entrance porch, Kitchen with no. 9 Stanley Range, Dining room, 2 bedrooms, mains electricity throughout, water from nearby spring well. The range of Out-Buildings include: Hay Shed with Lean-to, Machine Shed, 4 Loose Cattle Houses, Calf House, Garage, Tractor House, Cow House and Calf pens, Potato store and Barn. All buildings have electricity laid on and are in excellent condition.

Total area of land is 70 ¼ acres which has been carefully managed for a long number of years and is in great heart. The following crops are included: 6 acres barley, 12 acres excellent meadow and a ½ acre turnips. The remainder of the land is in grass with the exception of 6 acres of rough grazing. The owner is retaining a ½ acre plot of potatoes. All divisions are convenient size, easily worked and well fenced. The property is bisected by a road, giving easy access to all parts.

This is a first class holding which will be evident on inspection.

The auctioneer's notice reflects the changes that had begun to take place in rural Ireland, especially in Co. Wicklow. The wording of the sale notice, highlighting that the cottage was an hour's drive from Dublin, was aimed at a potential buyer who might only want the land and be looking at the option of selling on the dwelling house as a separate private residence. And indeed, that is what did happen. The purchaser who bought the farm planned to lease out the land to farmers from the surrounding locality needing extra grazing or tillage and she saw the potential of upgrading the farmhouse and reselling it as a holiday home or permanent residence for a non-farming family.

Two months after the farm sale, there was a clearance sale of the farm implements and stock.

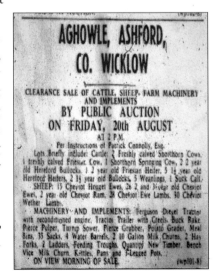

AGHOWLE, ASHFORD, CO. WICKLOW

CLEARANCE SALE OF CATTLE, SHEEP, FARM MACHINERY AND IMPLEMENTS

BY PUBLIC AUCTION
ON FRIDAY, 20th AUGUST
AT 2 P.M.
Per instructions of Patrick Connolly Esq.

Lots briefly include: Cattle: 2 freshly calved Shorthorn Cows, I freshly calved Friesian Cow, I Shorthorn Springing Cow, 2 2-year-old Hereford Bullocks, 1 2-year-old Friesian Heifer, 5, 1 ½ year old Hereford Heifers, 5 Weanlings, 1 Suck Calf.

SHEEP: 15 Cheviot Hogget Ewes, 26 2 and 3-year-old Cheviot Ewes, 2-year-old Cheviot Ram, 28 Cheviot Ewe Lambs, 30 Cheviot Wether Lambs.

MACHINERY AND IMPLEMENTS: Ferguson Diesel Tractor with reconditioned engine. Tractor Trailer with Creels, Buck Rake, Pierce Pulper, Turnip Sower, Pierce Grubber, Potato Grader, Meal Bins, 35 Sacks, 4 Water Barrels, 2, 10-Gallon Milk Churns, 2 Hay Forks, 2 Ladders, Feeding Troughs, Quantity Of New Timber, Bench Vice, Milk Churn, Kettles, Pans And 3-Legged Pots.

ON VIEW MORNING OF SALE

As a sign of the changing times in farming, some of the sale items such as the three-legged pots, old kettles, churn and box iron, were bought at the auction by the owners of local public houses and were destined to be displayed on the pub walls as decorative examples of farming in bygone times.

Lulu Goes out to Pasture

Listed in the above clearance sale notice are 26 2 and 3-year-old ewes - amongst these was our pet lamb Lulu. When the farm was sold in the summer of 1971, Lulu was a two-year-old ewe, but she still would come running across the field to greet us and she still had the occasional inclination to find a way into the farmyard and make her way to the kitchen door for her bowl of cornflakes.

On the day of the clearance sale all the sheep were sold, including Lulu and our father assured us that she had been bought by a very nice farmer who farmed down near the coast. My father told us that he had explained to this man that one of the ewes was a bit exceptional and that the farmer had promised to take good care of her for us. While I'm certain that Lulu must have lived out her days happily on this farm (because that's what the grown-ups had promised their three daughters), if by any slight chance she should have ended up in the butchers, her meat could have been legitimately sold as "corn fed" mutton.

A Short Move
On the day of the clearance sale, when everything had been sold and cleared away, we headed off to take up residence in the new bungalow at Slanelough crossroads about half a mile away. I am sure it must have been an emotional day for my parents, especially my father who had been born there in 1907 and whose father had come to farm there in 1898. But at least he still retained a small connection to the farm in the field around the new house.

In a way, his connection to that field stretched back much further than the land around the farmhouse. The Field Under The Crossroads had been part of the *Frank* Byrnes' family farm that my father's mother inherited in 1935 from her side of the family, so the field where the new house stood had belonged to his mother's people since at least the early 1800s.

A Century of Farm History Disappears in a Day
As the new owner wanted to upgrade and extend our old farmhouse with a view to reselling it, she had workmen move in very quickly to start the job. The farmhouse and outbuildings had originally been laid out in a courtyard style probably sometime during the nineteenth century and all of the farm buildings were built in a rectangle around the dwelling house. If the house was to be enlarged and sold as a stand-alone private dwelling, then all the farm buildings were now surplus to requirements and would not help the sale of the house.

A few weeks after we vacated the farmhouse a bulldozer came in and knocked and flattened all the farm buildings, with the exception of one small building at the entrance gate, thereby opening up the dwelling house to the main road. Many of these old stone buildings had stood there for more than a century, possibly having been built by the Edge or the Power family around the 1850s, or by James Doyle during his forty years farming here between 1858 and 1896. My grandfather and father would have maintained and upgraded some of them over their 70 years farming here.

I imagine my parents must have found this swift change very difficult.

Farmhouse c.1972 – upgraded, extended and farmyard and buildings removed

They were both very house-proud people who kept the farmhouse and farm yard immaculate. Each year on the first fine day in Spring, the whitewash buckets were taken out and the dwelling house and all the stone built farm buildings and all the stone walls facing on to the roadside were whitewashed. Then my mother would whitewash the walls around her flower garden in

The single small farm building that was left standing in 1971 still remains and is used by the current owners.
Also attached to the left side of the building is the original farmgate pier.
The OSI map from the late 1800s indicates a small farm building marked in this location.

front of the house. The neighbours passing by would often joke *"Oh God, it must be going to rain, May Connolly is out whitewashing again"*. Every year or two, my father would repaint the red corrugated roofs of the farmhouse and all the roofs of the farm sheds, as well as repainting his handmade green and white wooden gates leading into the farmyard.

To see all this vanish in a day was hard to comprehend and heart-breaking for them, but both of my parents were very philosophical people and they accepted life's changes and looked to the future. They were very happy with their new home and now freed from the strict routines and demands of the farming day, they had more time to relax and enjoy life.

A New Venture

They set up their market gardening business from the new bungalow at Slanelough crossroads, but while it was very successful, I feel it may have actually run at a loss due to their hospitable and generous natures.

During the busy season there would often be 10 or more people calling daily to the house for potatoes, cabbage plants and an array of other vegetables. As my father would take the customer's order, he would tell them *"sure you go on in along to May and get a cup of tea while I get these ready for you"*. In the kitchen, my mother would have the table set and the kettle on the boil and each caller sat down to tea and a table laden with cake, buns and apple tart. Outside, as my father prepared the ordered vegetables, cabbage plants or potatoes, he always threw in a few extra, *"just in case there might be a small one or a bad one in the order"*. Then my father would arrive in and sit down himself for a cup of tea and a chat with the caller and they would remain sitting there until the next caller arrived.

Nowadays, many garden centres run cafes or tearooms alongside their main business, but I think my parents were perhaps the original of the species. In their case, there should have been a sign on the gate outside advertising *"free tea and cake with every purchase"*.

House 5: O'Brien's

Here, Catherine O'Brien, the last member of the O'Brien family, recalls the final chapter of the O'Brien farmhouse:

> *Looking back, my childhood was idyllic. Perhaps we all think this from the selective memory of adulthood. Even though our family unit was small, we three were very close and I had my 6 Manning cousins in Ashford village. They came on their "holidays" to Aghowle*

and I was a regular in Auntie Nancy's. It wasn't all fun and games though. I had my jobs and helped where I was told, in particular with the sheep, because I loved them. I remember one year we had a lot of hoggets i.e. female sheep having their first lamb and if any of them were having "delivery problems", I had to help turn the lamb as my hands were small. I felt very important. Before school, I would go up to the sheep-fields and check on them. That meant Dad could get on with something else.

O'Brien family and relatives in the farmyard C.1965
L-R:Sheila Touchstone (nee O'Brien) with Galtee the sheepdog, Alec Hobbs and his wife Mary (nee O'Brien), Miley and Bridget O'Brien and their daughter Catherine in front.

When I was very small, I used to attach myself to Tom Sheane, who worked with dad a couple of days per week. I loved Tom and when I heard the 'putt putt' of his motorbike coming down the lane, I would race to get my coat and boots on. I can't say that Tom got much peace to get on with anything much, as I was constantly underfoot. Tom was very patient. He worked for our neighbours too and I was very jealous of them, as they got to spend time with Tom also.

I learned to drive our tractor when I was around 12. I would bring feed up to the stock in the field and in the autumn, bring home a small load of bales to put in the shed. In spring, we would make drills for the veg with a little drilling plough we shared with our neighbours the Smiths of Ballycullen. Dad also had old horse drawn machinery that he adapted for the tractor, some more successfully than others and we earthed up or "moulded" our potatoes with that. Our machine for making windrows in the hay field was also modified from a horse drawn machine. The 60s and early 70s were still a time of 'make do and mend.' There wasn't much money about and my parents came from a time where nothing was wasted.

In the Autumn, we would sell the large cattle that were ready for slaughter. This gave us a lump sum of cash to tide us over the winter. While it seemed a huge sum at the time, maybe 6 or 7 hundred pounds, by the time the feed bill and the vets bill etc. was paid, it shrank quite quickly. Over the winter there was no regular income and this money had to stretch till May or June of the following year, when a few surplus calves were sold. We grew potatoes for ourselves and sold some to local shops. We harvested them in October and made pits or clamps in the field near the house. These clamps were covered with a good coating of straw and sods. The potatoes were thus kept frost free over the winter.

We had lots of farm cats to discourage the mice and other wildlife who quite fancied a spud too. We had turnips which were kept in the same manner. They were put into a container and a handle turned which moved a blade to slice the turnips into big pieces like jumbo chips. These then fell into a big bucket and were fed to the animals. I put my hand in one day when the handle was turning and one of the blades neatly sliced the thumbnail from my right hand … lesson learned.

A source of income in the spring and summer was the sale of butter and eggs. Our hens were bought as "point of lay" pullets, at the gate of Ashford mart. We would have about a dozen hens, running free around the yard, usually Rhode Island Reds or White Leghorns. We would also have a couple of dozen broilers for the pot. We also got day old chicks from a company in Cork. They came on the CIE (now Bus Eireann) bus to Ashford and had to be collected. Lots of the neighbours seemed to get them at the same time and there could be 20 boxes of little day old fluffy yellow chicks sticking their tiny heads out of the airholes in the brown cardboard box and chirping in alarm and excitement.

The boxes were placed at the front near the bus driver and I'm sure the antics of the chicks provided great entertainment for the passengers. There were usually a couple of casualties, so when we got home the chicks were put beside the Range in an old wooden tea chest. There was a heat lamp suspended over the box and they were kept there for a few days until they got over the journey and grew a little bit. Then the youngsters were moved to their house and allowed out as they became bigger. They were truly free range, being outside from early morning picking and scratching.

We could have 4 or 5 dozen eggs per week to sell, once the hens started to lay. Mam would clean them with a damp cloth dipped in bread soda if necessary and the eggs would be sold in Synnotts' shop in Ashford. We also made butter in the summer and sold it too. These, together with early potatoes, (end July,) were our cash crops to keep things ticking over while we waited for the wool sales or the time to sell on sheep or cattle.

While I loved Aghowle and the country life, I was young and restless too. After finishing school, I went on to a course in Horticulture in An Grianan in Drogheda. I was always interested in plants and after college I found employment in a plant nursery and garden centre in Sandycove in Dublin. This was the late 1970s and Dad had semi-retired by then and most of the land was set to our neighbour, Larry Timmons of Ballycullen. Dad and I started to grow spring bedding plants, which my boss sold in the garden centre. This was a sort of hobby for Dad and he loved when we got a good order. He became interested in the different varieties and colours available and loved finding a new plant to grow.

My parents were enjoying this time of their lives. They were taking things easy and had the company of their neighbours and friends. They were involved in their community; my Mother was very active in the Moneystown branch of the I.C.A. They met once a month, (still do) which was a social outlet. Mam also loved her bingo and a game of cards. She was a good card player, having honed her skills in the nurses' home in St. Ita's hospital where she worked before her marriage. Those few years were a good time for the O'Briens.

On Holy Thursday 1986, Mam and I went to Wicklow to shop for the Easter weekend. A beautiful spring morning, we left home around 10am. Dad was out feeding his hens and doing his few jobs. On our return, around 12:30, we found him on the kitchen floor. He had suffered a massive heart attack and died. He was 73. Dad's funeral was on Easter Saturday, in the church he was baptized in. He was laid to rest with his parents, brother and infant son in Rathnew cemetery. Two years later, in March 1988, Mam became unwell. There followed the usual tests and scans, following which she was diagnosed with cancer of the lung. Mam was in St Vincent's University Hospital, Elm Park, awaiting surgery when she died on September 20th of that year. She was 67. She was buried in Rathnew cemetery beside dad and her baby son.

Aghowle was a lonely place without my family. The Aghowle community spirit was strong and the neighbours and my friends pulled me on through a very dark couple of years. The farm was still rented by a neighbour, Larry Timmons, so I had no active farming role. I was working for Wicklow Co. Council at this stage and in the spring of 1990, I made the decision to sell the farm. The sale was by public auction in Bel Air Hotel. A local auctioneer, Billy Clarke handled the sale. There were 2 lots, the dwelling and a small piece of ground and the Raheen, on the other side of the road. The house area was purchased by Larry Timmons, who sold on the house to Jim King and Noreen Keane, who continue to reside there. The Raheen was bought by a Christmas tree farmer.

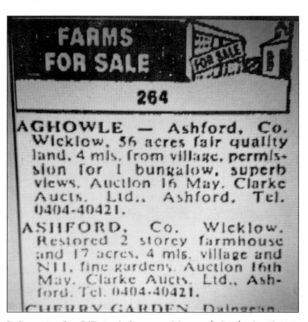

FARMS FOR SALE

264

AGHOWLE — Ashford, Co. Wicklow. 56 acres fair quality land, 4 mls. from village, permission for 1 bungalow, superb views. Auction 16 May. Clarke Aucts. Ltd., Ashford. Tel. 0404-40421.

ASHFORD, Co. Wicklow. Restored 2 storey farmhouse and 17 acres, 4 mls. village and N11, fine gardens. Auction 16th May. Clarke Aucts. Ltd., Ashford. Tel. 0404-40421.

CHERRY GARDEN, Dalnagan

Sale notice for O'Brien's farm and house (2 lots), April 1990

In the summer of 1990, we had the last family get together in our house. All the family came, Lar from the Potteries in England, Peg and Sheila from Cork, Mary from Wexford and Nance from Ashford. They brought the accordians and the tin whistles, the bodhran and the melodian. We sang, played our party pieces and told stories all through a summer Sunday. The house got a royal send off from the O'Briens, 2 generations of whom had lived, worked and raised their families there. It was a sentimental day, but also the beginning of the next chapter.

The O'Briens' farmhouse when it was sold in 1990

Chapter 15

A New Era Arrives

By the closing decades of the 20th century, it had come to pass that after centuries of farming families living in the townland of Aghowle, there was no working farmhouse or farmyard remaining in the townland. Some of the farmhouses and farmyards had disappeared slowly, slipping into ruin, other farmyards fell in a day beneath the bulldozer and six of the original farmhouses were sold on and given a new lease of life as homes for non farming families.

The farmland of course still remained, but was now either owned by farmers who lived outside of the townland and they used it as an extension of their existing farms, or it was leased out to farmers from further afield who needed extra land for grazing or tillage. So while sheep did still graze on some of the fields beneath Carrick, many of the little fields were knocked into much larger strips of land and planted with barley.

This poem written by Larry O'Brien in 1987, captures beautifully the changes that had taken place in the townland. Larry was born and reared in Aghowle and while he moved to England to find employment and settled there, he returned back home to Aghowle every year, into his old age. He saw clearly the disappearance of the way of life he had known as a boy and young man.

Larry O'Brien 1921-1996

More Production

LARRY O'BRIEN 1987

Everytime I come to visit
The old spot that I was born in
I see a countryside
That's changing year by year
That old familiar cottage
Or the hedge down by the river
All the little fields and paddocks
Somehow seem to dissappear

For the farms are growing bigger
As with JCB and digger
They level all the ditches
And the gripes are all filled in
There are no hedgerows and no bushes
And you'll find no nest of thrushes
For there isn't enough cover
For a mouse to shelter in

But I used to see the farms
Where the little fields lay scattered
Like a spread of coloured handkerchiefs
Along the valley side
But now the rotovator
Spoils the work of the creator
Every field is fifty acres
Every gate is twelve foot wide

In the early hours of morning
You can hear the tractors roaring
As they start their endless journey
That continues all the day
For they are clocking up the mileage
As they cut and pack the silage
In the little fields where years ago
We used to cock the hay

And I always will remember
Cutting corn in September
And the fields were full of neighbours
As we cut and stooked the grain
But today – through lack of patience
It's all one operation
And the buzzing of the combine
Drills a hole into your brain

Now to talk about a threshing
Is completely out of fashion
For the thresh it as they cut it
And the straw is left to rot
Sure it is only in your dreaming
That you'll see an engine steaming
In the name of more production
The big combine does the lot

But the people keep on telling me
That times are getting better
And the methods that we used to use
Are out of date they say
So don't mind about destruction
Concentrate on more production
And I have come to the conclusion
That this old dog has had his day!!!

From the 1970s onwards, the townland began to move into a new era. Some of the new owners of the farmland sold plots of land for house building and here and there new bungalows began to appear. The owners of these new homes, as well as the people who bought the old farmhouses, were not farming people and many of them commuted from the townland each day to work in Dublin or elsewhere – a concept that would have been unimaginable to those that had lived in the townland a century earlier.

But while the active farmyards may have gone, I feel that the townland of Aghowle retained the memory of the original farming community that had lived here, as a strong connected community formed amongst the new residents that had come to settle in the valley. The last two farming families still living here as the townland began to change were Miley and Bridget O'Brien and my own parents Patsy and May Connolly. I feel both of these families played their part in handing on that sense of community and history to the new residents who came to live here. They warmly welcomed each new family to the area with an open door, a friendly chat and a cup of tea.

The following are some of the memories retold to me by the families that came to live here in the 1970s:

- When Connollys' old farmhouse, No. 8, was renovated and upgraded in the early 1970s, the new owner decided to put it up for letting. One of the first people to rent it were Anne and John Lait, who were a young couple and new to Co. Wicklow. Anne recalls when they first moved in they were befriended by Patsy and May Connolly and when they would return home from work in the evening time there was often a few head of cabbage or some potatoes left sitting at the front door. Anne recalls this made her feel very welcome as it reminded her of what her own neighbours would do back in her own homeplace.

- Around 1973, Seamus Corcoran bought the Farrells' old farmhouse, House No. 6, which had fallen into disrepair. Over time he repaired and upgraded it and after a number of years moved in to live there. Seamus recalls that Bridget and Miley O'Brien who lived nearby were very welcoming. Miley would often drop in to say hello while he was out walking about his farm, often seeming to appear out of nowhere. On one of his first visits, he took Seamus down the road past the Raheen Lane to show him a spring well on his land that never went dry, so Seamus would always have access to clean water, if his own supply went dry. Seamus also has fond memories of Bridget O'Brien walking across the field to bring him some of her delicious homemade cakes.

- Diane and Graeme McHugh moved into Bradshaws' old farmhouse, House No. 4, in 1973. At that time, Patsy Connolly used to check on some livestock belonging to the family that rented the land behind McHughs house. Diane and Graeme were new to living in the countryside and used to marvel at Patsy's agility, then in his late 60s, in walking up to the top of the field under Carrick Mountain. Patsy would often drop in to say hello to Diane as he felt she might be lonely there on her own during the daytime, having moved to live in a new area. Diane recalls as she became friendly with the Connolly family, she would drop up to their house on Christmas Eve with a little gift and would always glide back home again after drinking a very generous measure of Christmas cheer.

- By the early 1990s, the only person still remaining in the townland from the original farming community was my mother May Connolly. When any new family arrived in the locality she would always call to welcome them to the area, usually bringing a little gift of a pot of her jam, or a bunch of flowers from the garden.

From only 7 inhabited houses here in the early 1960s, there are now 18 homes in the townland, almost back to the number of dwellings recorded here in 1851!

Some of the families who came to live here in the 1970s still remain, which means that they have actually now been resident for nearly half a century! They have formed their own community and traditions and in some cases they are now into their second and third generations living in the valley. Perhaps in years to come, they too will record their chapter in the history of the townland of Aghowle.

They were great people who lived and farmed here and now they have been remembered.

Appendix A – Aghowle Poetry

The Ballad of Dinny Byrne
By Larry O'Brien

Twas in the year of '98
When terror stalked the land
And cruel Yoes our deadly foes
Brought death at every hand
Then the men from county Wexford
Rallied to their leader's call
And vowed to fight for freedom
Or in freedom's cause to fall

But among those gallant pikemen
Some found death and some found fame
And when we speak of '98
We still revere their name
Men like Father Michael Murphy
And the men from Slaney Side
Men from Oulart and Kilmuckridge
We remember them with pride
The men from Forth and Shelmalier
And yet another band
Lead by Marshall Bagnall Harvey
And John Kelly from Killane

There were men from County Wicklow
Billy Byrne and Michael Dwyer
And the gallant young McAllister
Who drew the Yeoman's fire
In the misty hills of Wicklow
They still recall
And how he saved his comrades
In the glen of wild Imaal

One young man named Dinny Byrne
From the Wicklow Hills came down
To join with the insurgents
Close to Enniscorthy town
There to learn the arts of fighting

How to parry, guard and strike
And to do his bit for Ireland
With a twelve foot Wexford pike.

From the woods of old Shillelagh
Came the shafts of Irish ash
And when handled by the rebels
Were a weapon hard to match
With their shining blades all gleaming
Sure you've never seen the likes
And Mick Dempsey from Bellcarrig
Was the man who forged the pikes.

At New Ross and Tubberneering
And the route of Wexford Town
Dinny Byrne and his comrades
Saw the Redcoats mown down
But later came the shameful news
Of how the cause was sold
By the traitors and informers

For the lure of English gold
So homeward to his native hills
Young Dinny Byrne fled
With Yeomen troops upon his heels
A price upon his head

Near the slopes of Carrick mountain
Lived his sweetheart Mairin Ban
With laughing eyes and golden hair
Just like a summer dawn
With spinning wheel and comb and loom
She wove each Irish shawl
And sold them on a fair day
In the Rathdrum Flannel Hall
So to the valley of Aghowle

Young Dinny made his way
Through the woods of Ballycullen
Where he knew a welcome lay

He was dressed up as a tinker
Or so the story goes
A disguise to help him on his way
And foil the hunting Yoes
The harvest moon was rising
Over Carrick's misty cowl
When he knocked upon a cabin door
In the valley of Aghowle
There were decent people living there
Just like it is today
From the humblest door no man in need
Was ever turned away

But the Yoes were close behind him
And they knew of his disguise
The leader Captain Sinnot said
"We will take him by surprise
We will surround this cursed valley
In the early morning light

And we will have the tinker by the heels
Before the fall of night"
But the word had reached young Dinny
And in the dark of night
With Mairin Ban to guide him
To the mountain he took flight
And in a cave by Aghowle rock
On Carrick's lofty perch
They watched the Yeomen down below
Commence their deadly search

They saw the cabins burning down
In field and bog and wood
From Slane to Ballycullen
Not a single dwelling stood
But after all no trace of Dinny Byrne
*   could be found*
The captain of the Yeos declared
"He can't have gone to ground"
He stood on top of the Cobblers Rock
And swore upon his soul
"That the Devil ate the tinker
In the Valley of Aghowle"

The Eviction
By Margaret Connolly (2017)

Hugh Carey Counts His Blessings

It is a blessing father's body lay
Yonder in the graveyard clay
And he did not live to witness
The desolation of our eviction day

Although I know his heart remains
In our land beneath the hill
That he took from ferns and furze
To fertile field and ploughed drill
He would have cried bitter tears to think
That all his life was toiled in vain
And that one of kind Francis's kin
Could turn, throw us to the roads
And leave our fields grow fallow again.

It is a blessing too, that mother lay
There beside him in that graveyard clay
And she did not live to see our little house,
Her pride and joy, knocked and broken
down, by the agent's word
Empty now, that little room
Where she bore us all into life
Cold now, the kitchen's hearth of stone
Where she lived her days
Cooking and caring, by the turf firelight.

It is a blessing too, they did not see
Our poor simple sister, Bridget,
Sitting there sobbing by the empty shell
As she called their names through the fallen walls,
For their good hearts would have shattered
A thousand times, with splintered pain.
It is a blessing now at last
That dear Bridget has found some peace
As we gather here today
To lay her down to finally rest
Beside them in the graveyard clay

The Old School At Moneystown
By Larry O'Brien 1987

As I get a little older
And the years have dulled my brain
I often take a ramble
Down a place called Memory Lane
For I've got more past than future
As the time goes rolling on
And old memories are sweeter
Of the days that are long gone
But there is one place we all can meet
As that lane we travel down
It's the little grey stone schoolhouse
In a place called Moneystown

There were children from Kilmullen
From Tomriland and Lickeen
Parkmore Aghowle and Garryduff
And places in between
From Montiagh and from Parkroe
Ballycullen and from Slane
There was some from Castlekevin
And from Knockafrumpa Lane

We trudged for miles through rain and
    snow
And none were known to "mitch"
For we were better off in school than
    hiding in a ditch.
Sure there was no place we could hide
If someone chanced to pass
They would be sure to tell your Daddy
The next Sunday morn at mass
So when Mrs. Redmond called the roll
We moved not hand or foot
But sat up smartly in your desk
And answeared "Taim anseo"

Mrs. Redmond came from Kerry
That famed kingdom of the west

And I never met her equal
As a teacher she was best
She had some strong convictions
And enforced them with a cane
But she would teach a donkey logic
If he'd only half a brain
She thought the children Irish
Though we found it hard to grasp
But we spoke it like a native
When we finished in her class
Mrs. Timmons from Kilmullen
Taught the little ones at school
Though she was free and easy
Sure you couldn't act the fool

She was there with Mrs. Redmond
And they differed quite a bit
We respected Mrs. Redmond
But we all loved "Mrs. Kit"
She was there to take you by the hand
On your first day at school
And we all know that by nature
Little children can be cruel
But she understood and loved us
That was very plain to see
She was just as good as Mammy
When you fell and cut your knee

Yes they built the little schoolhouse
And a hundred years have gone
But for we who spent our childhood there
The memories linger on
Going barefoot in the summer
Trudging through the winter mire
With a Brassnagh from the wayside
Just to light the schoolhouse fire
And when the teacher kept us in
To clean and sweep the school

We did it in our turn
Because that was teacher's rule
But now I think I'll finish
For there is nothing left to say
But the memories are enduring
And will never go away
There is a younger generation

Full of plans and bright ideas
Bigger schools and modern methods
That the march of time decrees
But as the years roll onward
May God send his blessing down
On the pupils past and present
Of our school at Moneystown.

Echoes in Sunlight
By Margaret Connolly, 2016

For Mary Doyle, aged 6 years and her brother John Doyle, aged 2 years

We have come to re-call your names
From across the stillness of time
And to listen as they drift
Up into the sunlight

Those that loved you most and held you dearest
Could only endure the pain of your parting
By mourning you for their lifetime
In silence and solitude.

For they feared if they spoke your names again
They would be carried by a tide of grief
Down into the dark abyss
From which they could never return.

Those that shared in your young lives
Here in the valley, remembered you often
As they walked and worked,
Through field and farm.

And in gentle quiet moments
They passed on your story
To ensure your memory would live on
Long after their passing.

So Mary and John
We are come to re-call your names
From across the stillness of time
And to listen now as they drift
Up into the sunlight.

And the echoes that return to us
Are no longer of sadness and pain
But the sounds of soft summer evenings
And two children at play

As your young pure voices
Would drift from the house on the hillside
Down through the valley
In ripples of joy.

Appendix B – References

References

[AAI/GVR] Ask About Ireland, Griffith's Valuation Records, accessed through http://www.askaboutireland.ie/griffith-valuation/index.xml

[A/WMB] Ancestry.com Wicklow Message board accessed through www.ancestry.com/boards/localities.britisles.ireland.wic.general/3612/mb.ashx

[AJTT] Clarke Sheila, Ashford a Journey Through Time, Ashford Books 2003,

[C/NAI] Census records/National Archives of Ireland, accessed through www.census.nationalarchives.ie

[EPPI/C1841/51] Enhanced British Parliamentary Papers on Ireland, Ireland census 1841, 1851, accessed through: http:/ www.dippam.ac.uk/eppi/documents/13121/page/160542

[EPPI/DIPPAM/P696-708] Enhanced British Parliamentary Papers on Ireland, Law and practice in respect to the occupation of land in Ireland: minutes of evidence; part 11 accessed from: www.eppi.dippam.ac.uk/documents/11941/eppi

[FMP/CMOD] Findmypast/Cantwell's memorials of the dead, accessed through www.findmypast.ie

[FMP/IDLR] Findmypast, Ireland Dog Licence Registers, accessed through www.findmypast.ie

[FMP/IPCR] Findmypast, Irish Petty Court Registers, accessed through www.findmypast.ie

[FMP/LECR] Findmypast, Landed Estate Court Rentals 1850-1885, accessed through www.findmypast.ie

[FSTS] Byrne Kevin, *From Shadow to Sunlight – A History of St. Colman's Hospital Rathdrum, Co. Wicklow.* Wicklow Press Ltd.

[FUD] J.B.I. *Faithful Unto Death: A memoir of W.G. Rhind*, Primary Source Edition, William Yapp, 70 Welbeck Street, London, 1863

[IROI] Kane Robert, *Industrial Resources of Ireland*, Dublin, Hodges and Smith, 1845

[ITC1851] Immigrants to Canada 1851, immigration report, *From the British Parliamentary Papers, 1852 XXXIII (1474)*

[ITCT] Carey Michael, *If Trees Could Talk-Wicklow's Trees and Woodlands Over Four Centuries*, 2009 CONFORD

[IW1798] *Insurgent Wicklow 1798 - The Story as Written by REV.BRO. LUKE CULLEN*, edited by Myles V. Ronan, Clonmore and Reynolds 1948

[MUJ] *My Uncle John, Edward Stephens's Life of J.M. Synge*, edited by Andrew Carpenter, London Oxford University Press, 1974

[NAI/HMR] The National Archives of Ireland, Hearth Money Roll

[NAI/TAB] National Archives of Ireland, Tithe Applotment books, accessed through www.titheapplotmentbooks.nationalarchives.ie

[NAI/VOB/BC], National Archives of Ireland, Valuation Office Books 1824-1856, for the townland of Ballycullen. Accessed through www.nationalarchives.ie

[NFC/SC/GS] National Folklore Collection, Schools' Collection, Glenealy and Ballylusk School, accessed through www.duchas.ie

[NFC/SC/MS] National Folklore Collection, Schools' Collection, Moneystown School, accessed through www.duchas.ie

[NLI/EP/MS 41,997/2] National Library of Ireland, Estate Papers for Powerscourt, Ms 41,997/2

[NLI/HP/GEA] National Library of Ireland, Hatch Papers, Glanmore Estate Accounts, Ms 11,336

[NLI/LNLL/R] National Library of Ireland, Ladies National Land League of Ireland, Roundwood branch, Ms 17,794

[NLI/MSS/11996-11997] National Library of Ireland, Mss no 11996-11997, Hatch Papers

[NLI/MS/43,005/1] National Library of Ireland, MS 43,005/1 Powerscourt Estate Papers

[NLI/PR/A] National Library of Ireland, Parish Registers. Roman Catholic parish of Ashford, accessed through www.registers.nli.ie

[NLI/PR/G] National Library of Ireland, Parish Registers. Roman Catholic parish of Glendalough, accessed through www.registers.nli.ie

[NLI/PR/W] National Library of Ireland, Parish Registers. Roman Catholic parish of Wicklow, accessed through www.registers.nli.ie

[OSI/1839] Ordnance Survey Map 1839 Ordnance Survey Ireland

[OSL/W] *Ordnance Survey Letters -Wicklow*, edited by Christiaan Corlett & John Medlycott, published by Roundwood & District Historical Society and Wicklow Archaeological Society

[OSNB/W] Ordnance Survey Name Books, Wicklow, No. A 180.

[RAMPH] Roundwood and Moneystown - *An Essay in Parish History*, by M.G. Nevin, 1985

[RHJ/2009] Roundwood & District Historical & Folklore Journal, 2009, pages 14-18, *Wicklow & the Famine*, by Ken Hannigan

[THSOW] O'Rourke, Thomas *The Hedge Schools of Wicklow*, 20015

[TPN] Corlett, C. & Weaver, M. *The Price notebooks*, 2 Volume, Dublin, 2002

[TSBS] McCormack W.J., *The Silence of Barbara Synge*, Manchester University Press

[VOI/CB/AL] Valuation Office of Ireland, Cancelled Books, townland of Aghowle Lower

[VOI/CB/AU] Valuation Office of Ireland, Cancelled Books, townland of Aghowle Upper

[WCA/WR] Wicklow County Archives, Workhouse registers, housed at Wicklow County Council offices.

[WH&S] *Wicklow History & Society*, Ed. Ken Hannigan and William Nolan. Dublin: Geography Publications, 1994

Other Publications used as source reference for text and photographs:
O'Donnell, Ruan, *The rebellion in Wicklow 1798*, Irish Academic Press, 1998
Clarke Sheila, *A Pictorial History of Ashford County Wicklow. 1860s –1960s*, Ashford Books 2000
McNally Joseph, *A Pictorial History of Roundwood County Wicklow 1870-1970*, Martello Press Ltd., Blackrock Co. Dublin 2003
Corlett Christiaan, *Wicklow's Traditional Farmhouses: Rediscovering some of Wicklow's hidden treasures and a way of life that went with them*, Christiaan Corlett, 2014

Appendix C – Acknowledgements

Five years ago, when I set out to record the history of the farming community of Aghowle, I never envisaged that I would end up with an actual book. My idea was that I might end up with a small booklet of 30 or 40 pages and that I could run off a photocopy now and again for anyone who might be interested. But I soon discovered there was a lot more history to record about the townland and its people than I had first thought. This project could never have been completed without the assistance and goodwill of a great many people, to whom I am extremely grateful.

So many people helped me in so many ways: from passing on a vital piece of family or local history, to sourcing contact details for me, to tracking down old family photographs from biscuit tins in attics and from distant homes across the globe. A number of people very generously gave me permission to copy photographs from local histories they had already published themselves. Other people kindly invited me into their homes and sat patiently for hours while I recorded their memories of the townland and its people.

When I finally had all the research, photographs and memories down on paper, I realised I had no idea at all of how to then go about turning it into a book for publishing. But yet again there were more people willing to come to my assistance. A number of local Wicklow historians who had travelled down this road before me, went way above and beyond the call of duty to advise me, guide me, and assist me in turning my research into a published book.

To all these people I owe a huge Thank You. I have tried to record all your names below, but five years is a long time, so sincere apologies if I have omitted anyone - I hope at least I personally thanked you for your contribution at the time.

I want to single out for special mention my husband Brian Mathews, who for many years has suggested that I should record my childhood experience of growing up in Aghowle, and in a way, I feel this has at least partly been achieved in the book. All through this project, Brian has been so encouraging and supportive, and in recent months he has burnt many, many literal hours of midnight oil editing and reviewing the manuscript. Without his assistance, I feel this book might never have reached the publication stage.

So, my sincere thanks to all below for their roles in helping to record the history of the Aghowle farming community. Names are presented in alphabetical order.

Margaret Connolly, December 2017

Elizabeth Barratt, U.S.A.
Eilish Beirne
Roisin Beirne
Margaret Bloomer
Eric Bradshaw
The Bradshaw Family
Brendan Byrne
The Byrne Family, Moneystown
Jack Byrne
Kevin Byrne
Tommy Byrne
Sheila Clarke
Ann Connolly
Mary Connolly
Seamus Corcoran
Christiaan Corlett
Billy Crean
Robin Croughwell
Dudley Dolan
Rosaleen Durkin
Eleanor Fanning
Pat Fogarty
Michael Graham
Arthur Hall
Ken Hannigan
Richard Hatton
Joan Kavanagh
Liam Kelly
Johnny Kenneally
Anne Lait
Bernadette Lawler
Gerald Lawrence (Dorset)
Dick Mahon
Brian Mathews
Diane and Greame McHugh
Robbie McDonald
Joseph McNally
The Moran family, U.S.A.
George Murray
Jack Murtagh
Philip Higgins and the Staff of Naas Printing Limited
The staff of the National Archives of Ireland

The staff of the National Library of Ireland
The staff of the National Museum of Ireland
Derek Nielson
Agnes Noonan
Séighean Ó Draoi
The extended O'Brien family
Ellen O'Leary and family
Diarmuid O'Reilly
Sheila Owens
Catherine Power (*nee* O'Brien)
John Power
Jim Rees
Billy Rutledge
Ed Ryan
The Sheane family
Mary Slattery
Billy Smith and family
The Smith and Edge families, New Zealand
The late John Timmons
The late Larry Timmons
Liam Timmons
Terry Timmons and family
Carmel Toole
The staff of the Valuation Office Dublin
Catherine Wright -Wicklow County Archives

Index

Editor's Note: It is a common practice in Ireland for families to reuse parent and/or grandparent forenames in subsequent generations - hence the same person name will appear in multiple generations. While effort has been made to distinguish between different generations where possible, certain index entries below will actually reference more than one person.

Further, certain surnames are very common in Wicklow. Hence, not all forenames listed under a given surname will necessarily belong to the same immediate family.